After Thought

After Thought

The Computer Challenge to Human Intelligence

James Bailey

BASIC BOOKS

A Member of the Perseus Books Group

Designed by Elliott Beard

Library of Congress Cataloging-in-Publication Data

Bailey, James, 1946–
    After thought : the computer challenge to human intelligence /
by James Bailey. — 1st ed.
      p. cm.
    Includes index.
    ISBN 0-465-00781-3 (cloth)
    ISBN 0-465-00782-1 (paper)
    1. Computers and civilization. 2. Artificial intelligence.
I. Title.
QA76.9.C66B35   1996
303.48'34—dc 20   96-1050
                                               CIP

99 00 01 ❖/RRD 10 9 8 7 6 5 4 3

To Betsy

CONTENTS

REASSIGNING THE TASKS OF THE MIND

W hen Henry David Thoreau went to the woods of Concord, Massachusetts, he was seeking, among other things, to take back a set of muscle tasks that had long since been reassigned from humans to animals. Henry David suspected that it was a bad bargain. He saw his neighbors living in houses far smaller than the barns they built for their draft animals. He saw more of the crop being consumed in the barn than in the house. By hoeing his own beans with his own muscles, Thoreau showed that the reassignment was still reversible.

He succeeded because these muscle tasks had remained within human scale and under human control. A horse is more powerful than a person, but not vastly so, and it is difficult to apply even a dozen horses to the same task in parallel. The 5–10 horsepower that was conveniently available was enough to advance civilization but not enough to revolutionize it. Society eagerly adopted horses to transport its soldiers, oxen to pull its plows, and pigeons to carry its messages, but all of these tasks retained a human scale and character.

As he looked out across Walden Pond to the new railroad that skirted the far shore, however, Thoreau could see that something much bigger than himself was happening. Muscle tasks were making a *second* transition. They were moving to a whole new environment, to machines that embodied none of the human analogies that animals have. These new machines got cheaper every year at a time when nothing else did.[1] Soon they were ubiquitous. Far more significantly, they grew in performance without loss of efficiency. Over time, six-seat stagecoaches became hundred-seat passenger trains and then thousand-berth cruise ships, and life changed for good.

Life changed not only for those who used the new trains and cruise ships but also for those who had made their living building the old stagecoaches and farm wagons. These unlettered craftspeople saw their whole way of life being driven to extinction by the new methods of scientific engineering. Today, these rural networks seem almost quaint:

> A well-trained waggon-builder knew to a nicety how to arrange [each matter,] not by scientific calculation but by following the methods long ago learnt in his trade. . . . The nature of this knowledge should be noted. It was set out in no book. It was not scientific. . . . The lore was a tangled network of country prejudices, whose reasons were known in some respects here, in others there, and so on. In farm-yard, in tap room, at market, the details were discussed over and over again; they were gathered for remembrance in village workshop; carters, smiths, farmers, wheel-makers, in thousands handed on each his own little bit of understanding, passing it to his son or to the wheelwright of the day, linking up the centuries. But for the most part the details were but dimly understood; the whole body of knowledge was a mystery, a piece of folk knowledge, residing in the folk collectively but never wholly in any individual.[2]

During these same years, while Thoreau was at Walden making detailed records of the plants and animals of the surrounding woods and listening for the whistle of the steam engine across the pond, the Englishman Charles Babbage was designing a very different kind of engine, an Analytical Engine that would reassign the task of computing numerical tables from human minds to machines. Although Thoreau knew nothing of this development, his nearby contemporary Nathaniel Bowditch did, having corresponded with Babbage directly.

If the production of these numerical tables, "this toil of pure intelligence . . . [could] possibly be performed by an unconscious machine,"[3] the future would seemingly belong to thinkers like Babbage, who could exploit this new machine capability. Sure enough, during World War II, an electronic form of Babbage's unconscious machine, the ENIAC, was developed to compute tables of artillery ranges for the U.S. Army. Initially, some people worried about the alien nature of these scientifically designed "electronic brains." Those concerns have subsided as computers themselves have become domesticated. Today, our neighbors all have their own computers at home just as Thoreau's neighbors all had their draft horses at home.

The reason today's electronic computers seem benign is that the true electronic revolution has not happened yet. Our current phase of computerization is still akin to the stage of history when muscle tasks were moving from humans to animals. The tasks being reassigned from individual human minds to electronic circuits still retain all their old human structure and scale. Granted, they go faster: Entries in library catalogs are found in seconds instead of minutes. Financial transactions are completed in a single telephone call instead of the next day. Airline ticket prices change every few hours instead of every few years. But in each case, the underlying intellectual methodology remains the methodology of science as we have known it for centuries. We could, as Thoreau did with the muscle tasks, still take them back.

This short-term continuity, however, masks an important reality: Electronic circuits really *are* alien. Human minds and electronic circuits provide completely different milieus within which to carry out information-processing tasks. The difference is not just the obvious one of speed. The ways that information is encoded, remembered, organized, interchanged, and forgotten are also totally different. It is vain, therefore, to assume that the former tasks of the mind will remain unchanged after they are reassigned to electronic circuits.

It is no accident, of course, that these tasks in their current form are well adapted to the strengths and weaknesses of the human mind. Over many centuries, civilization has developed techniques of cognition that take advantage of what our brains do well and work around what they do poorly. We teach these techniques in our schools and practice them in our daily problem-solving tasks. We call them *thought*. When they involve mathematical symbols, we call them *scientific thought*. When they involve words only, we call the techniques *abstract thought*. Now, as more and more of these tasks become the responsibility of electronic circuits and as all information becomes uniformly encoded as bits,[4] they will change beyond recognition.

As it did in centuries past, science is leading the way. Science is the discipline in which our current methods of step-by-step thought were tested and proved first, before they spread to the humanities and social sciences. Scientific computing was, in turn, the very first mind task to be reassigned from human minds to electronic circuits, back in the 1940s and 1950s. Now it is the first discipline to enter the second stage. Instead of remaining on the path of traditional thought—pithy scientific "laws" and the old vocabulary of sequential equations and numbers—the electronic circuits are inexorably moving us to new ground. Symbolic numbers, equations, and the formulation of universal laws are what people and thought are good at.[5] Electronic circuits are good at different things.

For example, electronic circuits are proving themselves good at what Henry David Thoreau was good at: tasks such as tramping "eight or ten miles through the deepest snow to keep an appointment with a beech tree, or a yellow birch."[6] They are good at meticulously noting details about the world around them and carefully recording these details. Every time a satellite passes over Walden Pond or a credit card passes through the reader at the museum gift shop, new data are created within a computer. Because it is cheap to make an extra copy and save it, the computer always does so. No longer does it take the full-time attention of a Boswell to record the behavior of a single Dr. Johnson. Our traditional methods of thought were optimized to eke out conclusions from expensive and insufficient data. Yet today we are drowning in data, and there is unimaginably more on the way.

More astonishingly, electronic circuits are good at exactly what the society of rural wagon makers was good at: managing a "tangled network of country prejudices, whose reasons were known in some respects here, in others there, and so on."[7] Electronic circuits are good at letting higher level behavior emerge from the interplay of millions of tiny operations all interacting with each other in parallel, handing on each its own little bit of understanding but now linking up intervals of microseconds instead of centuries as the craftspeople once did. As a result, a whole new set of parallel intermaths is coming to the fore to challenge the sequential maths* of the Industrial Age, which had only humans to carry them out.

In a world with hundreds of millions of computers, these new intermaths have daunting potential. In concert with their bit-level data sources, they are more than just a replacement technology for numbers and equations. They are the milieu for a third level of evolution: *bit evolution*. It is by creating the fruits of electronic bit evolution, rather

---

*In British English, the reality that there are many types of maths has been scrupulously maintained. In American English, there is the tendency to refer to "math" as though it were a single homogeneous entity. This book follows English usage.

than just by speeding up the science of centuries past, that the new electronic computers will make their ultimate presence felt. And they will do it without any premonitory whistle blasts from across the pond. This change will come silently, because it will come—it is already coming—in software. It will be well underway before we are fully cognizant of it, just as cultural evolution was well underway before anyone was aware of its ability to augment biological evolution.

For tens of thousands of years, human evolution was limited to the slow pace of genetic evolution, which is unable to take advantage of what we learn during our lifetimes. Save for a rare mutation, the genes we pass along to our children are the same ones we received ourselves decades earlier. Cultural evolution is wonderfully faster, perhaps a hundred times faster,[8] because it allows much of what we learn to be passed on and combined with what others around us have learned via the medium of language. That is why we can do so much more than our historical ancestors could, even though our brains have not necessarily evolved at all in the interim. The power of cultural evolution comes in part from its ability to pick out best-of-breed techniques, but even more from its ability to mate these good ideas together in novel ways. People with different perspectives—carters, smiths, farmers, wheel makers, physicists, theologians, artists—contribute their own individual bits of understanding to the stew.

Cultural evolution really came into its own with the invention of written language and then of the printing press. At the folk level, the wagon trade remained stunted by the fact that its methodology "was set out in no book" and hence could not mix widely.[9] Today, as knowledge from millions of perspectives circulates in published form, to be contemplated and recombined in novel ways, cultural evolution is beginning to outrun even itself. Our culture is producing information faster than our processes of thought can absorb it and understand it, because the milieu of cultural evolution (you and I) has significant performance limits, too. For example, we are not skilled at sharing what we know until we can put it into high-level, symbolic form. Our early, tacit, inchoate insights on a subject tend to remain ours alone, even though they might profitably mate with a colleague's preverbal insights at a very low level. We must wait until we can put words to our ideas before we share them. More important, we are very poor at updating what we know, because we have no reliable delete key. New ideas, whether they be PCs or HMOs or new scientific truths, typically have to wait for the next generation before they are fully adopted by the culture, because, having learned the prior ways, we cannot forget them.

The only way behavior changes in science is that certain people die and differently behaving people take their place.[10]

Electronic circuits can share their tiniest insights, however, down as low as a few bits, and they can forget in an instant when it is to their advantage to do so. These are the abilities that allow, together with access to vast amounts of data, computer programs to evolve on their own initiative. Just as cultural evolution learned to operate independently of biological evolution, so too will bit evolution become autonomous. It is not necessary to tell computers to "get a life." They are already developing the ability to interbreed their programs, to check the results against the data they receive from the world, and to evolve and improve all on their own. This new *bit evolution* has the potential to yield another hundredfold speedup in the overall course of evolution on earth.

The impact of any such evolutionary speedup is immense. It was the more efficient written forms of cultural evolution that drove the earlier folkways into extinction. To the rural wagon maker George Sturt, this faster paced world of scientific thought was even more foreign than the New World that Thoreau's predecessors encountered in Plymouth and Boston. A completely different world emerged from this "discovery by science of an environment unknown to our forefathers. . . . [This] new environment, into which we were still stumbling blind, awaits us everywhere, and rests in Universal Law, in laws of Stress and Strain, of Combustion, and so on. . . . The Pilgrim Fathers had not found so new a world."[11]

For their first fifty years, electronic circuits have been put to work on precisely this established scientific tradition that "rests in Universal Law, in laws of Stress and Strain, of Combustion, and so on." Ported to electronics, these thought processes, the ones we have taught in our schools and used in our laboratories for four hundred years, have continued to prove effective. They have yielded important new insights into the behavior of the physical world: the earth, the air, the fire, and the water. They have, however, remained much less effective at helping us to understand the ever-changing patterns of cultural and biological evolution: the ecology, the economy, the society, and the mind itself. A new kind of parallel and evolutionary computing—computing analogous to tangled webs of country prejudices, computing that uses no numbers or equations—has now emerged to connect to this world. This is the true electronic computing revolution; its intellectual impact will be greater than anything since the Renaissance, possibly greater than anything since the invention of language.

- *Even scientists and specialists will increasingly be taking the word of electronic circuits for vital information on vital issues.*

Modern life demands that ordinary citizens defer to scientific specialists in more and more areas. To the general public, "the whole scientific inquiry starts from the familiar world and in the end it must return to the familiar world; but the part of the journey over which the physicist has charge is in foreign territory."[12] Soon it will be the turn of the scientists to display such commendable maturity, deferring to electronic circuits that have evolved their own formulations based on their own analyses of trillions and trillions of pieces of data and that will be "foreign territory" even to the expert. Not even specialists will know how these answers actually come about, because the ways of bit evolution will not be our ways.

- *By processing information adaptively, computers will open up important new vistas for us in the social and life sciences.*

The fixed maths of the Industrial Age curriculum are powerful tools for investigating the fixed world of the physical sciences, where events recur. Just as the maths of geometry supported the ancient astronomers in mapping the heavens, the maths of algebra and calculus have supported modern physicists as they clocked the changing motions of objects here on earth. The fruits of these investigations are exactly the universal laws of stress and strain and combustion and so on that physicists and engineers use to predict the behavior of nonliving objects.

The biological and cultural worlds, however, are worlds of "perpetual novelty," where fixed universal law does not apply. They are more nuanced worlds, where events recur in ways that are similar but not identical. They are worlds whose entities, whether they be desert ecologies or new market segments, take much of their reality from the interaction of their constituent parts rather than from within the individual component parts themselves. Behavior emerges in ways that thought cannot grasp. The economist John Maynard Keynes underscored the gulf between his subject matter and Newton's:

It is as though the fall of the apple to the ground depended on the apple's motives, on whether it is worthwhile falling to the ground, and whether the ground wanted the apple to fall, and on mistaken calculations on the part of the apple as to how far it was from the center of the earth.[13]

The new evolutionary maths are the right match for this world of perpetual and emergent novelty because they themselves learn. When tomorrow turns out to be a little different from today, they absorb the differences from the data and adjust themselves accordingly. Such mutable maths are, of course, difficult to communicate in books, because books, this one included, are a rigid medium. These maths are much more appropriately passed from computer to computer than from book to book, because information within computers is free to change.

• *With the growing role of computing in the life and social sciences, numbers will become less ubiquitous.*

Since the Renaissance, numbers have been the physical scientist's abstraction of choice for thinking about and expressing the world. Most social scientists have adopted numbers as well, believing with Joseph Schumpeter that certain behaviors are "made numerical by life itself" in ways that are not even true for physics.[14] Other social scientists argue that the very process of imposing numbers onto life causes us to misread and even corrupt meaning and to see things that are not actually there.

> Take, for example, the 1911 Federated Malay States Census. . . . It is extremely unlikely that, in 1911, more than a tiny fraction of those categorized and subcategorized would have recognized themselves under such labels. . . . One notices, in addition, the census-makers' passion for completeness and unambiguity. Hence their intolerance of multiple, politically "transvestite," blurred, or changing identifications. . . . The fiction of the census is that everyone is in it, and that everyone has one—and only one—extremely clear place. No fractions.[15]

Some observers of the murder trial of O. J. Simpson made the same point about media polls that arbitrarily categorized respondents into one of two races—no fractions—and then used the resulting numbers to draw conclusions about the role of race in the whole society. Alfred North Whitehead saw it as the role of philosophy to critique such choices of abstractions and to help society to burst through them when necessary.[16] The new electronic abstractions will aid this process because they are dependent on abstracting neither life into numbers nor behavior into equations.

- *In a world with hundreds of millions of computers (with billions of hours of spare time available each night to support the processes of bit evolution), the maths we teach in school must change.*

The designers of the first electronic computers deliberately designed them to carry out the same numerocentric operations of algebra and calculus that had been developed back when all computers were people and when available computing capacity was minuscule. These equational maths came to prominence in the Renaissance, replacing the circles and diagrams of geometry. Their entry into the schools almost three hundred years ago was the last substantial change in the secondary mathematics curriculum.

In an age when computing power is abundant, these maths are obsolete. At a minimum, it is time to transfer responsibility for teaching geometry to the history department. If students should be introduced to the maths of the ancient Greeks, it should be in the same way they are introduced to the political theories and the art of the Greeks. The problems for which geometry originally entered the schools have been either solved or taken over by other methods.

Reassigning responsibility for geometry opens up room in the curriculum for new evolutionary intermaths, maths with still-unfamiliar names like *cellular automata, genetic algorithms, artificial life, classifier systems,* and *neural networks.* These are maths that would have made no sense in previous centuries because they are maths that no people in their right minds would ever try to carry out "by hand."[17] They are maths that flourish in an environment where all information is uniformly encoded as bits. These are the maths with which electronic computers will evolve their own versions of scientific theories and formulations.

- *Because the new maths are parallel, learning them will change the way we ourselves experience the world and our appropriate role within it.*

When the world is presented to us in books, it is perforce presented sequentially, so that we see only one set of realities at a time. We see, for example, more isolated facts and fewer relationships. The philosopher Suzanne Langer drew the distinction quite clearly in the 1940s:

Words have a linear, discrete, successive order; they are strung one after another like beads on a rosary; beyond the very limited meanings of inflections, which can indeed be incorporated in the words themselves, we cannot talk in simultaneous bunches of names. . . .

Visual forms—lines, colors, proportions, etc.—are just as capable of articulation, i.e., of complex combination, as words. But the laws that govern this sort of articulation are altogether different from the laws of syntax that govern language. The most radical difference is that visual forms are not discursive. They do not present their constituents successively, but simultaneously, so the relations determining a visual structure are grasped in one act of vision. . . . An idea that contains too many minute yet closely related parts, too many relations within relations, cannot be "projected" into discursive form.[18]

Sequential thought is thought with an attitude. For example, in a test of problem-solving ability that has been used for many years, college students have been faced with the dilemma of a doctor whose patient has a malignant stomach tumor.[19] The doctor has no surgical tools but does have a radiation source sufficiently powerful to destroy the growth. Unfortunately, a source this powerful also destroys the healthy tissue en route to the malignancy.

Because students typically are unable to come up with a solution to this dilemma on their own, they are given one of two versions of a story about a military commander who is attempting to storm a fortress. Mines in the roads leading to the fortress prevent a large force from simply marching in. In one version of the story, the commander splits the forces and sends a few in over each road. In the other version, the commander discovers and uses an unmined road.

The story of the unmined road resonates immediately. Only 10 percent of the students who are given that analogy are still able to see that the doctor should think in parallel and split up the radiation source into many small, individually harmless rays that meet at the malignancy, as a modern gamma knife does. The more popular, brute-force proposal is to aim the radiation source down the esophagus, perhaps inserting a tube first to straighten it out. This authoritarian tendency to ram a singular solution down the problem's throat is a hallmark of sequential thought. Sequentialism allows for only a single action at a time, often obscuring more cooperative, parallel, and adaptive approaches.

- *Because these computers will be free to evolve in whatever way works for them, the odds are high that they will evolve a process of*

*intelligence that is not the same as ours, or even understandable by
ours.*

Notwithstanding a few observers who believe that human brains
became large because they are sexy and, like peacock tails, offered an
advantage in mating,[20] most conclude that brains, and the information
processing that goes on within them, are valuable to life in general.
The process of biological evolution has been augmented by the
process of cultural evolution to bring our information-processing ability to the level it is at today. Whenever information is encoded at a very
primitive level, as it is in biological chromosomes or electronic computer memories, it becomes possible, indeed inevitable, for that information to evolve on its own. As bit evolution takes hold, it will allow
electronic circuits both to carry out traditional mind tasks and to flourish at whole new ones.

To the extent that the tasks that these computers take on are tasks
that require intelligence when *we* do them, we will refer to them as
intelligent as well.[21] However, the capabilities they develop may bear
no relationship to the "intelligence" we have developed. More likely,
the capabilities will be different because the information-processing
milieu is sharply different and so are many of the tasks that need
doing. The result will not be "artificial intelligence" in the sense that
scientists in that field attempt to replicate human intelligence electronically. It will be something quite new. In the years after Galileo first
trained his telescope on Jupiter, the Latin language had to add something it had never had before: a plural form of *luna,* or "moon." In the
coming years, we will have to add plural forms to words like *intelligence,* because humans and computers will exhibit different intelligences. And they will be peer intelligences.

We can choose to involve ourselves in this process or we can just
watch it happen. Fueled by the ubiquity of hundreds of millions of
computers with billions of hours of spare time on their hands, bit evolution will ultimately pick up the pace in areas where traditional
modes of cultural evolution cannot keep up. Bit evolution is not yet,
of course, any match for cultural evolution. The most powerful computer programs are still ones that have been written sequentially by
teams of human programmers rather than ones that have been evolved
and bred at the level of bits. The Cartesian process of programming,
however, is straining the limits of the cultural-evolution process. Individual human programmers are barely able to understand what other
programmers have done and stay consistent with it. In addition, the

processes of life on earth continue to unfold in ways that are beyond the abilities of humans, or humanly generated computer programs, to absorb or predict. That is why there are already some modules in the Windows operating system that were evolved rather than coded.[22]

Even as tasks that used to belong to our minds are reassigned to electronic circuits and then evolve into completely new forms, we have the responsibility to be active partners in the new world that emerges. None of this is very far away in time. The individual building blocks of bit evolution are mostly in place. Computer scientists have been breeding and evolving programs successfully for over a decade. The techniques are increasingly well understood. Ultimately, it may take millions of computers evolving their programs based on trillions of pieces of information to be successful at large problems, but a million computers is no longer a large number. Nor in the age of satellites does a trillion describe a large number of pieces of information. Whether we prepare them for it or not, children born today will grow up to live in a world where computers outnumber them,[23] where bit evolution plays a prominent role, and where thought no longer holds the exclusive franchise.

2

$\mathcal{T}$HE MASTER THOUGHT PROCESS OF THE MODERN WORLD

The contest between the age-old ways of the rural wagon makers and the new "laws of stress and strain and combustion" of the scientists was a mismatch because only one afforded a view into the future. The wagon makers knew how to function adaptively in the world they were used to, but they could not *predict* where that world was going; they could not process their tangled web of country prejudices fast enough to get out ahead of events.

The advantage of the methods of Universal Law was that they could be abstracted into high-level mathematical symbols that could be both printed and manipulated. Because they could be printed, these mathematical symbols and the information they encoded could be widely disseminated and taught to us all in school and then augmented from one generation to the next. These symbols could also be manipulated at a theoretical level. Scientists could step them ahead in time and examine the effects of forces and tensions before they happened. By manipulating these mathematical symbols, they could, in Galileo's beguiling phrase, "trace the future history" of physical objects in the world.[1] They could write the history before it happened, something rural craftspeople had not learned how to do.

The first examples of scientific prediction appeared in the ancient world. During the Renaissance, these predictive thought processes received a powerful boost from a new mathematical methodology. To some observers, the new predictive techniques of the Renaissance have been at the center of world history in the period since then.

> The advantage which European man gained over the rest of humanity is based on a new method of prediction. . . . before this intellectual explosion took place five centuries ago, the great civilizations of the world differed [inappreciably] in the level of intellectual or moral attainment.[2]

Whether captured in the circles and lines of Greek geometry or the numbers and equations of Renaissance algebra and calculus, these methods of prediction are what we now know as *scientific formulations.* They are among the crown jewels of thought. A society that can successfully predict the future history of the physical world is a much more efficient society. Soon these powerful ways of thinking spread. Humanists such as Goethe encouraged all students to model their thinking after that within scientific formulations: to think step by step just as mathematical prediction unfolds step by step.

> This prudence of arranging in order, or rather deducing the next from that near, we must learn from the mathematicians; we must always proceed as if we were obliged to give an account to the most rigid geometer.[3]

These techniques of thought have been so universally taught and are so well adapted to the strengths and weaknesses of human minds that we take them for granted. Symbolic versions of the world's behavior have come to assert a peer relationship with life itself.

> There is hardly anything that I know that is as exciting as finding that the great events that move history, the forces that determine the destiny of empires and the fate of kings, can sometimes be explained, predicted or even controlled by a few symbols on a printed page.[4]

In fact it has been rare for symbols on a printed page to predict, much less control, the future history of empires, because empires, like economies and ecologies and embryos and environments and ebola viruses, adapt. Traditional symbolic formulations are not designed for behavior that adapts.

Early on, scientists developed a step-by-step, sequential strategy for doing their physical science predictions. They looked for ways of taking a current situation and transforming it into the situation a very short time into the future. Such a method might, for example, take the current position of a planet and move it ahead one degree of arc or take the current state of the weather and move it ahead ten or fifteen minutes of time. These small predictive transformations have little practical value by themselves, but they can be repeated.

The practical value comes from repeating the operation hundreds of times. The weather fifteen minutes into the future can immediately be used as the basis for predicting the weather half an hour into the future and so on out to several days. The first uses of scientific formulation as a source of prediction were suggested by Plato. He set the agenda, very limited at first, as "saving the appearances of the heavens."[5] By that he meant that astronomers were to invent symbolic methods of matching the motions that we actually see when we look up into the skies. Once such methods are in place, they can be used to foretell the astronomical events that intrigue or alarm the citizenry. In Plato's day, it was a fear of eclipses. Today, it seems to be a fear of comet collisions.

Over time, scientists have changed their terminology from "saving the appearances" to "capturing the phenomena" and "scientific visualization," but the basic idea of using a formal process of thought to foresee today what will not happen until tomorrow remains the same. The twentieth-century computer architect John von Neumann simply added a footnote to Plato when he said that the sciences "mainly make [predictive] models. . . . The justification of such a mathematical construct is solely and precisely that it is expected to work—that is, correctly to describe phenomena."[6] Similarly, the economist Milton Friedman asserted that "the only relevant test of the validity of a hypothesis is comparison of its predictions with experience."[7]

Today, the best-known instance of "saving the appearances" is the so-called Turing test. Each year the Computer Museum of Boston, Massachusetts, tests the ability of new software routines to fool interviewers into believing they are conversing with people. These interviewers type messages to an unseen correspondent and receive typed messages back. They are then asked if their fellow conversationalist was human or electronic. The computer is considered to have passed the Turing test if it saves the appearances of a person well enough to fool the interviewer. The computer scientist Alan Turing proposed in the 1950s to call such circuitry "intelligent."

One of the pleasures of predictive models in the physical sciences is that the basic formulation does not change as one moves ahead degree by degree or cycle by cycle. A division of labor becomes possible. The scientist need only invent the formulation, or "model," for a single cycle. Then the process can be delegated to somebody else to do over and over again. That somebody else was a "computer." Until very recently (the 1940s), all computers were people. Computing was a career path no different from accounting or library science or any other job that uses the mind. As these professional computers improved their skills, they moved up the ladder and made more money:

> The $1440 position carries the title of Junior Computer, while the better salaried position ($1620) would be for an Assistant Computer, and finally a Computer would be the title corresponding to the $1800 bracket. A Head Computer earns $2000.[8]

Because they were often the weakest link in the chain of scientific investigation, these human computers have played a role in the history of thought all out of proportion to their numbers. Over the centuries, methods of work that suited them went into general scientific usage and gained enormously in prestige and influence. Methods that did not fit the computers, and these include the controversial methods of the Renaissance astronomer Johannes Kepler, atrophied without influencing the wider culture at all. Ultimately, the intellectual strengths and weaknesses of these professional computers became the design specification for the electronic computers that have spread throughout society in the past fifty years. Theirs were the first mind tasks to be reassigned to electronic circuits. By the late 1950s, all of those Junior Computer, Assistant Computer, Computer, and Head Computer job descriptions were completely gone from the personnel department. The reason we do not hear much about this transition is that it involved no particular hardship or dislocation. The last professional computers became the first professional programmers, with higher status and better pay. As their last act, these computers bequeathed to their electronic heirs the very methods of sequential, step-by-step thought that are now being challenged.

As this transition from human to electronic computers took place, there was not even a thought of replacing, along with the human computers, their age-old sequential ways of looking at the world. The first job of any new computer is to run all the software of the old ones. Computer architects of the 1940s were quite clear about this right from the beginning: "We may now be more precise about what is meant by the digital approach. It is the realization that a machine can be built up to imitate the human method of calculating."[9] Four hundred years of intellectual property were at stake.

Computer architects styled their circuits anthropomorphically to meet an existing market. The approach worked, but only because of the astounding computing capacity that electronic circuits turned out to have. When Western science began, its total computing capacity was probably on the order of a hundred human beings, mostly clustered in Greece and Babylon. Today, the world's computing capacity is perhaps a trillion times larger, with most of the increase coming in our lifetime. The reaction of users has been predictable and not unlike that of a lottery winner: same diet, bigger appetite. Normally, this sort of gluttony is self-limiting; beggars, once mounted, ride their horses to death. The new electronic mount was different, however. It kept getting stronger every year. Thus, the speed of the new computers gave new life to the age-old corpus of human-optimized formulations. Even today, most of what supercomputers do all day, like most of what high school mathematics departments teach all day, was originally published in Latin.

Electronic circuits, however, are very different beasts from the human minds for which these formulations were originally devised. The differences go way beyond simple speed. Electronic circuits can, for example, memorize amounts of information that to us are mind-boggling. A single equation as long as a book would be no problem. No human can retain such a sprawling formulation. Circuits can also keep vast amounts of intermediate data active and changing all at once. Psychological studies put the capacity of active human memory at about the size of one local phone number. Before we can go on to a new local phone number, we need either to forget the current one or consciously to impress it into our longer term memory. Human computers have always underscored the necessity of keeping just one piece of data active at a time:

The key to mental calculation lies in registering only one fact at a time, the strain in calculation being due to this work of registration.

Thus, in a complex multiplication he goes through a series of operations, the result in each operation being alone registered by the
memory, all the previous results being consecutively obliterated
until a total product is obtained.[10]

Von Neumann–architecture computers do the same thing, even
though the electronic circuitry itself is perfectly comfortable with billions and billions of intermediate values, all active and changing at
once. Electronics provides a naturally parallel computing environment. Human minds, at the level of conscious thought, provide a very
sequential environment.

It is ultimately even more significant that electronic circuits have a
delete key that works. No matter how much effort it has expended to
memorize information, an electronic memory can let go of it all in an
instant and start afresh. Human memory cannot. As poor as we are at
remembering, we are even worse at forgetting, a fact that has constrained the choices of scientists since sailing-ship days.

A proper formula, once adopted . . . ought not hastily be got rid of.
. . . it is a very mischievous innovation to disturb the technical memory of an old seaman, and to unsettle his familiar rules of computation. Every one, man of science or not, knows, from his own experience, the great value of fixed rules.[11]

We are all old sea dogs in this respect. We are very resistant to having our familiar rules unsettled. When faced with fundamental change,
we are like the wagon makers. We can feel its presence, but until we
delete some old prejudices, we cannot come to grips with it. To see
what is happening to thought today, we must be willing to peer
through new intellectual telescopes.

We must, for example, look past the myth that the mathematical
vocabularies in which scientific formulations and universal laws have
been written have somehow existed since the Creation, like buried
treasures waiting to be "discovered." If this view were reality, there
would be little relationship between the "discovery" of new maths and
the contemporaneous needs of the wider world. In fact, as many scientists have noted, there is a very strong correlation. In the ancient
Greek world, when the focus of science was on determining where
objects such as stars actually were, the dominant form of math was
geometry. Since the Renaissance, when the focus of mathematical science has been on the rate of change, or speed, of physical objects, the

dominant maths have been algebra and calculus. Isaac Newton established both the science of mechanics and the mathematics of calculus; they are fraternal twins. Today, the focus of science has shifted from the rates of change of physics to the patterns of biology. Not surprisingly, we are now seeing the rise of the new pattern-finding maths that are the subject of this book. Once again, mathematicians are inventing the maths that scientists need.

Meanwhile, just as we are tempted to see maths as eternal, we are equally tempted to see scientific theories as disposable, as tools that are used until they wear out, at which time they are discarded without a trace and replaced by fresh ones. In its extreme form of "gotcha and forgotcha," this myth is a caricature of the original notion of scientific paradigm promulgated by Thomas Kuhn.[12] In Kuhn's analysis, a shared set of assumptions, a *paradigm,* guides a field of inquiry until the weight of contradictory evidence becomes too great and science is forced to develop a replacement theory, which then becomes the organizing paradigm.

The possibility of such paradigm shifts has now motivated scientists to try actively to bring them about as rapidly as possible and to shorten the shelf life of truth. Toppling a current paradigm, a heady prospect, forms the "gotcha" phase. The "forgotcha" phase follows, with the belief that all influences of the toppled paradigm cease as soon as it is discredited. The previous paradigm can be safely ignored as soon as the new one is enshrined. Thus, for instance, the existence of the current paradigm of electronic computers supposedly makes it safe to forget—even deny the existence of—the previous age of human computers. In so doing, of course, we also forget that the designers of these electronic computers designed them explicitly as copies of human computers, making myriad unfortunate compromises as a result.

These two myths contribute to an overall belief that the process of understanding can go straight to a "bottom line" or a "punch line." In the numerocentric processes of the Industrial Age, it often could. If the bottom line is a scalar 5, it cannot matter whether it came about by starting with a 7 and subtracting a 2 or by starting with a 2 and adding a 3, or by having an unchanged 5 all along. The resulting 5 is the same in all three cases, so why clutter the mind with the preliminaries? For example, it used to take a human computer about twelve hours to step through the trajectory of an artillery shell and determine where it would land. Once the landing spot was determined, however, all those intermediate steps could be thrown away. Only the punch line itself needed to be kept.

Life, however, is different from the artillery shell trajectories for which the first ENIAC computer was designed. In life, history matters. Rather than being governed by unswerving universal law, its future path is conditional on the path by which matters arrived at their present state. If an artillery shell were, like Keynes's economic apple, unsure whether it was worth falling to the ground and confused about how far it was from the center of the earth to begin with, it would no longer be possible to cut to any bottom line. We would have to pay attention to the intermediate steps along the way.

Economists offer the extreme example of the traditional QWERTY typewriter key layout to illustrate how much history can matter.[13] The design is a rather low-caliber intellectual offering, an unlikely candidate to achieve permanent orbit. The original reason for its clumsiness was to slow down typists and thus reduce jam-ups. This rationale has long since faded and far better alternatives are now available, but QWERTY shows no signs of falling to the ground. It is not feasible to improve the layout a few keys at a time, and it has seemed too disruptive to change it entirely, as the Dvorak layout does.

More typically, new ideas can and do graft onto old ones, allowing novelty to enter incrementally. History influences the trajectory but does not totally dictate it. The way that a novel future is built up out of existing building blocks can be seen from two-word phrases such as "information highway" or "home page" or "iron horse" or "bit evolution." Often this interbreeding of past and future is deliberate:

> I had to go to Washington to try and explain to some folks from [the government agency] DARPA what our research was about. I needed a word that would convey to a bunch of people who understood FORTRAN programs that what we were doing was different. . . . I figured "inference engine" was in the right spirit.[14]

Because they are disciplines in which history matters, the social and biological sciences have reopened the old contest between the tangled webs of the country wagon makers and the step-by-step thought of the physical scientists. This time, however, the tangled webs win, for two reasons. First, they incorporate history and adaptation in ways that numbers and equations do not. Second, they are a close fit to the strengths and weaknesses of electronic circuits. This time the contest is not for the hearts and minds of human beings, as it was before. Now it is a contest for control of the future generations of electronic circuits that will be called on to predict economies and immune systems among many other mind tasks.

One of the reasons we find it hard to imagine computers having their own thought processes is that we have not gone back and looked afresh at the circumstances and pressures that led human thought to develop as it has. Those who are unaware of the sound bites of the past are doomed to rebreed them into their own thoughts over and over again. In the pages that follow, the still-potent voices of history are frequently quoted directly: They are the genetic material of our current habits of thought. There is no steering our whither without explicitly acknowledging our whence. History matters.

3

THE BOOK OF NATURE

The success of the traditional symbolic mathematical vocabularies at predicting Nature has always been a source of both delight and perplexity to scientists. Why this "unreasonable effectiveness of mathematics in the natural sciences"?[1] Was it one of God's gifts that could be taken away at any time? Did God have no choice, because the mathematical basis of the world was somehow bigger than God? Or did the truth lie somewhere in between?

When the number of successful mathematical formulations was few, it was possible to view them as happy coincidences. According to the rules of logic, a totally false premise may still lead to a true conclusion. Therefore, a totally fallacious formulation could still produce a valid prediction. Medieval theologians such as Saint Thomas Aquinas held that even the most successful formulation must be viewed as interim; a completely different one might come along to replace it at any time. For this reason, no conclusions about the world itself could be drawn from the methods that happened to be in current use for predicting its future history. God could change the ways of the world tomorrow and render all the predictions false.

God, however, did not seem to be so capricious. Over the centuries, the physical world continued to work as it always had. New predictive formulations were discovered that proved to be even more reliable than the earlier ones. By the time Charles Babbage began to build his Analytical Engine, it had come to be popular wisdom that Nature and even God were somehow "constrained" to operate within the very mathematical "laws" that scientists used to predict them. Babbage had no worries that God would change the rules of the game during the fifty years he spent building his machines, because, in his mind, "the minutest changes, as well as those transitions apparently the most abrupt, have throughout all time been the necessary, the inevitable consequences of some more comprehensive law impressed on matter at the dawn of its existence."[2]

Between these two extremes of total serendipity and total compulsion lies a more subtle position first articulated by Galileo. He imagined a "language" through which God declared the world. Because humankind was part of God's creation, we were also imbued with this language. Scientists were able to say sensible things about the world because they inherently spoke the language in which the world itself was expressed:

> Philosophy is written in that vast book which stands forever open before our eyes, I mean the Universe; but it cannot be read until we have learned the language and become familiar with the characters in which it is written. It is written in mathematical language, and the letters are triangles, circles, and other geometrical figures, without which means it is humanly impossible to comprehend a single word.[3]

Galileo's view allowed for surprises. God could alter Creation by, for example, acceding to Joshua's plea to hold the sun still. But whatever God did, scientists could potentially catch up to in their understanding, because the new reality would still be expressed in the old language. God was omnipotent, but not polyglot. God could change what was said in the world, but not the language in which it was said.

The idea of an inherent language introduced a coadaptivity between science and nature. Scientists asked a certain range of questions about the world and used a certain mathematical language in which to ask those questions. The world responded by being predictable in those particular ways, so that mathematical predictions formulated in that language often proved to be correct. The correctness of those predictions led scientists more and more to look at the world through the vocabulary of the language, thereby locking in the relationship even

further and making it harder to change any one of the supporting elements without replacing them all.

Science has already developed through two such eras and is now,
with the new preeminence of biology and the advent of the new evolutionary intermaths, entering its third. Each constitutes a separate
unit in the Book of Nature. Each such unit has its own particular set
of questions that scientists tend to ask. Each has its own mathematical
language, suited for posing those particular questions and formulating
the solutions. Each has its own set of technologies that support the use
of that language. Each also has its own immense influence on the wider
culture, reshaping our perceptions of heaven as well as earth.

A new unit opens either when scientists start to ask new questions
or when changes in technology make the old language untenable. It
happened in the Renaissance, and it is happening again now. Part One
of the Book of Nature, the one that Galileo knew, was focused on
answering questions of *place*. Scientists sought to predict the places of
the sun, moon, and stars as a necessary step in determining what their
own proper place in the universe was. For Arab scientists, there was
the particular need to know the place of Mecca relative to each new
place in the growing Moslem empire. Star by star and planet by planet,
the first scientists set out "to compute, by ways of observations and
calculations made with the utmost certainty that human diligence can
attain, what . . . [the heavenly object's] place was."[4]

As Galileo noted, the vocabulary used to write Part One was geometric. Questions about place are naturally framed in geometric terms.
The solutions that scientists came up with to bring place under their
own control were also geometric. They were the circles and lines of
Euclid extended out into the Heavens:

> *For of Meridians, and Parallels,*
> *Man hath weav'd out a net, and this net throwne*
> *Upon the Heavens, and now they are his owne.*[5]

Galileo saw himself as part of this tradition, carrying on a dialogue
with nature in its very own language of geometry. In fact, science, and
the mathematical language for expressing it, were both changing dramatically during his lifetime. Once indifferent to time, Europe had
finally obtained the technology with which to measure it. Scientists
were starting to ask new questions framed in terms of "speed." Part
Two of the Book of Nature changed the focus from *place* to *pace*.
Physics replaced astronomy as the central science. Today, computa-

tional scientists routinely predict the rate at which fuel will burn in various parts of an engine cylinder or the rate at which vortices will shed off a helicopter blade. They no longer do it, however, in Galileo's language of geometric figures. By the time of Isaac Newton, the behavior of the world was coming to be routinely expressed in numbers and equations. Even traditional geometric objects like the moon were being reinvented into the vocabulary of pace and number.

> *At last we learn wherefore the silver moon*
> *Once seemed to travel with unequal steps,*
> *As if she scorned to suit her pace to numbers—*
> *Till now made clear to no astronomer.*[6]

Soon the language of numbers and equations was as ubiquitous, and as mandatory, as the language of circles and diagrams had ever been: "In any scientific or technological field, such as astronomy, chemistry, engineering, physics, etc., the formulation of a natural law is regarded as completely precise and definitive only when it is expressed as a mathematical equation."[7] The new orthodoxy spread even beyond the physical sciences.

> Mainstream economists believe proper [theoretical] models—good models—take a recognizable form; presentation in equations. . . . While students are also presented with verbal and geometric masterpieces produced in bygone eras, they quickly learn that novices who want jobs should emulate their current teachers rather than deceased luminaries.[8]

The impact of this new unit, focused on pace instead of place, has been profound. The whole Industrial Age, with its "laws of Stress and Strain, and Combustion, and so on," is a product of the new mechanistic way of thinking, a way of thinking that overwrote the words of Galileo with those of Robert Boyle: "Mathematical and mechanical principles are the alphabet in which God wrote the world."[9]

Now, in the late twentieth century, the questions scientists ask are shifting again, this time from questions of *pace* to questions of *pattern*. As computer architect Seymour Cray has noted, this new focus on pattern also represents a move away from number: "Adding two and two together is no longer the issue: it's pattern recognition, pattern generation, and interpretation."[10] Computational scientists are focusing on pattern because they now want to save the appearances of immune systems, of economies, of politics, of ecologies, and of the mind. They recognize that "when you're talking about things like genes and genotypes and gene pools, you're talking about information . . . they're patterns."[11]

Biology and biological evolution are central subjects of this new Part Three of the Book of Nature. The fruits of cultural evolution are also prominent topics because they, too, create complicated patterns of behavior. Industrial Age technology, for example, interacts strongly with the environment, affecting, among many other things, the behavior of the earth's ozone layer. Information Age technology interacts strongly with the economy, affecting among other things the rate of new product innovation. As the late economist Kenneth Boulding pointed out in the early 1990s, such patterns are beyond the expressive reach of geometry or algebra.

> One of the great opportunities I think for the next few decades is the development of a mathematics which is suitable to social systems, which the sort of eighteenth-century mathematics which we mostly use is not. The world is topological rather than numerical. We need non-Cartesian algebra as we need non-Euclidean geometry, where minus minus is not always plus, and where the bottom line is often an illusion.[12]

Technology itself was critical in the transition from Part One to Part Two, and it is critical again today. For classical scientists, the vocabulary of rate of change, or pace, was out of reach because they had no clocks. Similarly, for Industrial Age scientists, the vocabulary of adaptation was out of reach because they had no electronic computers and few data to train on. The new adaptive maths presuppose massive amounts of computing power, far more than was available even fifty years ago, when all computers were still people.

More fundamentally, the new intermaths presuppose computers that are willing to change their minds over and over again, holding nothing constant. Human computers never could operate this way. Human minds seem to need something constant to hold on to.

> The mind of man doth wonderfully endeavor . . . that it may light upon something fixt and immoveable . . . which may, in some measure, moderate the fluctuations and wheelings of the understanding; fearing, it may be, the falling of their heaven.[13]

The whole evolution of mathematical vocabulary, from geometry through algebra and now into adaptive intermaths, reflects the slow, grudging relaxation of the human need for constancy. The Greek forms of astronomical prediction, like their ideals of Perfection itself, were particularly "fixt and immutable." Both the figures in their astronomical diagrams and the motions around their circular orbits—what today we would call their programs and their data, respectively—were fixed for each planet. Greek orbits never changed, and Greek planets never speeded up or slowed down. Then, during the Renaissance, as scientists gradually opened their minds to objects, including planets, that speeded up and slowed down, the old vocabulary died. The language of numbers and equations offered a much more natural, convenient, and concise way to incorporate ever-changing data values into the formulations. More than that, the use of variables allowed a single formulation to serve multiple situations. The Greeks had a separate diagram for each planet; Kepler and Newton offered single equations that sufficed for all. Formulations that used to be specific now became "universal," leading natural philosophers to believe that the world, and perhaps God as well, was governed by universal law. Data changed, but the programs remained steadfastly the same. This Renaissance-era view of the world is still wired into modern multiuser electronic computers at the hardware level. Such computers have two memory-address spaces. One is for program instructions (sometimes called *I-space*) and is shared by many users because, of course, instructions never change. The other (*D-space*) is for data, which is allowed to be different for each user.

The success of Newton's *Principia Mathematica* focused scientists on behaviors that could be successfully predicted within the constraints of fixed formulations. Newton himself was a prime example. Having retreated to the countryside during the plague years, he developed the whole framework of the calculus that is still in use today. It was then, for example, that he invented the techniques of infinite series by which, he admitted sheepishly, he computed logarithms to more than sixty digits. So great was his achievement that it may be churlish to note that he could have stayed in town instead and worked to understand the plague. Had he done so, he would have encountered phenomena that do not lend themselves so readily to description by invariant formulation. Immunity to plague, for example, changes from time to time and from place to place. While Europeans were being exposed to one disease in Newton's time, they were spreading another to native Americans. Over time, both behaviors changed. Immune systems in both populations ultimately changed and adapted, but in ways that no fixed equation has ever described.

Evolution and adaptation present a world where more than just the data parameters change. Program formulations themselves must be pliable. Numbers and equations, unfortunately, cannot be gracefully changed because they are too compacted. The very brevity that makes them so popular with human minds makes equations brittle and hard to evolve. Changing a single "+" to a "–" or a "√" turns an equation into something radically different, and probably something false. As the biologist and evolutionary theorist Stuart Kauffman has pointed out, "the more compact [a formulation] becomes, the more violently [it] changes at each minimal alteration."[14] Equations are not a good language for expressing behaviors that adapt the way immune systems do.

The electronic computers of today, meanwhile, care not a jot about the wonderful compactness and fixity of algebra. They store all their information as bits. They can remember, and change, a thousand-page formulation as easily as a phone number. These vast sprawling formulations may then be adapted and changed in tiny, but persistent, ways. A whole new set of such sprawling maths is now being created. Collectively called *evolutionary maths* or *intermaths* or *emergent behavior maths* or *net maths,* they *presuppose the electronic computing milieu.* They take full advantage both of the elbow room and the erasability of modern computer storage as they do their work. Each tiny piece of an intermath formulation may be meaningless by itself, but the changing aggregation of millions of them interacting in parallel is proving able to save the appearances of phenomena heretofore unserved by numbers and equations:

> The premise of emergent computation is that interesting and useful computational systems can be constructed by exploiting interactions among primitive components, and further, that for some kinds of problems (e.g., modeling intelligent behavior) it may be the only feasible method. . . . Emergent computation is potentially relevant to several areas, including adaptive systems, parallel processing, and cognitive and biological modeling.[15]

These new intermaths have still-unfamiliar names like *neural networks, genetic algorithms, simulated annealing, artificial life,* and *cellular automata.* Pioneered by the computer scientist John Holland in the

1960s and 1970s, they blossomed with the advent of parallel computers in the 1980s. Like the community of wagon makers, these techniques use myriad tiny individual operators all of which can be active
and all of which can be evolving themselves, simultaneously, in parallel. Freed of the size and frequency-of-update constraints of the
human mind, this new form of computing puts no premium on either
compression or invariance. Every piece of data, and every possible
point of view about the data, is potentially valuable, and potentially
disposable, in its own right. These differing aesthetics can be seen in
the observations of two professors at French universities, Pierre-
Simon Laplace and Albert Tarantola, writing almost two centuries
apart:

An Intellect who at any given
instant knew all the forces that
animate nature and the mutual
position of the beings who compose it, were this Intellect but vast
enough to submit his data to
analysis, could condense into a
single formula the movement of
the greatest body in the universe
and that of the lightest atom; to
such an Intellect nothing would
be uncertain, for the future, even
as the past, would be ever before
his eyes.[16]

As soon as you write an equation,
it is wrong, because reducing a
complex reality to an equation is
just too simplistic a view of things.
Large parallel computers, with
large amounts of memory, may
allow us to develop an entirely
new sort of physics where, instead
of reducing the facts to equations,
we can just store in the computer
the facts. Then we can extrapolate
and we can predict. That's what
physics is about: extrapolating
and predicting.[17]

In the simplest cases, the data are just fed in and delivered back out,
as Tarantola has envisioned. More typically, new data-driven and adaptive formulations will go to work on this trove of bit-level data, evolving their own patterns and predictions and inexorably improving their
own performance over time.

These intermath formulations, formulations that change themselves
as they compute, mark the opening of Part Three of the Book of
Nature. They increase our ability to grasp the world and extend that
ability beyond the limits of the traditional exact sciences. In so doing,
however, they take over central roles that used to belong to human
thought alone. They create their own programs. With emergent computations, expressed in the new intermath vocabularies, there is no
direct way for the human mind to understand where the answer came

from, because the formulation itself is constantly changing along the way. Like a Jackson Pollock drip painting, the formulation does not know exactly where it is going until it gets there: "He didn't know where he would end up when he started. . . . Pollock allowed the form to emerge out of the materials and out of the process. For me, as a student, this idea of allowing the form to emerge out of the process was incredibly important."[18] An emergent formulation is also parallel. Like the street scenes described by the urban sociologist Jane Jacobs, an emergent formulation depends on many component parts all interacting at once.

> Under the seeming disorder of the old city, wherever the old city is working successfully, is a marvelous order for maintaining the safety of the streets and the freedom of the city. It is a complex order. Its essence is intricacy of sidewalk use, bringing with it a constant succession of eyes. This order is all composed of movement and change, and although it is life, not art, we may fancifully call it the art form of the city and liken it to the dance—not to a simple-minded precision dance with everyone kicking up at the same time, twirling in unison and bowing off en masse, but to an intricate ballet in which the individual dancers and ensembles all have distinctive parts which miraculously reinforce each other and compose an orderly whole. The ballet of the good city sidewalk never repeats itself from place to place, and in any one place is always replete with new improvisations.[19]

The similarity between how emergent computations work and how living processes work is, of course, not serendipitous. Geometry was effective because it worked in ways that were analogous to the positioning of the stars it was asked to predict. Algebra and calculus have been effective because they work in ways analogous to the rates of change of the motions they are asked to predict. Intermaths are effective because they work in ways analogous to the adaptivity of the biological and social behavior they are asked to predict. In fact, there will be no Part Three of the Book of Nature in a literal sense. The inert pages of a traditional book will be superseded by the vast memory banks of a Tarantola-style network of computers. Because the formulations inside will be incomprehensible to humans anyway and will be changing all the time, there will be no point in printing them out for inspection. Unable to read the details of Part Three as we could of earlier chapters, we will simply work with the outputs and decide whether or not to trust them on the basis of how accurate previous outputs turned out to be.

Inevitably, it will take time for such startling new techniques to enter the mainstream. Algebra, too, was once an obscure and faintly disreputable technique, referred to ignominiously as the *ars rei,* or "art of the thing." The Renaissance astronomer Johannes Kepler found it "gauche"; Galileo ignored it. There were important problems even within early astronomy, however, that could not be solved in diagrams but *could* be solved with the art of the thing. Thus, the author of the astronomical tables carried by Christopher Columbus interrupted his otherwise orthodox geometric discussion of triangles to draw on the new way:

> This problem has to this day admitted no solution in the geometric way, but we will try to achieve it through the art of the thing and its power[20] [what René Descartes would later refer to as] a certain kind of arithmetic called algebra, which performs with numbers that which the ancients did with figures.[21]

Today, the orthodoxy of numbers and equations is at least as strong as the orthodoxy of circles and diagrams was in Columbus's time. But once again there are problems, even in the classical domains of forces and mutual attractions, that cannot be computed with the orthodox approaches but can with the art of the tangled web. For example, drug designers need to predict how a string of molecules will curl up into a protein. Traditional algebraic techniques can require years of computer time. Thus, a contemporary team of biologists interrupt their otherwise orthodox paper on one of the molecules of blood to draw on the new way:

> We present a method for determining the tertiary structure of α-proteins through computer simulation. . . . The optimization consists of a Monte Carlo simulated annealing procedure combined with a genetic algorithm.[22]

This change in mathematical vocabulary, just like the one that occurred in the Renaissance, matters to all of us, because the description inexorably becomes the reality. Perhaps it should not, but it does. When, for example, a high school class uses a computer to generate predictive movies of an upcoming impact of a comet into Jupiter, the students should not care whether that behavior is computed by means of the geometry of the ancient Greeks or the numbers and equations of Isaac Newton or even by genetic recombination. Indeed, Plato insisted that this should be the case. The methods were to be considered purely fictional. Throughout history, other scientists have held this same view:

> The question whether atoms exist or not has little significance in a chemical point of view: its discussion rather belongs to metaphysics. In chemistry we have only to decide whether the assumption of atoms is an hypothesis adapted to the explanation of chemical phenomena. . . . I have no hesitation in saying that, from a philosophical point of view, I do not believe in the actual existence of atoms. . . . We may, in fact, adopt the view of Dumas and Faraday, "that whether matter be atomic or not, this much is certain, that, granting it to be atomic, it would appear as it now does."[23]

In fact, the cultural impact of the change to new evolutionary maths will be vast, just as the cultural impact of the new method of prediction of the Renaissance was vast. As humans, we simply cannot maintain the levels of detachment demanded by Plato. If a formulation saves the appearances, we feel that there must be something more to it. *The vocabulary of the mathematical fiction inexorably becomes the vocabulary with which we describe the reality.* This is the reason that a change from sequential equations to parallel matings and breedings is so seminal. It affects all of us, not just scientists. It will literally change heaven and earth because it will change the way we conceive of them.

It was, for example, precisely this kind of intellectual–computational transition that brought Galileo into conflict with the Renaissance Church. When the conflict arose, the Church demanded merely that he restrict himself to saying that the world operated "as if" the earth moved, that the moving earth was just a Copernican contrivance to make the computations easier:

> To say that by assuming the earth in motion and the sun immobile one saves all the appearances better than the eccentrics and epicycles ever could is to speak well indeed. This holds no danger and it suffices for the mathematician.[24]

Galileo felt compelled to go the fateful step further, however, and murmur that "nevertheless, it does move." He could not accept that a scheme that worked so well was just a fiction: "Just so should it be granted that a system that agrees very closely with appearances may be true."[25] In more colloquial language:

> *His notions fitted things so well,*
> *That which was which he could not tell.*[26]

Galileo wanted to let the computational fiction become the scientific reality. Conversely, Albert Einstein sought to keep the success of randomized "Monte Carlo" computing techniques from leaking over into his overall worldview. He did not want to believe that God might play dice. Other scientists have tended to the view that if computers got the right answer using random chance, then God was somehow constrained to doing the same.

Einstein notwithstanding, Monte Carlo techniques have become a staple of modern computer prediction. They were the very first mathematical children of electronic computing, being methods that no persons in their right mind would try to carry out by hand. More interesting than random numbers, however, are the computational potentials of entities like neurons and chromosomes. Clearly, these mechanisms have accomplished much over time. Large arrays of neurons, for example, are able to recognize patterns in ways that no geometric or algebraic formulations can. Unfortunately, it can take them years to learn how. The same is true of the genetic recombination of chromosomes. Wondrous results have emerged, but over millions of years. Neither were viable candidates for computing before computing became electronic. Now, more and more scientists are heeding the advice of the physicist Stanislaw Ulam: "Ask not what mathematics can do for biology. Ask what biology can do for mathematics."[27]

In the abstract, nobody is likely to quarrel with Ulam. The reality, however, is new enough and different enough to be scary. René Descartes encountered the same kinds of entrenched resistance as he promoted the use of numbers and equations instead of the incumbent circles and lines of geometry. Not the least of the sins of a new equational view was that "it turns away the young from the study of the old and true Philosophy. . . . An imprudent youth can deduce from it certain opinions which are opposed to the other disciplines and faculties and above all the orthodox Theology."[28]

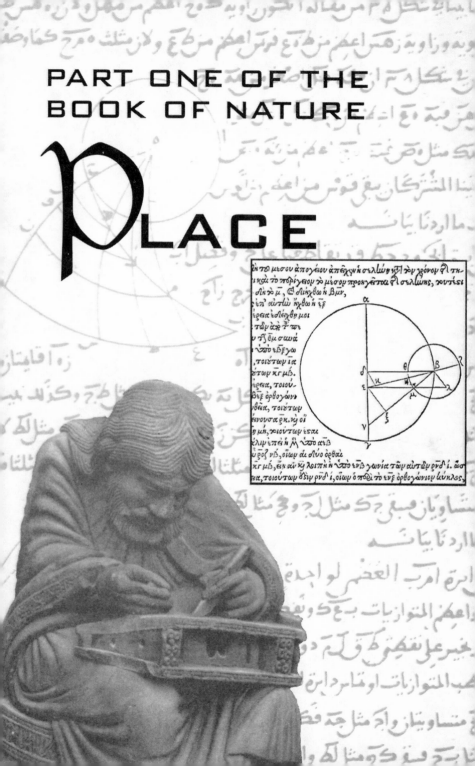

PART ONE OF THE BOOK OF NATURE

PLACE

4

THE FIRST FICTION

Most students learn that Archimedes, in trying to explain the principle of leverage, said, "Give me a place to stand and I will move the earth." Earlier Greeks, faced with the more basic question of where the earth actually was, might equally well have said, "Give me a reliable reference point and I will locate everything in the universe." The reason the Greeks were successful in mathematically orienting themselves in their universe, but not in physically moving the earth, was that the reference point did not have to be real to be effective. It was enough to create a fictional reference. As Friedrich Nietzsche noted more than two thousand years later, we can *compute* our way forward once we have that starting point:

> No more fiction for us: we calculate; but that we may calculate, we had to make fiction first.[1]

Inventing a new fiction is hard, which is why we often recycle old ones, as computer scientists are now doing with the Internet. They have borrowed the ancient fiction of *place* to help themselves and potential users to feel more oriented. Internet providers use pixels to draw elaborate virtual shopping malls where data is accessed with tools called *navigators*. The entire entity is called *cyberspace.*

The ancient Greeks were initially just as disoriented as they looked up into the sky at night. They had to start from scratch however. First, they had to invent the concept of *place,* itself. Then, they had to develop a set of mathematical fictions with which to define and under-stand it. Finally, to move forward and test their ideas, they had to invent the whole predictive art of computing. As the computer scien-tist David Cooper has observed, "We have to go back at least to Euclid for the concept of a stored program—for what else is his various con-structions for performing given tasks using only a pair of compasses and a straight edge?"[2]

It was not possible to determine the places of the individual stars using direct observation. The sky is too big, and the stars do not stand still. The Greek achievement lay first in establishing reliable refer-ences—the meridians and parallels—in the immensity and then in cre-ating a geometric vocabulary for describing how far and in what direc-tion everything lay from these reference points. Today, the predictions of the paths of heavenly objects such as comets—Will one smash into the earth?—still require extensive amounts of supercomputer time, even though our scientists start with accurate knowledge about the places of the fixed stars already in hand. The Greeks had a much harder problem: determining the places of the sun and moon without first knowing the places of the stars.

The Greeks believed in an orderly universe, a "cosmos," and used that belief as a central ingredient in their notion of place. When they looked up in the sky, they did not see a random scattering of stars all shining in parallel. In accordance with Aristotle, they saw "the ordered system of the heavens and the march of the stars and the sun and the moon. . . . Even all the unexpected changes which occur in it are really accomplished in an ordered sequence."[3] The audacious Greek solu-tion to their inability to understand the heavens by sight alone was to create a fictitious, well-behaved, computational sun and moon and use them, rather than the visible sun and moon, to determine the places of the stars. Such fictitious worlds could take the form of an actual mechanical solar system, as Virgil described:

> When Jove looked down and saw the heavens figured in a sphere of glass he laughed and said to the other gods: "Has the power of mor-tal effort gone so far? Is my handiwork now mimicked in a fragile globe? . . . Here the feeble hand of man has proved Nature's rival."[4]

More typically, the Greek models of the universe were purely abstract, existing only as geometric diagrams on sheets of papyrus and parchment. From those pages, the astronomers could learn the places of the sun and the moon far more accurately than by looking up into the sky or using mechanical models. However, to have a computational sun to work with, they first had to define the following:

- A vocabulary in which to formulate and express the synthetic behavior of this synthetic, computational, sun.
- A resource within which to carry out the manipulations that would move the synthetic sun accurately on its appointed rounds.
- A fiction about how the computational sun and moon were to behave.

For their grammar, the Greeks needed to choose between geometry and arithmetic. They chose the language of geometry even though the school of Pythagoras had kept alive the philosophy that the universe was somehow constituted of number and hence, perhaps, could be manipulated arithmetically. The Greeks, however, never became power users of numbers. Their use was akin to that of the sports page scores: no negatives and rare fractions. Geometry, on the other hand, was used with confident abandon. Initially, the Greeks even recorded the results of their computations as geometric angles. Only gradually did they become comfortable expressing angles as numerical ratios to the angle of a full circle. Thus, the size of the full moon was expressed as 1/180th of the whole circle, where today we would just say two degrees or, more accurately, half a degree. This practice of measuring or enumerating only relative to something else was already being experimented with in Homer's time:

> *if both sides were to be willing, Achaians and Trojans,*
> *to cut faithful oaths of truce, and both to be numbered,*
> *and the Trojans were to be counted by those with homes in the*
>   *city,*
> *while we were to be allotted in tens, we Achaians,*
> *and each of our tens chose a man of Troy to pour wine for it,*
> *still there would be many tens left without a wine steward.*
> *By so much I [Agamemnon] claim we sons of the Achaians*
>   *outnumber*
> *the Trojans.[5]*

The adoption of numerical ratios to record results was fortuitous for us. The figure of an angle is impossible to record and replicate with accuracy. If books of astronomy had contained only drawings of the observed angles of the star positions, the process of copying these diagrams would have forfeited accuracy almost as soon as it was gained.

The second choice, the selection of a resource with which to carry out the formulations, was easy. People were the only resource available. To complete the method, the Greeks needed only to solve the third problem: defining a fiction with which to describe the apparent motion of their computational sun and moon. The fiction they chose was that the irregular motions were actually regular ones with a super-imposed adjustment factor, which they called an "additosubtraction." This two-component strategy was a direct reflection of the two-level way they viewed their world as a whole: an apparent maelstrom but containing a deeper level of constancy, or "order." To the extent that this strategy seems self-evident, it is because it is still widely used today even though our view of the world has fundamentally changed since Greek times. When the Greeks used additosubtraction correction factors, the accepted wisdom was that reality itself was ordered and regular. The irregularities were not part of the essence. They were artifacts of the way that viewers were looking at the world. Only the regular, ordered behavior actually existed.

This adjustments-to-an-unchanging-core computing strategy worked well because the constant component of the motion in fact dominated. The additosubtractions were quite small, especially for the sun, which is where the Greek process of computing the places of the universe began.

Two classical diagrams, illustrated in figure 4.1, lay at the heart of Greek astronomy. Both formulations directly express a constant core modified by a correction factor. The eccentric formulation assumed that we, on earth, were viewing the motion of the sun from a position slightly removed from the actual center of its circular orbit. Observers were like the operator of a carousel, who stands inside all the circling horses but not quite in the middle. An operator who took the trouble to mark out four right angles against the background would find that an individual horse moved through some of these right angles more expeditiously than others. Exact observations and skilled geometry would allow the off-center, or "eccentric," position of the operator to be worked out. Thus, the standard eccentric diagram showed two circles of equal size, one centered on the earth, and the other centered on the true center of the sun's orbit. Observers on the earth experienced the sun as if it were moving irregularly on one circle, but according to their worldview, it was in fact moving regularly on the other. From the diagram, astronomers computed and recorded the size of the angle between the place where the sun appeared to be on one circle and

harum ſtellarum latitudines, quod fieri non poteſt, niſi etiam orbes illorum in obliquitate ſua librētur. Sed ut antea diximus in his quæ librantur, oportet medium quoddam extremorum

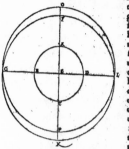

accipere. Quæ ut aper‑ tiora fiant, Sit orbis ma gnus, qui in plano ſigni feri A B C D, centrum ha‑ bens B, ad quem incli‑ nus ſit orbis planetæ, q̃ ſit F G K L, mediæ ac per‑ manentis declinationis, cuius limes latitudinis Boreus F, Auſtrinus K, deſcendens ſectionis no dus G, aſcēdens L, Sectio cōmunis B E D, quæ exte datur in rectas lineas G B, D L. Qui quidem qua‑ tuor termini non muten tur, niſi ad motum abſi‑

dum. Intelligatur autem, quòd motus ſtellæ longitudinis non feratur ſub plano ipſius F G circuli, ſed ſub alio quodā obliquo

um F G, in quo terra uertetur, omniaĩ̃ in eodem plano zodiaci.

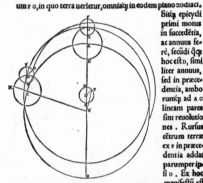

Sitĩ epicycli primi motus in ſuccedētia, ac annuus fe‑ rè, ſecūdi q̃q̃ hoc eſt D, ſimi liter annuus, ſed in præce‑ dentia, ambo rumĩ̃ ad A C lineam pares ſint reuolutio nes. Rurſus cētrum terræ ex F in præce‑ dentia addat, parumper ipſ ſi D. Ex hoc manifeſtū eſt

quòd cum terra fuerit in F, maximum efficiet Solis apogeum, in G minimum: in medijs autem circumferentijs ipſius F G epi‑

Figure 4.1. The scientific thought processes of the ancient Greeks were expressed in circles and lines instead of the numbers and equations we use in our maths today. Their understanding of the peculiar behavior of the planets, for example, was summarized in two classic diagrams. The eccen‑ tric diagram, on the left, sets the circular orbits of the planets slightly off‑ center from the view point. The epicyclic diagram, on the right, places the planets recursively on circles that themselves revolve on circles. Fifteen hundred years later, these two basic formulations retained all the expressive power needed to support Nicholas Copernicus's great work, *de Revolutionibus*. When it was published in 1543, however, printing was already well established. Diagrams like Copernicus's, so welcome in the scriptorium, were anathema to the composing room. Geometric maths were already being replaced by algebraic maths that could both express rates of change and be typeset. Diagrams from the first edition of *de Revolutionibus* courtesy of the Boston Athenaeum.

where it truly was on the other. These angles, computed for each day of the year, were the additosubtractions for the sun.

Once the place of the sun had been determined, this information was used to determine the place of the moon. (To eliminate distortion, the determination was done only at the rare moment of a lunar eclipse, when each of the two bodies was known to be exactly half of a full circle—180 degrees—away from the other.) Because the moon's behavior was more complicated than the sun's, the second diagram, the one using epicycles, was generally used for the moon. In the epicyclic formulation, the object was assumed to be on a small circle that moved on a larger one. The motion around the larger circle was the constant component. The motion around the smaller circle was the additosubtractive correction factor. Later, Greek astronomers added further refinements to the epicyclic diagram and with them a second table of additosubtractions.

Only after the behavior of the synthetic moon had been formulated in an epicycle and its places computed and tabulated could this moon be used as the reference point by which to determine the places of individual stars. Such was exactly the procedure recorded in classical astronomy texts. First, the fictional sun and moon were used as more tractable substitutes for the visible sun and moon to determine the places of key reference stars. Only then could these stars be used to help work out the places of the planets and ultimately to make predictions about future events such as solar eclipses.

We no longer believe that the irregularities of the world are illusions caused only by how we look at things. We now believe that the irregularities are real, but scientists still use a numerical version of the additosubtractive computing strategy. This strategy had a direct role in the design goals of the first electronic computers in the 1940s, which were invented to solve the problem of aiming artillery guns. The approach involved first producing a table of average values, which represented the behavior of an artillery shell in the absence of any interfering parameters. These core values were then followed by a series of correction tables, the additosubtractions, which accounted for factors such as wind and elevation. The tables produced by these electronic computers, although generated by means of numbers and equations rather than circles and lines, are indistinguishable in structure from those produced by astronomers in Greek and Roman times.

The reason the additosubtractive strategy worked for ballistics was that the corrections, like those for the sun and the moon, were comparatively small. The method is also still in use, however, in situations in which the additosubtractive element actually wags the supposedly constant dog, as it does in many weather computations, for which the average (mean) is known as the "general circulation":

> Before the equations can be used, the mean values must be precisely defined. If the earth wore the mean motion, called *the general circulation,* as a recognizable garment, with a sort of embroidery of turbulence or lumpiness, then all would be well; but as more and more observations became available the embroidery grew until now it seems that the weather over most of the earth consists mainly of embroidery and the main garment of the general circulation, if it exists, is completely obscured over vast areas, of which the North Atlantic ocean and Europe form one.[6]

The original fiction has been turned inside out. The additosubtractions are now the reality. The unchanging mean only exists because of how we look at the problem and our human need to "light upon something fixt and immoveable . . . fearing, it may be, the falling of [our] heaven."[7] One of the key differences between the new intermaths and the traditional geometric and equational ones is that the new adaptive approaches dispense with the need for the constant core that was introduced into computing by the Greeks. Emergent methods allow the formulation itself to change, without fear that heaven will fall as a result. They do not require that nature come clothed in a mean or an equilibrium.

Inconstancy has always encountered resistance within the classical mind. Even at the very end of the Middle Ages, the Polish astronomer Nicholas Copernicus was rejecting the possibility of planets that moved faster in some parts of their orbits and slower in others. "The mind shudders," he said of an explanation that served only "to unhinge the understanding."[8] Keeping the understanding securely on its hinges, Copernicus made one last, glorious use of pure geometry in his book *The Revolutions.* He died the day it returned from the printer, and with him the era of creative geometric computing died, too. Inside the book, however, were two lasting bombshells.

The first bombshell was the interchanging of the earth and sun in Copernicus's diagrams. The swap saved the appearances with fewer epicycles, but it moved the earth off the center stage of the universe, and humankind along with it. The resulting controversy has overshadowed the second bombshell, whose impact was also immense. By also asserting in *The Revolutions* that his new fictions were not fictions at all (he claimed that they were *true*), Copernicus began to give a new centrality to thought. Admittedly, other astronomers had been using tables and direct observations interchangeably. Thus, the Austrian astronomer Johannes Kepler cheerfully acknowledged that instead of making new observations, he was using a colleague's tables of Mars "to be my eyes."[9] Copernicus, however, was not talking only about tables of results. He was talking about the circles-on-circles fictions themselves. In the words of his student: "The hypotheses of my learned teacher correspond so well to the phenomena that they may be mutually interchanged, like a good definition with the thing defined."[10]

Plato's dictum that computations spoke only to appearances, not realities, had in fact been a boon to the early practitioners. It gave them the freedom to innovate, grow, and mature. Within a few constraints, which they tended to agree with anyway, they could try out all manner of weird formulations, justifying them not on their merits but simply on the results they produced. The result was a thousand-year dual track for science. On one track was astronomy and on the other track everything else, including physics, biology, and medicine. On the astronomy track, there was an ever-increasing reliance on computation and prediction. On the other track, there was no computing at all. On the astronomy track were a few dedicated astronomers; on the other track were arrayed all the Aristotelians and, with the coming of Christianity, all the clerics as well. Confident in their monopoly on truth, these Scholastics humored the astronomers and even dipped into their fictional wares as needed to carry out their own roles as teachers. Peaceful coexistence prevailed.

> The assumption of such eccentrics and epicycles is sufficient for the astronomer qua astronomer because as such he need not trouble himself with the reason why. . . . That investigation concerns the physicist.[11]

> What could be more useful for research, better suited to teaching . . . ? But in the sky there are no such lines and intersections. They have been thought up by extraordinarily ingenious men with a view to teaching and demonstration.[12]

Copernicus broke this truce at a very nervous time. Martin Luther's Protestant challenge to Rome was spreading throughout Germany. For a while, the Catholic tradition of openness to scientific speculation held; it was Luther who first denounced Copernicus's theory as blasphemy. By Galileo's later years, however, the Catholic Counter-Reformation, the militant Society of Jesus, and the establishment of the Inquisition added up to a much less tolerant environment:

> The churches lost their nerve. . . . Throughout the early and medieval times [ongoing] faithfulness was achieved by a dynamic process of rethinking the past in the light of current experience and of the best knowledge available. On the whole, the most creative minds were the leading thinkers of the church. They did not experience the Christian faith as any more restrictive of their freedom to think honestly and openly than scientists today feel restricted by the methods and expectations of the scientific community.[13]

The issues about the relationship between computing and truth first raised by Copernicus and Galileo remain unresolved today. The new technology of scientific visualization is making the question even more compelling. No matter how precisely Copernicus's tables saved the appearances of the heavens, they were still quite clearly tables of numbers and not of stars and planets. With modern high-resolution display screens, even the visual distinction between natural result and computed result blurs. For objects like molecules, the version on the display screen is the only version humans have ever seen. If seeing is believing, the rendition chosen by the visualizer becomes "true" by default. With the advent of virtual reality, the question of computing as truth is heating up anew.

Although Copernicus's book was not banned outright at the time of Galileo's trial, changes into the subjunctive were mandated. Thus, phrases like "hence I feel no shame in asserting," had to be changed to "assuming." (Galileo made the changes to his copy himself in longhand.) Faced with an uncertain market, the book itself went out of print for two hundred years. By the time the next edition came out, it was a book for the historian, not the practicing scientist. The whole world of science—and computing—had been completely reinvented by a wave of new technology.

Not until the twentieth century would the world of computing experience a similar convergence of new hardware and software technologies. This first convergence came together initially in the small region of southern Germany around medieval Nürnberg and Augsburg. Home to skilled mechanics, the towns were already producing some of the best astronomical instruments available in Europe. An exceptionally promising young scientist growing up in the region, Johannes Müller had access to instruction in astronomy unavailable in most parts of Europe. Müller continued his training in Italy and acquired the Latin name Regiomontanus, by which he appears in the history books. Returning to Nürnberg, he produced, among other works, the astronomical almanac used by his contemporary Christopher Columbus on the first voyage to America. He also found himself at the center of three new technologies: two hardware and one software.

The first of the new hardware technologies was the printing press. Regiomontanus was one of the first to participate in the new printing and publishing industry, deciding "to practice the wonderful art of making printing type for making lasting records, and may God prosper it."[14] Using the new technology, the citizens of Nürnberg hoped to leverage their intellectual assets into a thriving knowledge industry:

> There have always been men in our city devoted to the mathematical sciences. . . . And thus since goods are exported from here to nearly the entire world, what also prevents the writings of the most learned men preserved by the most excellent men from being published from here to the entire world?[15]

Had Regiomontanus not died prematurely, he would have witnessed a second major hardware transition in the region: the fabrication of mechanical clocks. These new clocks did more than just "tell time." They changed the working definition of what time was and how it entered into thought. In the ancient world, two very different definitions of time competed. To Aristotle, time was the measure of the motion of the heavens: *numeros moti,* or "the number of motion." Plato, meanwhile, suggested that time was the motion of the heavens—*motus caeli*—itself. The first definition was numerical, the second geometric. Since Newton, we have taken it for granted that time is something independent of motion, and we always express it by means of numbers. The geometric meaning of time, however, survives in everyday language. Questions about time are still phrased in terms of "how long" rather than "how much." A "great time" is still something very different from a "long time" or a "short time."

It was the geometric definition that the astronomers used: "What is time? Time is the slow movement of the celestial bodies."[16] It was unthinkable that the heavens go faster or slower, because they were the definitions of time as well as of motion. The two competing conceptions of time, one geometric and the other numerical, manifested themselves explicitly in the forerunners to the mechanical clock. The most famous of these early devices, known as the di Dondi clock after its designer, was a miniature version of the heavens themselves. All the major motions of the planets were carried out in obsessive detail. The planets moved on physical epicycles, expressed as trains of gears. What makes this device so jarring to the modern sensibility is that such clocks were "only very incidentally time-telling devices. . . . What was important was the enormously elaborate gear-work of the many dials to display all the motions of the stars and planets and the course of the calendar."[17]

The time-telling devices that later came to be made in Nürnberg and Augsburg, and soon throughout Europe, were full-fledged versions with the focus increasingly on the hands and dials that "tell time" in the modern numerical sense. Using these new tools, scientists could access concepts like "velocity" for the first time. Mechanical suns and moons and planets, the tellers of geometric time in the original sense, gradually receded into a purely decorative role. Regiomontanus missed this emergence of a new form of clock and with it a new role and meaning for time in computation. He did not, however, miss the new software technology of the period. He was at the very forefront of it.

While Regiomontanus was a young man working as the royal librarian in Budapest, Constantinople fell to the Turks. Large numbers of Greek scholars made their way west, carrying ancient manuscripts, some unknown in Christian Europe at the time. Regiomontanus, in Hungary, was the first to intercept and study this new wave of software. Among the works was a book about arithmetic by Diophantus, unique among Greek works for its focus on numerical manipulations rather than geometric ones. Today, this book is best known as the one in which Fermat wrote the marginal reference to his Last Theorem. It was, however, also the vehicle by which the ideas of "algebra," including the concept of an "unknown," entered Christian Europe.

As is clear from the purely geometric work of Copernicus half a century later, the impact of the new algebraic technology was not immediate. It was integrated in halting and tentative steps. For example, at the time Regiomontanus was absorbing Diophantus, he was preparing his own treatise on triangles. Twice in this book, he departed from geometric orthodoxy. In an almost apologetic manner, he made Europe's first use of *ars rei*, or art of the thing, to do what he could not do with geometry.

In so doing, Regiomontanus flouted Aristotle's dictum that arithmetic could never be used to demonstrate things geometric, or vice versa. It would take another hundred years, however, for this barrier to crumble completely in the minds of European scientists. The technology of printing helped tip the balance. It had already, in fact, brought the reprinting of mathematical works to a dead halt. Decades after the invention of the printing press, there were still none in print. The publisher of the first one, an edition of Euclid, explained why in his introduction to that work:

> I was puzzled why the enormous output of the printers of Venice has included so few of the mathematical works of the ancient masters. I have discovered the reason: the extreme difficulty of including the diagrams without which the most significant works are incomprehensible. I committed myself to the labors of binding text elements and geometric figures together in the press.[18]

In the manuscript era, when it could take a year to copy a text file the size of the Bible, diagrams were a boon. A circle was made as quickly as a single letter "o" and in exactly the same way. If a diagram saved a thousand words, it was a wonderful economy. With the changeover to printing, diagrams became an expensive burden. They had to be specially carved out of wood and carefully fitted into the type. The thin lines of geometry were particularly ill-suited to woodcuts, because everything but the line had to be cut away. No longer could astronomers casually flip back and forth between their word-processing environment and their draw environment. Even textbook editions of Euclid's *Elements* of geometry came to be published without full sets of diagrams in order to make them cheap enough for students to buy. As the diagrams were suppressed, the formulations themselves became incomprehensible. The coming of the printing press "canonized the primacy of text over pictures."[19]

Numbers and equations, meanwhile, rode the tide of the new economies of print. Perhaps they also changed the relationship of computers and mathematicians to the symbols they worked with. Until the time of Regiomontanus, numbers and letters had been distinct markings on a page. Was it harder, perchance, to conceptualize using one such ink marking to stand for the other as the techniques of algebra require? When numbers and letters became individual slugs of type, physically interchangeable in the hand, did it become mentally easier to conceive of substituting one for the other in the sense of the modern algebraic variable?

Such speculations are relevant today because the medium of scientific communications is changing again, for the first time since the Renaissance. It has shifted from typewriters and printing presses to pixels and laser printers. The classical balance between the cost of text and the cost of diagrams has been restored. An integrated Postscript® word-processing and drawing program, like a medieval monk, creates a circle on a piece of paper or a display screen in exactly the same way as it creates a letter *o*. Maths that make heavy use of noncharacter elements are economically viable again in ways that they have not been for five hundred years. It is far easier, as Langer has emphasized, to communicate parallel ideas with a draw program than it is with a word-processing program. Traditional algebra, which uses only one relation at a time, is easily projected into discursive form. Adaptive intermaths, which involve myriad simultaneous relations, are not. They require the expressive capabilities of the draw program.

The potential influence of these changes in technology is immense. It was only during the five hundred years of the printing press that we came to believe that numbers were the way to express both times and computations. Imagine that, a hundred years from now, the Smithsonian Museum's replica of the fourteenth-century di Dondi clock is displayed next to its twentieth-century Cray™ supercomputer. Will visitors view them both in the same bemused way? Will they wonder why nine-tenths of the Cray's circuitry is taken up with manipulations of obscure objects known as "floating point numbers" just as nine-tenths of the clock's mechanisms are taken up with manipulations of planet places?

5

AN EMERGENT FABLE OF ASTRONOMERS AND STARS

There is a sentence that the cognitive scientist Jordan Pollack uses to illustrate how the human brain brings prior knowledge to bear on language processing. The sentence is: "The astronomer married the star." Given the context of astronomy, our minds initially are led to the conclusion that *star* refers to something up in the sky. In the competition between meanings, however, this initial understanding of the sentence loses because we "know" that an astronomer is a human being, whereas a star up in the sky is a physical object. If we are to talk sensibly of marriage, we must search through memory again, looking for another kind of astronomer or another kind of star.

Human astronomers and inert stars cannot marry or even collaborate. The star's job is simply to be a star. It is the scientist's job to describe the behavior of that star, to have "weav'd out a net, and this net throwne/Upon the heavens and now they are his owne."[1] If the astronomer gains a measure of dominion thereby, then that is only the fulfillment of the biblical pronouncement that humans should stand above the world and its other creatures. We deserve to own the heavens because we wove the net and threw it out there. These controlling formulations of astronomy were created by the succession of brilliant individual scientists we read about in the history books. Johannes Kepler, for example, labored for many years to "triumph over the motions of Mars and fetter him in the prison of tables."[2] Sir Isaac Newton developed a theory of the moon, which "till then never submitted to the bridle of calculations, nor was ever broke by any Astronomer."[3] The mythology of a sequence of sole-practitioner scientists is an important element of Western culture. When Newton professed that if he had seen further, it was by standing upon the shoulders of giants, he was not talking about the view from the mosh pit. He was imagining something more like a totem pole.

The new intermaths assert that such formulations *can* well up out of a computational mosh pit, not just be added atop the totem pole or spring full grown from the head of Zeus. They show that "tangled webs of country prejudices" can produce valuable science as well as valuable wagons. Galileo foresaw that many small efforts, acting in parallel, could combine in a mighty way, so that "a vast number of ants might carry ashore a ship laden with grain."[4] Adaptive evolutionary computation adds the conviction that a vast number of tiny, individual insights might carry ashore the ship of science, laden with predictive formulations.

A typical adaptive computation operates very much like the culture of the wagon builders of rural England, none of whom knew the whole art but all of whom collectively carried it forward from generation to generation. In the beginning, there were no wagons, there were no wagon builders, and there were no roads. There was only a need to move things, and it was from that driving need that wagons, wagon builders, and roads all emerged. The same could have happened with Greek astronomy. Its formulations could perhaps have emerged computationally from inside one of today's parallel supercomputers. Galileo provided some hints of how this might happen when he imagined astronomy coming about within the life of a single mind:

> It is to be supposed that the first observers of Heaven knew no more but one motion common to all the stars, as is this diurnal [i.e., daily] one; yet I believe that in few days they perceived that the Moon was inconstant in keeping company with the other stars; but yet, withal, many years must have passed before they distinguished all the planets. . . . Many more years ran out before the stations and retrogressions of the three superior planets were known, as, also, their

approximations and recessions from the Earth, which were the necessary occasions of introducing the eccentrics and epicycles, things
unknown even to Aristotle, for he makes no mention thereof.[5]

Galileo's imagery oversimplifies, however, by starting the story in
the middle. His "first observers" are skilled and motivated scientists
right from Day 1. They know exactly what they are looking for and
why there would be value in finding it. Greek astronomy did not start
that way. It started from nothing. It emerged at a time when there was
no science, and there was no understanding of what science would
potentially be valuable for. The power of the adaptive view is that it
offers an explanation of how such an intellectual process might start
from nothing.

We know that Greek astronomy was prefaced by the development
of a large stew of almost random statements about the world. Only a
few of these pre-Socratic fragments have survived, but there may have
been many more. A modern adaptive computation typically starts in
the same place, with thousands of random statements. Electronic computers keep such statements in the form of imperative commands;
human societies put them in the form of declarative sentences. Otherwise, the thoughts of the pre-Socratic Greek philosophers are, as illustrated in figure 5.1, very much like the soup of random, unpromising
prattle that characterizes the early stages of an emergent process.

Although more thoughtful than "the moon is made of green
cheese," these statements were no more useful scientifically. Their
weakness, as pointed out by Cyril Hinshelwood in a different context,
lay in the fact that scientific information in this form could not be profitably combined: "The poetic simile, except in a strictly ancillary
capacity, is certainly the wrong idiom for science. . . . The poetic vision
relates the elements of the external world to the human mind, but not
in a way which helps to relate them in any general or consistent way to
one another."[6]

Vast repetitive recombination of individual ideas or statements is
exactly what many adaptive intermaths depend on. They take the first
half of one sequence and mate it with the second half of another
sequence to see if the result turns out to be an improvement. New
combinations of these early Greek pronouncements were, unfortunately, no more valuable than the originals. When tested against the
actual behavior of the stars, these pronouncements were able to predict virtually nothing.

Even in this first batch of utterances, however, there were two that were just slightly less hopeless than the others, one because it contained the idea of "all" and the other because it contained the idea of "first." In the actual behavior of the stars at night, what is true for one star is true for all, so statements that contain the *all* word are minutely more likely to be valuable than statements that do not. Much of the behavior was also sequential, so the word *first* also had value. Adaptive methods include a mechanism for evaluating the "fitness" of every single utterance. Each one, even the ones that are total nonsense, is treated as potentially being the full and ultimate answer. Each one is given a fitness score, even though most of those scores are zeros.

Eventually, the recombination of these utterances may create one that chances its way into a successful match with some trivial piece of real-world behavior. In emergent computing processes, elements that receive even slightly better fitness scores receive preference in the next round of recombinations and matings, as illustrated in figure 5.2. Over thousands of generations of matings, these utterances continue to receive preference, and useful concepts such as "all" and "first" spread, rather like the way new slang words spread through the speech patterns of teenagers.

At this stage of the process, it is still hard to imagine that anything of value could ever come out of such an unpromising start. Adaptive methods also include random mutations, however, so that ideas like "number" could, over long periods of time, enter or be borrowed from other contexts. New statements such as "all is change" or "all is number" eventually sprang up. "All is number" would have been particularly promising because it could easily mate with a preexisting body of Greek knowledge about multitudes and arithmetic. For a while, "all is number" flourished, indeed dominated. But then came a slightly different version, "all is circle," which could mate with the even larger and more energetic body of knowledge built up by the geometers. In just a few hundred generations, it was perhaps able to match some additional part of what was actually seen in the heavens. Even a slight advantage would have been enough to drive "all is number" from the field.

For Galileo, this was the level of the first day, the level at which the whole process started. He correctly noted that once the process had reached this stage, it could be (and historically was) carried forward by individual scientists stacking up their individual improvements totempole style. It is instructive, nonetheless, to see how evolutionary techniques would carry forward and solve the same problems. Even with all the theorems of Euclid's *Elements* to interbreed with, "all is circle"

Pre-Socratic Greek Version	Computational Version	First "Interbreeding"
"All things are one."	Set all bits to 1.	Set all bits to tension.
"The harmony of the worlds is tension."	Set harmony equal to tension.	Set harmony equal to 1.
"Infinite air is the first principle."	Initialize air to infinity.	Initialize air to brow sweat.
"The sea is sweat of the brow."	Set sea equal to brow sweat.	Set sea equal to infinity.
"Swift sun and kindly moon."	Combine swift with sun and kindly with moon.	Combine swift values to infinity.
"The first principle is infinity."	Initialize all values to infinity.	Initialize all swift with sun and kindly with moon.
"We are and we are not."	Set all 1's to 0 and all 0's to 1.	Set all 1's to 0 and all 0's to 1.

Figure 5.1. The early sayings of the pre-Socratic Greek philosophers seem to lead nowhere, yet they were the seed corn of science itself. Somehow Greek culture evolved them forward into increasingly sophisticated and accurate descriptions of the universe. Genetic intermaths start out at a similarly primitive level, with thousands of individually random formulations. Then they interbreed these formulations over and over again, taking the first part of one and putting it together with the second part of another to see if the result is an improvement.

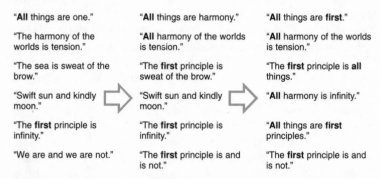

"**All** things are one."	"**All** things are harmony."	"**All** things are **first**."
"The harmony of the worlds is tension."	"**All** harmony of the worlds is tension."	"**All** harmony of the worlds is tension."
"The sea is sweat of the brow."	"The **first** principle is sweat of the brow."	"The **first** principle is **all** things."
"Swift sun and kindly moon."	"Swift sun and kindly moon."	"**All** harmony is infinity."
"The **first** principle is infinity."	"The **first** principle is infinity."	"**All** things are **first** principles."
"We are and we are not."	"The **first** principle is and is not."	"The **first** principle is and is not."

Figure 5.2. The key to the genetic approach to computing lies in its ability to recognize and then proliferate tiny incremental improvements across a large population of candidate formulations. Since, for example, the fixed stars all moved across the sky in the same order and along the same circular trajectory, early fragments containing words like "all" or "first" would be slightly more effective in describing that behavior. Such building blocks then spread to the whole population of a genetic formulation because they receive preference in the breeding cycles. Slowly, but surely, the formulation learns.

by itself could explain only a small fraction of the appearances of the heavens. The next step required the statements breeding with themselves recursively to produce, after many false starts, statements like "all is circles of circles" and eventually "all is circles nested within circles." With these more powerful statements, the system would finally be able to start saving appearances as complex as the retrograde motions of Mars, Jupiter, or Saturn.

At this stage, the method of evaluating the fitness of individual formulations became significant for the first time. An adaptive system evolves its answers in the direction of a "fitness criterion." An important component of any such computation is the feedback it receives from its environment. A baby notices that the approval ratings for noises like "mama" or "papa" are higher than those for gibberish and adapts its behavior accordingly. Unfortunately, organisms that learn must often do so in the face of conflicting criteria and reward systems. The criteria for Greek astronomy embedded two such conflicting goals. On the one hand, the Greeks wanted their astronomical theories to save the appearances accurately. On the other hand, they wanted the theories to fit well with the theories of physics and theology that were developing at the same time. When environments give conflicting feedback, organisms often divide, or speciate, so that each can exploit a specific niche. That is, in fact, what classical astronomy did, with one branch optimizing its fit to physics and the other continuing the drive for ever-greater accuracy. That is also what the wagon makers of old England did, so that the wagons of Suffolk could not be used in Gloucester, where the road ruts were a different gauge. That is also what adaptive methods of computation do.

Once the formulations of Greek astronomy split, with one favoring fit-to-physics and the other favoring fit-to-the-stars, there was no payoff in mating the two branches back together again because neither had what the other subenvironment valued. They became like diverging subspecies and lost the ability to interbreed. Already well adapted to the general environments of physics and theology, the somewhat sloppy "all is circles nested within circles" branch stopped evolving altogether. Meanwhile, the more restless subspecies, having found a protected niche that valued accuracy no matter where it came from, gradually evolved into amazing formulations laden with tricks such as "all is circles riding atop circles, or circles next to circles, or both in combination" in ways that bore less and less resemblance to classical "truth." In the final Copernican step, the sun and the earth swapped places in the formulation.

It was not the swapping of earth and sun that drove the two species back together again during the Renaissance; it was the inclusion of an assertion of truth. Truth had always been a major element of the main-line environment. Therefore, formulations such as those of Copernicus that professed truth would be able to breed back into the mainline population. The result, of course, was ecological crisis. Somnolent all this time, the "all is circles within circles" formulations were no match for the battle-hardened offspring of the accuracy niche. They were swept away, leaving physics and theology to defend the status quo. (Thus, the scientists chartered by Pope Gregory to reform the calendar based their work on Copernican tables because they were the most accurate. All the while, they insisted that the heliocentric formulation itself was false and blasphemous.) When the computational formulations of circles and lines proved able to breed into physics and save the appearances of falling bodies here on earth, the transition was complete. Theology alone could not keep the new methods from establishing themselves in the wider scientific environment and ultimately changing our whole way of looking at the world.

In addition to showing how a mind task such as astronomy might be created from scratch, either within a society of human beings or within a network of computers, this fable offers useful insights about (a) specific elements of the development of astronomy, (b) the possibility that astronomy could have developed in completely different ways, and (c) the actual relationship between astronomers and stars. All three of these topics provide perspective on the current interplay between the new evolutionary maths and the incumbent numbers and equations.

First, the evolutionary interpretation offers insight into the long-standing tension between diagram and number in classical astronomy. Numbers entered the process as the means of recording the results. They proceeded to work their way back into the formulation process, taking over some parts that once were purely geometric. Thus, astronomers often stopped their geometry to tabulate the intermediate results in numbers. These numbers saved the scientists from having to repeat all the geometry for subsequent analyses. But the numbers worked their way back only so far. When they stopped aligning with the spirit of the geometry, an immune system was activated. A dialogue between two medieval scientists, recorded by Regiomontanus, captured this immune system in action:

FIRST SCIENTIST: The numbers in the table are not the true latitudes?
SECOND SCIENTIST: Of course not. These numbers are used to divide

other numbers. Large numbers at the beginning of the table thus actually result in a smaller latitude.

FIRST SCIENTIST: You have convinced me that his chapter on latitudes contains nothing but intolerable absurdities.[7]

The first scientist could accept the substitution of numbers for geometric angles of latitude as long as the substitution was literal and the physical reality continued to shine through in the tables. Specifically, the scientist wanted to be sure that bigger numbers always meant bigger angles of latitude. Any attempt to abstract the numbers away from the geometric reality, even if it made production of the end result easier, was "absurd" and hence "intolerable," that is, unable to be tolerated by the mind of the first scientist. It was rejected. Time and again in science and computing, techniques are rejected not because they are wrong but simply because they "unhinge the understanding."

A second benefit of the adaptive view of classical astronomy is its ability to frame the question, "Could it all have developed in a completely different way?" If the process were run from scratch on seventy large parallel computers, would they all end up with epicycles and eccentrics, or even geometry, just as the seventy translators of the Septuagint were said to have independently arrived at identical results? Fortunately, an answer to this question need not await a new generation of parallel supercomputers. Scholars have learned that indeed it could have happened differently, because it actually did. In Babylonia, before the Greeks perfected their eccentric and epicyclic formulations, astronomers were saving the same appearances without any geometry at all. The historian Otto Neugebauer described what happened.

> A theoretical astronomy existed from the Persian time to the first century A.D. operating with methods entirely different from the Greek ones which were based on the combination of circular motions. . . . The earliest existing mathematical astronomy was governed by numerical techniques, not by geometrical considerations. . . . The development of geometrical explanations is by no means such a "natural" step as it might seem to us who grew up in the tradition founded by the Greek astronomers of the Hellenistic and Roman period.[8]

Neugebauer found it hard to imagine Greek geometry being the parent of the Babylonian arithmetic methods or vice versa; indeed, "the inverse influence is practically excluded since it would mean the transformation of the arithmetical methods into a simple geometrical argument; but this is not feasible in a simple fashion."[9] In this context, the technology issues of the medium of scientific communications may have played a decisive role. Unlike the Greeks, the Babylonians used cuneiform. In the words of the historian George Owen:

> The clay tablet lends itself most readily to an abstracted shorthand notation, whereas, while well-drawn geometric figures may well have had their aesthetic appeal, they could not be consistently produced in clay. Algebraic problems were well suited to the writing media.[10]

The ancient Babylonians, like the Europeans of the past five hundred years, used a character-based communications medium. Operating within that environment, both developed a numerocentric mode of scientific formulation. The ancient Greeks used a stroke-based communications medium; they developed a nonnumeric mode of formulation. As the science of the 1990s reverts to a stroke-based communications medium, how will that change in medium serve to influence the content?

Finally, the evolutionary approach challenges age-old assumptions about the controlling and adversarial relationship between astronomers and stars and between scientists and nature in general. At times, it seemed that Johannes Kepler wanted nothing more than to marry nature:

> *Galetea seeks me mischievously, the lusty wench:*
> *She flees to the willows, but hopes I'll see her first.*[11]

He went on to say that "it is perfectly fitting that I borrow Virgil's voice to sing this about Nature. For the closer the approach to her, the more petulant her games become. . . . She never ceases to invite me to seize her, as though delighting in my mistakes."[12] From the beginning, the process of predicting has been a process of taking behavior out of the wider world and dragging it into a fictional context in which the scientist feels more in control. To the Renaissance philosopher Thomas Hobbes, "when we calculate [computamus] the magnitude and motions of heaven or Earth, we do not ascend into heaven that we may divide it into parts, or measure the motions thereof, but we do it sitting still in our closets or in the dark."[13] Today's closet is a computer monitor. Scientists awe their colleagues, and sometimes society as a whole, by bringing nature into these high-resolution closets:

My colleagues and I stayed up most of one weekend to get our first hexagonal model experiment running. . . . We froze the simulation, left the display on, and went home. The next morning I found a group of scientists, many of them fluid experts, standing in the doorway of my office staring silently at the screen in total shock, disbelief, and awe.[14]

The desire to save the appearances inevitably lapses into the desire to play God: "When, therefore, the mind of the astronomer composes a correct representation of the heavens and their movements, he resembles the Artisan of all things creating the heavens and their motions."[15] In the case of the medieval king Alfonso, it was not enough just to be Nature's successful rival. He wanted to go God one better. Echoing the lament of the consultant in every age, Alfonso said that the world would have come out much better if God had brought him in on the process of Creation. In his recent book *Earth in the Balance*, Vice President Al Gore asks whence comes the belief that mankind is somehow "so powerful as to be essentially separate from the earth?"[16] The seeds of that perspective were already being sown in the computational culture of the ancient world.

Had the Renaissance shifted to adaptive forms of prediction that interact with nature and draw their answers from the data itself, this mind-set might have weakened instead of intensifying. Adaptive formulations, however, require the enormous amounts of cheap computing power and cheap training data that have only recently become available. The whole way of thinking about the world did, in fact, change during the Renaissance, but in the direction of the only resources that were available at that time: human minds.

6

The Computer Within Living Memory

When he said, "I think, therefore I am," René Descartes was refusing to define himself by any realities of the universe outside his own mental processes. If his very existence stood as an outgrowth of his ability to conceive it, then clearly the way to understand the world was to start with the specific qualities and abilities of the human mind. Thus, a hundred years after Copernicus eliminated *place* as a basis of the human claim to centrality in the universe, Descartes replaced it with human thought. What other information-processing resource was there in the universe to contest the claim?

On the other hand, René had a point. The traditional geometric ways of thinking about the world were needlessly taxing on the human mind. By the time Charles Babbage was designing his Victorian Analytical Engine, it never occurred to him that the machine need carry out geometric operations. It was strictly a number mill. Babbage found geometry to be confusing and complicated for students when compared to algebra: "The facility of comprehending their algebraic demonstrations forms a striking contrast with the prolixity of the geometrical proofs."[1]

The ancient Greek scientists had never really focused on the processes of thought that lay behind their formulations. They drew their abstractions from what they saw in the world around them rather than from an analysis of how their own minds seemed to work. The result was a language, geometry, that was a poor match because it is not strictly sequential. A geometric proof is peppered with the "meanwhiles" and "alsos" that ask the mind to keep multiple steps in mind in parallel. A comparatively simple theorem of Galileo's illustrates how taxing geometry can be to humans. Galileo proves that two balls rolling down separate ramps from the top of a circle will reach the circumference of the circle at the same point in time.

> Since the triangles FA.AE and FA.AD are respectively equal to the squares of AC and AB, while the rectangle FA.AE is to the rectangle FA.AD as AE is to AD, it follows that. . . . But since . . . it follows that . . . and hence also. . . . But it has been previously demonstrated that . . . ; but this ratio. . . . Therefore . . . [and] the ratio of those times is therefore unity.[2]

Whew. Galileo, like the Great Geometers of the ancient world such as Archimedes and Apollonius, could keep all this going in his mind at once. He was even able to add in more parallelism. Not content with his original result, he suggested two very beautiful extensions. First, he imagined myriad ramps at all angles, with balls being released simultaneously on all of them. The balls, he noted, would form a circle as they descended. Then he imagined balls descending in three dimensions, forming a sphere. Not just that, but "there may be some great mystery hidden in these true and wonderful results, a mystery related to the creation of the universe (which is said to be spherical in shape), and related also to the seat of the first cause."[3] In the hands of a Galileo, the humble compass and straight edge of Euclidian geometry provided a tool set sufficient to support a theory of an expanding universe, as illustrated in figure 6.1.

One of the reasons that Galileo's own geometry became so taxing on the human mind was that he was applying it to the field of physics for the first time, and for that he had explicitly to incorporate time. He used lines in his diagrams to stand for lengths of time as well as lengths of travel. He was successful in gaining insight into "paces sometimes a little more swift and at other times more slow,"[4] but in so doing he pushed the vocabulary of circles and diagrams beyond what it was designed to do.

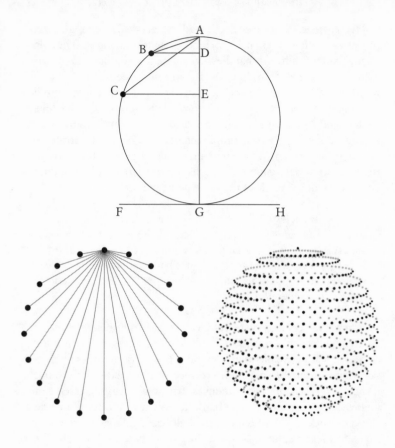

Figure 6.1. Advanced geometry typically requires multiple relationships to be kept in mind in parallel, which only the best minds could do. Advances in the field, therefore, were the province of a few "Great Geometers" who worked out their answers personally instead of employing computers. Inside the minds of these few gifted individuals, however, it was a vocabulary of great versatility. Galileo, for example, used circles and lines to develop a very lovely theory of an expanding universe based on his recognition that myriad balls, all rolling down their own ramps from the same starting point, would form an ever-expanding sphere.

It was this prolixity that Descartes sought to alleviate. He made it his mission to doubt, and ultimately to discard, all the knowledge that had been handed down to him by previous generations. As one component of this process of doubting, he ultimately concluded that numbers and equations must replace circles and diagrams. His wider goal, however, was to define a general process of thought that aligned with the strengths and weaknesses of his own mind. He started with an analysis of how his brain actually went about its business. His analysis formed the Renaissance equivalent of the modern field of computer science: the study of how information processors do what they do. His description of how the human mind is organized was in many ways parallel to John von Neumann's description of how the first electronic computers were organized:

> In the matter of cognition of facts . . . there are four faculties only which we can use for this purpose, viz., understanding, imagination, sense, and memory.[5]

> For the purposes of our discussion we shall distinguish the following [four] organs of a digital computer: The memory, i.e. the part of the machine devoted to the storage of numerical data; the arithmetic organ, i.e. that part in which certain of the familiar processes of arithmetic are performed; the logical control, i.e. the mechanism which comprehends and causes to be performed the demands of the human operator; and the input–output organ which is the intermediary between the machine and the outside world.[6]

The two faculties that were most critical to the development of Descartes's science were the understanding and the memory. They were inextricably linked because the understanding was inherently sequential. Unlike the imagination, it could not happen "all at once." The subject matter of understanding had to be stored away, in memory, and then dealt with piecemeal, with the knowledge that "though we attend to only a few simultaneously, we shall yet cover them all in time, taking one after the other."[7]

Descartes was not the first to note that human memory was sequential. The Romans had compared knowledge stored in memory to houses lined up along a street. Accessing this information was akin to walking down memory lane, remembering one fact per house. Nor was Descartes the first to note the codependency between sequential memories and maths. Aristotle had rejoiced in the fortuitous fact that "whatever has some order, as things in mathematics do, is easily remembered. Other things are remembered badly and with difficulty."[8] Aristotle failed to note that maths that were highly parallel, and hence were remembered badly, would have had very low survival prospects.

Descartes was quick to sense this resonance between the order of numbers and the sequentiality of living memory. He reveled in this "double function of numbers ... which use the same symbols to express now order, and now measure."[9] The very process of getting information ready to be stored away was identified with numerical order: "We give it the name of enumeration or induction, because it cannot then be grasped as a whole at the same time by the mind, and it certainly depends to some extent on the memory."[10]

The slowness of sequential memory clearly created a bottleneck, especially when compared to the imagination, which could process information all at once but could deal only with a limited amount of data. Once again, Descartes looked for ways to modify the form of the information itself to make it more amenable to sequential processing. In particular, he felt that if information in memory could be artificially smoothed out, it could be run through the mind at very high speeds and become almost the same as imagination. The historian Emily Grosholz summarizes Descartes's view as follows:

> Whereas deduction involves running through ideas successively in time and retaining some of them in memory, intuition grasps a nexus of ideas all at once. However, if the mind runs through a chain of reasoning quickly and easily enough, deduction can be converted to intuition.[11]

The very same concept occurred to supercomputer designers such as Seymour Cray in the 1970s. If sequences of computing instructions could be somehow smoothed out and regularized, they could be run through specialized circuitry at much higher speeds. These high-speed circuits became known as "vector pipelines." If a sequence of instructions can be put into a specific homogeneous format, a vector pipeline can carry it out at many times the speed it would otherwise achieve, "moving continuously in such a way," said Descartes, "that while it is intuitively perceiving each fact it simultaneously passes on to the next."[12] In both cases, the impact was the same. Scientists became motivated to stylize their formulations to fit the requirements of the higher performance circuitry.

Descartes was among the first to teach this idea: that the efficiency of information processing was contingent on how one set up the problem, and that how one set up a problem was in turn influenced by how one chose to view the world. Viewing the world in ways that made the subsequent mental effort surer and easier was the essence of Descartes's famous Method: "By a method I mean certain and simple rules, such that, if a man observe them accurately, he shall never assume what is false as true, and will never spend his mental efforts to no purpose."[13] The whole key was to arrange one's thoughts into ordered sequences and to "follow obstinately such an order."[14] Obstinate he was:

Rule V: Method consists entirely in the order and disposition of the objects towards which our mental vision must be directed if we would find out any truth.[15]

Order is what is needed: all the thoughts that can come into the human mind must be arranged in an order like the natural order of numbers. [16]

We must banish from the ideas of the objects presented whatsoever does not require present attention, in order that the remainder may be the more readily retained in memory.[17]

Descartes drilled this methodology into the collective psyche of Europe. He had a phobia of processes that proceeded in a nondirected way, comparing them to travelers lost in a forest who wander around when the only hope of exit lies in picking a direction and staying with it resolutely. It frustrated him, as it has frustrated schoolmasters ever since, that useful results could, in fact, be gotten that way: "We must principally beware of wasting our time in such cases by proceeding at random and unmethodically; for even though the solution can often be found without method, and by lucky people sometimes quicker, yet such procedure is likely to enfeeble the faculties and to make people accustomed to the trifling and the childish."[18]

Based on his analysis of how his mind worked, Descartes proposed a new dual track for science. Plato and Aristotle had divided science into astronomy and everything else. Now Descartes redivided it on the basis of whether the subject matter could be sequentialized or not. On one side would be those sciences that were amenable to arbitrary delineation; they were to be considered mathematical because they could align with the strengths and weaknesses of the sequential human mind:

All those matters only were referred to mathematics in which order
or measure are investigated, and that it makes no difference whether
it be in numbers, figures, stars, sounds or any other object that the
question of measurement arises.[19]

On the other side of the divide were those aspects of nature that
could not be so delineated. With these, claimed Descartes, success
should not even be expected and so should not be attempted. Modern
computer scientists sometimes take an equally passive stance:

Though many problems may present themselves, from the solution
of which this rule prohibits him, yet . . . if he is reasonable, this very
knowledge, that the solutions can be discovered by no one, will
abundantly satisfy his curiosity.[20]

The only problems we can really solve in a satisfactory manner are
those that finally admit a nicely factored [i.e., hierarchical] solution.
At first sight this view of human limitations may strike you as a
rather depressing view of our predicament, but I don't feel it that
way. On the contrary, the best way to learn to live with our limitations is to know them.[21]

Descartes's boldest and most treacherous step was to pretend that
the world outside his mind conformed to his dictum of sequentiality
even when it demonstrably did not. In his third rule for the right con-
duct of the mind, he said that, in order to understand nature, scientists
should feel free to sequentialize it artificially, "assigning in thought a
certain order even to those objects which in their own nature do not
stand in a relation of antecedence and consequences."[22]

Without this overt sequentialization of reality, many of the parts of
nature that most interested Descartes would have fallen outside the
reach of his beloved Method. Even astronomy would leave the field if
one saw the stars as all shining at once, in parallel. Better to believe,
with Aristotle, that stars were "units with a serial order indeed."[23]
Sequentialization was firmly entrenched by the time the philosopher
Kant made the obvious point that "the order and regularity in the
appearances, which we entitle nature, we ourselves introduce. We
could never find them in the appearances, had we not ourselves, or the
nature of our mind, originally set them there."[24]

Modern scientists use the terms *linear* and *nonlinear* to distinguish
behavior that can be understood one piece at a time from behavior

that cannot. If the behavior is genuinely linear, then "by studying the parts in isolation, we can learn everything we need to know about the complete system." With nonlinear systems, "their primary behaviors of interest are properties of the interactions between parts, rather than being properties of the parts themselves, and these interaction-based properties necessarily disappear when the parts are studied independently."[25] The city as described by Jane Jacobs is nonlinear and hence beyond the reach of step-by-step Cartesian thought.

Sequentialization was the first of two potentially distorting Cartesian steps in aligning thought with the strengths and weaknesses of the human mind. Descartes also recognized that he had to abbreviate. Data could be set off to the side because "art has most opportunely invented the device of writing."[26] A scientific formulation, however, needed to be stored right in living memory. Doing so required compression as well as sequentialization.

When Regiomontanus first dipped into algebra to solve a specific problem, he never intended it as a general replacement technology for circles and lines. To him it was still just a clever trick, not a true math at all at the level of geometry. Much had changed by Descartes's time, however. Scientists had begun to wonder why the ancients had "allowed almost no numbers other than integers; nor did they allow the material of arithmetic to be infinitely divisible like that of geometry."[27]

Descartes gave a new prominence to equations. For him, the equation was no longer just one possible ratio—the ratio of equality—among many. It was explicitly an identity; a relationship between two magnitudes. He urged scientists to work through a problem "until we find it possible to express a single quantity in two ways. This will constitute an equation, since the terms of one of these two expressions are together equal to the terms of the other."[28] Equations were wonderful because they were both compact and potentially universal. Regardless of the branch of science an equation came from, it could be manipulated, and ultimately perhaps solved, using the same rules and techniques. Students could be taught the art of manipulating equations independently of the science that gave rise to them.

Descartes's enthusiasm for his new method was boundless. Having invented the method for the purposes of mathematical problems, he then denied that he had done so and asserted that his was a method much more general than mathematics:

> It was not the case that this part of our method was invented for the purpose of dealing with mathematical problems, but rather that

mathematics should be studied almost solely for the purpose of
training us in this method.[29]

Influential pedagogues such as John Locke helped to ensure that
the new methods of sequential thought did indeed spread from math
to other parts of the curriculum: "I have mentioned mathematics as a
way to settle in the mind a habit of reasoning closely and in train."[30]
The sequential processing of information soon became much more
than a pragmatic way to carry out computation. It was the way to do
"good thinking" in general. As Descartes's method became more
widely taught in schools, "orderly thinking" became the ideal, and
alternatives to sequentiality became increasingly invisible. We sequentialize without being aware of it. For example, we all know how Christmas gift giving actually works. All over Christendom, parents shop for
presents and hide them in the attic. On Christmas Eve, all those parents, in parallel, bring all those presents down from the attic and put
them under the tree so that Christmas morning, all over Christendom,
children wake up to toys under the tree. Yet when asked how it all
happens, we insist that a single old agent from the North Pole, perhaps
in a gallium arsenide sleigh, has somehow gone from house to house
to house sequentially and delivered all those toys before dawn. Our
preference for explaining even the most patently parallel processes of
our world as though they were sequential began with Descartes.

7

LISTENING TO DATA

Science and computing both developed at a time when facts, or "data," about the world were a great luxury. The desire of the Greeks to know their own place in the universe was stymied by a lack of data about the places of even straightforward objects like the stars. Trustworthy facts about the place of the moon were especially precious because they could be gathered only at the rare moments of a lunar eclipse, and what were really needed were pairs of eclipse observations in opposing sectors of the sky. It took over a thousand years to assemble three solid pairs of facts about the moon. The great accomplishment of geometric computing, of course, was to leverage these three precious facts—in geometry, it requires three points to determine a circle—into a synthetic moon whose position might be known throughout time.

Only in the final decade of the twentieth century has this chronic shortage of facts about the world turned into a glut. The whole economics of data has been reversed. Little electronic Thoreaus and Boswells are all around us, whether we like it or not. The computers that capture data are creating an enormous challenge for the computers that seek to understand data. The culture of thought, developed to survive on a trickle of information, is being asked to deal with a flood.

Like the convergence of new hardware and software technology in the late twentieth century, the availability of too much data is a situation that has a singular precedent in history. For one brief lifetime, a great scientist (and skilled computer) found himself drowning in data. The approaches he used, and the way these approaches were subsequently held up to ridicule, hold important lessons for the scientific formulations of the twenty-first century. The scientist was Johannes Kepler. When he left his home in Austria and traveled to Prague to join the aging astronomer Tycho Brahe, he found a lifetime of observations that had been carried out by Tycho and his assistants. Nothing like Tycho's corpus of raw astronomical data had ever existed before. The Babylonians had accumulated a large body of observations, but they did so in the course of a thousand years. As information trickled in, it was studied by generation after generation of scientists. The Greeks added more observations, but again it was a comparative trickle. Tycho, on the other hand, had filled a large notebook every year for twenty-five years.

All Tycho had planned to do was to publish the data in the form of tables. This Kepler ultimately did, but he never felt that simply publishing the data was enough. He was driven to somehow do something more with it. What that "more" might be was unknown. There were no precedents, beyond the traditional diagrams, for the form an "explanation" of data might take. The instinctive response of the educated person today is to look within the data for some "relationships." In Kepler's time, scientific relationships as we now know them had not yet been invented. Relationships involving time in its current form made no sense at all because, back then, the motions and the times were the same thing.

Perhaps the closest model was astrology, in which events on earth were related to and predicted by events in the skies. Kepler himself had had success with astrology and never disdained it. Early in his career, he had prepared a horoscope for his prince that predicted both a bitter winter and renewed invasion by the Turks. Both came to pass. Throughout his life, Kepler dabbled in and defended astrology. It was one potential source, among many, for explanatory relationships. No such source, in his mind, should be ruled out.

Prior to encountering Tycho's database, Kepler had one other signal success. He had wondered whether any other geometric object held the same spatial ratios as those of the orbits of the planets. It was like looking for a needle in a haystack: "If, for the sizes and the relations of the six heavenly paths assumed by Copernicus, five figures possessing certain distinguishing characteristics could be discovered among the infinitely many, then everything would go as desired."[1] Against all odds, he found what he was looking for, as illustrated in figure 7.1. Somehow, he conjured up an image of all the regular geometric polygons nested one inside the next—a result that algebra could never have produced—and noticed that their relative sizes corresponded to the relative sizes of the orbits of the planets.

With these two successes behind him, and Tycho's mass of data in front of him, Kepler began an unprecedented search for ways that would help him make sense of it all. The very breadth of his search is exhausting to retrace. He drew all he could from classical astronomy, priding himself on being an integral part of the linear, totem-pole-like tradition. When he made a modification to a specific length within the eccentric diagram, he took pains to push his assumptions onto the stack of historical development: "Ptolemy set [the eccentricity] down as very large; Regiomontanus reduced it; Copernicus halved it and transposed it. . . . Tycho Brahe got hold of it and claimed a part for the equant circle."[2] He plunged into formidable works of advanced geometry such as the *Conics* of Apollonius, although its insights did not pay off for many years. He carried on his own observations in the cold German night, taking readings with a glowing coal when the wind made candles unusable. Like Regiomontanus, he reached out to numerical techniques when geometry failed him, although he found them "gauche and ungeometrical"[3] and wished to be able to get the results he needed "with more finesse."[4]

The search was eclectic and frequently playful. Kepler did not hesitate to engage "in a clown show"[5] or to "summon up from tragedy a *deus*, or rather a sort of *ratio ex machina*."[6] He wondered if the planets perhaps had minds, and he pictured such a planetary mind carrying out its appointed rounds computationally, "as if it were obtaining the values right from the Prutenic or Alphonsine tables."[7] When the first study of magnetism was published, he decided that the "relationship with the sun can now be maintained without a mind, by the constancy of the magnetic faculty alone."[8]

What constrained Kepler's helter-skelter process and made it ultimately productive was his iron commitment to the facts themselves, the data, which was "not false,"[9] and his willingness to recognize contradiction when it arose. The data, like the data pouring Tarantola-style into a modern parallel computer memory, were true, and truth was incapable of contradiction; within these twin constraints, any approach was permissible. Over the course of decades, he surfaced, one at a time, the three nuggets now known as Kepler's laws of planetary motion. In Wolfgang Pauli's view, laws in the form he ultimately promulgated them were not even what he was looking for; he was looking for musical harmonies.[10]

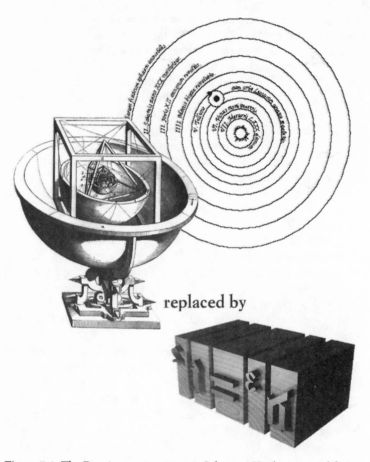

Figure 7.1. The Renaissance astronomer Johannes Kepler spent a lifetime looking for patterns in the astronomical data he inherited from Tycho Brahe. He was willing to consider anything. His first result had the distances of the planets from the sun determined by the sizes of nested polygons, a formulation that can only be expressed geometrically. His last major finding, the Third Law, can be expressed in the vocabulary of numbers and equations. It is this latter version that has endured within the culture of science; his geometric version died out. So, too, did Kepler's whole method of searching for formulations down at the level of the data itself. Only with the arrival of parallel electronic computers in the late twentieth century have these data-level approaches returned to prominence. Drawing of Kepler's nested figures courtesy of the Boston Athenaeum.

Scientists ever since have been both dazzled by his achievement and appalled by his methods. Kepler's methods have been trivialized as being "like the child who having picked a mass of wild flowers tries to arrange them into a posy this way, and then tries another way, exploring the possible combinations and harmonies."[11] Arranging data into a posy, first this way and then that, is exactly how the new intermaths seek out patterns in large amounts of data. These maths depend on being totally uninhibited, just as Kepler was. An adaptive math must be like Galileo's description of Kepler, "a free mind, perhaps even too much so,"[12] even willing to entertain "occult properties and such-like trifles."[13] Kepler was successful in creating something from nothing precisely because he did not constrain the form of the answer. With benefit of hindsight, we know that Isaac Newton was later able to express Kepler's insights in a more satisfying way and then to carry those ideas far beyond. Newton, however, not only had Kepler's three laws themselves to build on, he also had Kepler's very concept of scientific law to build on.

Although he was willing to rearrange his data into first this posy and then that, Kepler was also willing to compute indefatigably when he saw an arrangement that he found promising. It was only after heroic computational effort that he finally pinned down the elliptical orbit of Mars. Unlike ancient astronomers, Kepler had a surplus of facts about Mars in front of him. He recognized that any set of three data points should yield the same circular orbit. When he found a fraction of a degree (eight minutes) of discrepancy, he pursued the causes until, as he ultimately proclaimed, "these eight minutes alone will have led the way to the reformation of all of astronomy."[14] But success came only because he and his computer were willing to do backbreaking computations that he worried would exhaust his reader just in the retelling:

> I can't imagine anyone reading this not being overcome by the tedium of it even in the reading. So the reader may well judge how much vexation we (my calculator and I) derived hence, as we thrice followed this method through the 180 degrees of anomaly, changing the eccentricity each time.[15]

He did it by breaking the orbit in half and then dividing each half into 180 single-degree segments. He computed each of the 180 orbit pieces individually and then added them all together to get an orbit. It was a vexatious method because, when it did not match the data, it had to be done all over again from the beginning with a new set of assumptions. Kepler and his computer together went through this long process dozens of times. Gradually, he found himself on new ground, forced to let go of the assumption of a circular orbit because the assumption could not be made consistent with the data. Having no mathematical vocabulary to describe what the data were telling him, he reached out to the marketplace for the words he needed. He imagined the orbit being reshaped "in much the same manner as, if one were to squeeze a fat-bellied sausage at its middle, he would squeeze and squash the ground meat, with which it is stuffed, outwards from the belly towards the two ends, emerging above and below from beneath his hand."[16]

In retrospect, the step from fat-bellied sausage to mathematical ellipse seems a trivial one. Kepler even lamented on how much easier it would have been if his sausage *were* an ellipse, because then all the math could have been borrowed directly from Archimedes. Instead, his process took him searching through all the other possibilities first. It was only when he had ruled out every option except an ellipse that he finally proclaimed that, therefore, "no figure is left for the planet to follow other than a perfectly elliptical one."[17] In so doing, of course, he demonstrated for all time that circles and lines were *not* the vocabulary of the Book of Nature after all.

> Lover of the circle as of the Sun, Kepler long took for granted that the planets must inevitably move in that perfect form. . . . When gradually the mathematician was forced to the conclusion that the planets moved in ellipses, the mystic was bewildered. . . . Reluctantly and against his own desire Kepler broke the perfect Circle in the heavens.[18]

When Kepler broke the circle, he created a window of opportunity for the young vocabulary of numbers and equations to move in and provide a replacement. Galileo, meanwhile, had opened up the fertile field of dynamics, which needed the new vocabulary in order to reach its potential. Thus, the whole table had been set for an Isaac Newton.

Was it true, as John Stuart Mill later asserted, that "the ellipse was in the facts before Kepler recognized it"?[19] Was the ellipse prior to the data itself, and did it force the data to be what it was? If so, Kepler's decision to operate down at the level of the data might indeed have been the waste of a fine mind. And if so, Isaac Newton was much shrewder in the way he invested his time in the search for a law of gravity. Newton started by framing the hypothesis of a single mathematical relation that would hold for both the fall of an object, perhaps an apple, near the earth's surface and the motion of the moon above it. Knowing what he was looking for, he required very little supporting data. A few parameters for the moon and for the distance of the earth's surface from the center of the earth sufficed. He derived the radius of the earth from the value of sixty miles per degree of latitude that was commonly used in navigation at that time. An acquaintance of Newton described the result:

> He was, in some Degree, disappointed, and the Power that restrained the Moon in her Orbit, measured by the versed Sines of that Orbit, appeared not to be quite the same that was to be expected, had it been the Power of Gravity alone, by which the Moon was there influenc'd. Upon this disappointment . . . he threw aside the Paper of his calculation, and went on to other Studies.[20]

Later in life Newton claimed he had, in fact, found them to "answer pretty nearly."[21] Whatever the reality, disappointment or near success, he did set the whole issue aside for twenty years. Kepler, whose original orbits for Mars answered far more nearly than Newton's results, had been nowhere near so casual. He stayed doggedly on the question until he found a way to answer to the data exactly. Newton ignored the data and spent the next two decades developing the new mathematical language of calculus. The result was a whole new body of insights expressed as exact equalities, or "equations."

First, he extended the equational vocabulary to values that had previously been thought to be only very similar, asserting that quantities that "approach nearer to each other than by any given difference, become ultimately equal."[22] Then he developed never-ending sequences of numbers that became closer and closer to values such as logarithms, allowing them to be computed very accurately, as illustrated in figure 7.2.

Finally, and most influentially, he showed that an exact, idealized equation could be a more accurate expression of nature than the approximate equalities that raw data tended to produce. As a subsequent historian noted, this discovery gave great impetus to the new belief that truth could be sought at the level of the formulations, not down at the grubbier level of the data, where Kepler operated:

> He was unaware that the sun and earth exerted their attractions as
> if they were but points. How different must these propositions have

Hanc seriem transformare licet in fractionem continuam sequentem:

$$X = \cfrac{\frac{4}{3}}{1 - \cfrac{\frac{6}{5}x}{1 + \cfrac{\frac{2}{5 \cdot 7}x}{1 - \cfrac{\frac{5 \cdot 8}{7 \cdot 9}x}{1 - \cfrac{\frac{1 \cdot 4}{9 \cdot 11}x}{1 - \cfrac{\frac{7 \cdot 10}{11 \cdot 13}x}{1 - \cfrac{\frac{3 \cdot 6}{13 \cdot 15}x}{1 - \cfrac{\frac{9 \cdot 12}{15 \cdot 17}x}{1 - \text{etc.}}}}}}}}}$$

Figure 7.2. The new algebraic maths were more than just a good tool for answering the new questions of "rate of change," or "pace," that scientists started to ask during the Renaissance. They were also the schoolmaster's tool of choice for shaping young minds and teaching them to always "think in train."

Equations are an excellent fit to the strengths and weaknesses of human thought. Unlike circles and lines, they were welcomed by both printers and hired computers. The word "etc." in an equational formulation marks the point where the work of the scientist ended and the work of the hired computer began. Courtesy of the Trustees of the Boston Public Library.

seemed to Newton's eyes when he realised that these results, which he had believed to be only approximately true when applied to the solar system, were really exact! . . . Imagine the effect of this sudden transition from approximation to exactitude in stimulating Newton's mind to still greater efforts. It was now in his power to apply mathematical analysis with absolute precision to the actual problems of astronomy.[23]

The idealized point was not just easier to work with; it was more true as well. Galileo had made a similar assertion: "Things shall jump no less exactly than arithmetic computations. The errors therefore lie neither in abstract nor in concrete, nor in geometry, nor in physics, but in the calculator, who does not know how to adjust his accounts."[24]

For those who still clung to the primacy of data, this inversion of formulation and data was as incomprehensible as Copernicus's swapping of the earth and sun once had been. Newton stunned the astronomer royal John Flamsteed by suggesting that Flamsteed's observational data would most advantageously be presented to the world as a side dish to Newton's latest formulations. How dare Newton assert that "to have the theory of the moon published with my observations, would be a great proof of their accuracy"![25] Flamsteed clung to the belief that "theories do not command observations; but are to be tried by them."[26] Unfortunately for Flamsteed, in the contest between the pesky particularity of data and the sweeping universality of the new breed of equations, the human mind was opting for the compact equation. If the ellipse were in the data all along, perhaps it could be found without spending one lifetime (Tycho's) gathering raw data and a second lifetime (Kepler's) sifting through it. Furthermore, if the ellipse were universally present, then only a small amount of data would be required to confirm its presence.

To Flamsteed's dismay, that is what Newton did. It is also what the twentieth-century economist John Maynard Keynes habitually did. When statisticians, operating at the level of the data as Kepler had, found some of Keynes's hypothesized parameters within their data, Keynes's patronizing reaction was "isn't it nice that you found the correct figure," together with an admission that perhaps his confidence in the data had risen "slightly."[27] Einstein was also certain that the formulations were in the data ahead of time. When asked what would happen if measurements failed to corroborate one of his theories, Einstein said, "Then I would have felt sorry for the dear Lord. The theory is correct."[28] Like Keynes, he had come to share the radical new belief of the astronomers that "when we have thus obtained a simple law, . . . we may regard it as more exact than the observations themselves."[29]

Two decades after Newton made his first attempt at a theory of gravity, he tried again. In the meantime, French surveyors had done a very careful measurement of a degree of latitude and found it to be almost seventy miles, not sixty. When Newton updated this one piece of data, the answers all clicked into place. The same formulation of gravity that saved the appearances of the apple also saved the appearances of the moon. Newton then showed that his inverse square law for gravity resulted, of necessity, in Kepler's elliptical orbits for the planets. When Edmund Halley, who subsequently discovered the orbit of Halley's comet, first heard of this, he was amazed: "Struck with joy and amazement, Halley asked him how he knew it? Why, he replied, I have calculated it; and being asked for the calculation, he could not find it, but promised to send it to him."[30]

Fortunately, Halley channeled this joy and amazement into persuading Newton to publish his findings. The result, the *Principia Mathematica*, completed the transition to a new unit in the Book of Nature, a transition that had been initiated by Galileo, Descartes, and Kepler. Prior to the *Principia*, all serious mathematical work had been geometric. Even the *Principia* itself was written geometrically, because that is the form its audience expected:

> By the help of the *New Analysis* Mr. Newton found out most of the Propositions in his *Principia Philosophiae:* but . . . he demonstrated the Propositions synthetically, that the Systems of the Heavens might be founded upon good Geometry.[31]

The *Principia* set the agenda for much of science and just about all of computing down to the present day. Formulations, not data, became the starting point for inquiry. Within certain constraints, it became possible to go straight from one scientific formulation, such as the law of gravity, to another, such as Kepler's law of elliptical orbits, without going back through the data at all. King Alfonso's wish was coming true: The world was being recast into a form that was much more pleasing to human understanding.[32]

Lurking in the background of Newton's universal formulations, of course, was "time." If a formulation were to remain true for all time, then time itself could not be permitted to change. Newton simply asserted that time existed unblemished and independent of all else: "Absolute, true, and mathematical time, of itself, and from its own nature, flows equably without relation to anything external."[33] Not even the discoveries of Einstein change this assumption that our everyday life plays out in the context of constant and unblemished time. Earthly processes such as evolution may leap ahead in some eras and then remain static, but that is not interpreted to mean that "time" has slowed down or speeded up.

The net result of Newton's work was a way of looking at the world so new and so different that it rendered the old way incomprehensible and, ultimately, ridiculous. Having made forces an essential part of all planetary behavior, for example, scientists then wondered, with Newton, how their predecessors had dealt with these forces: "We do not know in what manner the ancients explained the question, how the planets came to be retained within certain bounds."[34] The answer, of course, was that the ancients had no need to deal with these forces because the old diagrammatic formulations did not require them. A circle does not require a force to keep its circumference in place around its center.

It was not possible for the human mind to maintain two such different formulations of the heavens at once. As the universal numbers and equations came to predominate, they were used to overwrite old astronomy as well as to invent new physics. When asked what one should read to prepare for the *Principia*, Newton suggested a mix of traditional geometric and modern algebraic works. Within a few generations, the geometric works he recommended had been completely replaced by new versions using only algebra, as illustrated in figure 7.3. Inexorably, the whole era of geometric computing became invisible. Students today are led to believe that even the Greeks worked in equations. Twentieth-century translations of early astronomy texts use the equals sign (=), not because it existed when these books were written, but because it helps make the material intelligible to modern readers.

As he was closing the door on Part One of the Book of Nature, Newton also closed it on Kepler's nascent method of learning by swimming around in data. Newton's vanity left him no choice. In terms of the planetary orbits, nothing in the *Principia* changes Kepler's simple realization that the orbit of Mars was a perfectly elliptical one. Worse yet, nothing Newton said about universal gravity changed what Robert Hooke was already saying:

> The same rules of motion that make out the curved motions of heavy bodies on the earth will make out all the celestiall motion, and give a physicall ground mathematically to calculate tables for

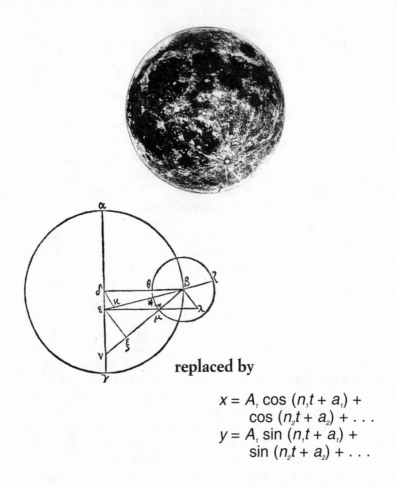

replaced by

$$x = A_1 \cos (n_1 t + a_1) + \\ \cos (n_2 t + a_2) + \ldots \\ y = A_1 \sin (n_1 t + a_1) + \\ \sin (n_2 t + a_2) + \ldots$$

Figure 7.3. At first the transition to a new vocabulary does not affect the way we understand the world itself. The epicycles of the moon's behavior, for example, were simply reexpressed with sines and cosines instead of with circles and lines. Soon, however, a change of vocabulary is accompanied by a much deeper change in *understanding*. Scientists choose underlying fictions that are well-adapted to their vocabulary. Where once they looked up into the sky and saw epicycles, for example, they—and we—came to see fields of gravitational force instead. Geometric diagram courtesy of the Trustees of the Boston Public Library.

them which I could easily doe had I time to spend in that employ, but I hope there will be found others that will save me the labour.[35]

It was to Hooke that Newton had addressed his famous, and uncharacteristically modest, comment that if he had seen further, it was by standing on the shoulders of giants. Now Newton was determined to show that the shoulders he was talking about did not include Hooke's, or even Kepler's. Newton proceeded to make a firm distinction between computing and guessing. His method, at the level of the formulations, was true scientific computing, he said. Kepler's, down at the level of the data, was unscientific guessing. Hooke's was beneath dignity, being connected to neither: "For as Kepler knew the orb to be not circular but oval, and guessed it to be elliptical, so Mr. Hooke, without knowing what I have found out since his letters to me, can know no more."[36] Newton was at pains to remind the world that he had not just invented a computational path to these results, he had also put in the effort to follow that path through. He not only produced the formulation, he personally produced the answer in a step-by-step way that was reproducible by other human minds and hence was, in modern terminology, "tractable."

He [Hooke] has done nothing, and yet written in such a way, as if he knew. . . . For 'tis plain, by his words, he knew not how to go about it. Now is not this very fine? Mathematicians that find out, settle, and do all the business, must content themselves with being nothing but dry calculators and drudges.[37]

Descartes, of course, had drawn a very similar distinction between "orderly method" and "guessing." In this respect, he and Kepler offered totally opposite models for the modern age. Descartes "never examined aught except in order." Kepler insisted that "I cannot submit to strict order."[38] Galileo was less dogmatic than Descartes but not so radical as Kepler. He wrote "by way of dialogue, which, as not being bound up in the rigid observance of mathematical laws, gives place, also, to digressions that are sometimes no less curious than the principal argument."[39]

To Descartes, as to Newton, Kepler's approach was not thought at all. It was something inferior to thought, something down at the level of "mere guessing." Only at the end of the twentieth century is it becoming clear that Kepler's method may be more useful than thought. Mated with a suitable computing resource, it can go where thought alone cannot.

From the European Renaissance through World War II, exact scientists focused on questions of pace and used keyboards and printing presses as their communications technology. To compute the rates of change of behaviors from trajectories to turbulences, they have used sequential thought processes based on numbers and equations. At the very end of this four hundred year period, sequential electronic circuits replaced human computers and provided a very significant speedup, but little change in the formulations themselves. For fifty years we have been trying to teach electronic circuits to process information the same way we always have. Photo of human computers courtesy of UPI/Bettmann. Photo of Cray Y-MP courtesy of Cray Research Inc. Background text courtesy of the Boston Athenaeum. Equational formulation courtesy of the Trustees of the Boston Public Library.

iam determinationem elementorum ex f'', r, r', θ'' fit $\log \eta'' = 0{,}0005i9$

II copiose .explicatum hic apponere sup

Tandem habemus per art. 146

e per art. 144 obtinemus

$$\tfrac{1}{2}(u''+u) = 205^\circ\ 18'\ 10''\ 53$$
$$\tfrac{1}{2}(u''-u) = -5\ \ 14\ \ 2{,}02$$

$\log r$.........0,5500178

$\log \sin$

C. $\log \dfrac{}{n}$ .. 9,5552971

$2f'' = 5^\circ\ 29\ \ ''05$

Hanc seriem transformare licet in fractionem continuam sequentem:

$$X = \cfrac{\frac{4}{3}}{1 - \cfrac{\frac{6}{3}x}{1 + \cfrac{\frac{2}{5.7}x}{1 - \cfrac{\frac{5.8}{7.9}x}{1 - \cfrac{\frac{1.4}{9.11}x}{1 - \cfrac{\frac{7.10}{11.15}x}{1 - \cfrac{\frac{5.6}{15.15}x}{1 - \cfrac{\frac{9.12}{15.17}x}{1 - \text{etc.}}}}}}}}}$$

C. $\log \dfrac{}{n''}$ ...9,4125969

$\log \sin 2f''$......8,8555599

$2f'' = 4^\circ\ 6'\ 45''\ 28$

gatum $f' + 2f''$ hu a $2f'$ tantummodo $0''01$ differt.

PART TWO
OF THE
BOOK OF NATURE

PACE

itaque ogarithmi quantitatum θ, θ'' recti 9,2343153 et 9,3134225. I

iam d mina one ementorum ex f, r, r'', θ prodit $\log \eta = 0{,}0002$

e ex f, r, r, θ'' fit $\log \eta'' = 0{,}0005191$. Hunc calculum in Libri p

II cop se explicatum hic apponere supersedemus.

oportet. **Ecce calculum**

itaque logarithmi quantitatum θ, θ'' correcti 9,2343153 et 9,3134225. I

iam determinationem elementorum ex f, r', r'', θ prodit $\log \eta = 0{,}0002$

le ex f'', r, r', θ'' fit $\log \eta'' = 0{,}0005191$. Hunc calculum in Libri p

III copiose explicatum hic apponere supersedemus.

Tandem habemus per art. 146

ue per art. 144 obtinemus

$$\tfrac{1}{2}(u''+u) = 205^\circ$$
$$\tfrac{1}{2}(u''-u) = -5\ \ 1$$
$$f' = 5\ \ 4$$

$\log \sin 2f'$......9,1218791

$\log r$............500178

C. $\log \dfrac{n'r'}{n}$ ..5

dem ha

art. $\tfrac{1}{2}$

f'......9,1218791

$\mathcal{T}$HE MATHS OF THE INDUSTRIAL AGE

Not until the middle of the twentieth century would technology open up new opportunities for intellectual discovery on the same scale as it had in the Renaissance with the simultaneous emergence in Europe of clocks, printing, and algebra. At the end of World War II the electronic circuits originally pressed into service to aim artillery shells and decipher codes became available for wider scientific use. Scientists like Charles Darwin and Sigmund Freud (and soon Rachel Carson) had opened up whole new disciplines that were, like the field of quantum mechanics, well-aligned to these inherently parallel electronic circuits. Philosophers such as Langer, writing in the early 1940s, had made clear the need to break through the old sequential, discursive mechanisms of thought.

> So long as we admit only discursive symbolism as a bearer of ideas, "thought" in this restricted sense must be regarded as our only intellectual activity.[1]

Electronic circuits, operating in parallel, offered the epochal possibility of a second intellectual activity, able to complement sequential thought and, for the first time in history, to go beyond its limits.

It did not happen. In the years immediately following the war, electronic computers grew unimaginably in both speed and influence, but not at all in their intellectual scope. They were used simply to mimic the methods and processes put in place centuries earlier for human computers. For sure, "instead of being just a matter for practitioners who didn't seem to be in the mainstream, computing now [became] the Queen of Technology."[2] But even in the 1990s, this newly crowned Queen of Technology remains faithful granddaughter to the "array of women cranking out firing tables" in the ballistics computing halls of World War II. Instead of being used in parallel to open up the intellectual activities of the next four hundred years, the circuits were constrained to operating sequentially and recapitulating the intellectual activities of the past four hundred. Nobel Laureate Kenneth Wilson summarized the reality for a Congressional subcommittee in the 1980s:

> Embedded in the current worldwide economic competition is a human undertaking of staggering scope. The undertaking is to embody four hundred years of scientific inquiry and wisdom into computer programs. . . . For example, Newton's Laws of mechanics are the basis for "structural analysis" programs widely used throughout industry. . . . All of this encyclopedic wisdom is potentially harnessable for practical use via the computer.[3]

The warning of an eighteenth-century observer was continuing to be borne out: "that which happened to Aristotle has happened to Newton; his followers have bowed so implicitly to his authority, that they have not exercised their reason."[4] The users of the new electronic computers looked back instead of forward.

How have the methods of thought that were put in place so long ago maintained their control even into the 1990s? Much of their staying power is narcissistic. Sequential thought is what *we* do, and it feels good to see electronic circuits doing exactly what we do, in the same way we have always done it. The real source of their continuing influence, however, is cultural. Equational maths were able to establish themselves at the very core of Western thought because they were in the right place at the right time. Equational maths appeared just when they were needed to support Europe's new wave of global navigation. Circles and lines could not provide the accuracy needed to keep Europe's sailors out of harm's way; numbers and equations ultimately did. Navigational ephemerides were the "killer apps" that ultimately propelled equations into the core curriculum of schools worldwide.

Biologists and analysts of the personal computer software industry are both very familiar with so-called "founder effects," where the first species, or the first technology, on the scene reaps overwhelming competitive advantages that often block out fitter, but later-arriving, alternatives.[5] Even in the late twentieth century the maths of Newton's *Principia* remain the sole criteria for advanced placement tests for high school mathematics students.

The timing for numbers and equations could not have been better. It was in exactly the same years that Regiomontanus was taking his first halting steps down the course of algebraic manipulations that Prince Henry the Navigator of Portugal was taking his first halting steps down the coast of Africa. When his followers reached the equator and lost sight of the Pole Star, they had to switch to the non-stationary sun and moon as reference points, adding major new complications that geometry alone could not resolve with sufficient accuracy. The field of practical navigation was absolutely fundamental to the ascendancy of the new maths and thought processes because it provided clear feedback and the inexorable pressure to improve. Purely academic uses do not provoke the same level of urgency. When the Pope, for example, picked a line of longitude out in the Atlantic and arbitrarily gave Portugal everything to the east and Spain everything to the west, it did not much matter that nobody had any idea where that line actually lay. On the other hand, when the publisher of the American nautical almanac for the year 1800 made the seemingly innocuous mistake of treating it as a leap year in the computations, sailors along the Atlantic coast were thrown almost thirty miles off course, leading to shipwreck and loss of life.[6]

In the quest for better and better navigational accuracy, four basic methods competed. The first and purest was to use Newton's formulations to work out, for all time, the exact positions of the sun, moon, and stars and then to use them as the basis for navigation forevermore. The second approach was to update annually the almanacs and ephemerides on the basis of current observational data rather than trying to make them correct perpetually. The third avenue was to tune the practices of navigation adaptively. The fourth approach was to build better clocks.

Initially, adaptive solutions prevailed. Sailors just tuned their methods until they gave the right results. They took no note, for example, of the textbook correction of the length of a degree from sixty miles to almost seventy, the adjustment that was so crucial to Newton's theory of gravitation, because they had already factored it in tacitly. Ships carried knotted ropes with logs on the end. Sailors tossed the logs overboard and, using a sandglass, counted the knots as the line paid out to determine speed. When they kept getting the wrong answer, they reknotted their ropes, changing the spacing between knots, or took a little sand out of their sandglasses. In so doing, they even managed to incorporate rough corrections for the curvature of the earth.[7]

In the end, it was the technology of clocks that solved the problems of practical navigation. This practical outcome, however, did not mollify the scientists, who were determined to show that their step-by-step methods of computing the sun's and moon's locations could be carried out once and for all time. Sequential algebra and planetary orbit calculations were made for each other, perhaps literally. The motion of the moon takes place one place at a time. It was in this context that Laplace first asserted his ideal of an Intellect that could condense into a single formula all the movements of the heavens, past, present, and future. As the mathematician John Couch Adams recalled:

> Wishing to see astronomy founded exclusively on the law of attraction, only borrowing from observation the necessary data, Laplace induced the Academy of Sciences to propose for the subject of the mathematical prize which it was to award in 1820 the formation, by theory alone, of lunar tables as exact as those which had been constructed by theory and observation combined.[8]

Soon afterward, Laplace's fellow countryman Urbain-Jean-Joseph Leverrier, along with Adams, took this computational capability to even greater heights of authority. In the single most influential computing event between the publication of the *Principia* and the powering up of the ENIAC, they independently guided astronomers right to the previously unseen planet of Neptune.

It was not yet nightfall for Henry David Thoreau, at his cabin at Walden, when the telescope of the Berlin Observatory showed what Leverrier had already seen in his mind: the planet Neptune. Both Leverrier and Adams had studied the inexplicable behavior of Uranus and decided that an unseen planet must have been tugging at it. They had determined computationally where such a planet needed to be in order to have the necessary effect. Sequential thought proved able to "realize in this her highest triumph, a discovery made with the mind's eye, in regions where sight itself was unable to penetrate."[9] The homework was considerably more prosaic, of course, as Adams's brother related: "Night after night I have sat up with him in our little parlour at Lidcot, when all the rest had gone to bed, looking over his shoulder, seeing that he copied, added and subtracted his figures correctly, to save his doing it twice over."[10]

Adams's parlour work was greatly expedited by the availability of logarithm tables, whose production had become a small industry of its own, organized just like weaving or toolmaking and destined to have enormous impact on the design of sequential electronic computers. A post-Revolutionary logarithm project in France involved almost one hundred workers. At the top of the organizational hierarchy were some of the best mathematicians in France, including Legendre. Their job was to choose the overall formulations. Working under them were mid-level mathematicians whose role was much like that of contemporary programmers. They created computing forms that broke the formulation down into a series of individual steps. These were in turn passed to a staff of dozens of full-time computers who carried out the actual computations.[11]

Who were these computers, these "martyrs of Science . . . who without hesitation, and with an indomitable perseverance, devoted so many years of their lives to this irksome and herculean task"?[12] In the case of the French project, they were hairdressers rendered surplus by the passing of the *ancien regime*. Their specialty was subtraction, but they were also able to carry out additions. Others were moonlighters, like the "highly skilled computers, most of them elderly Cornish clergymen, who lived on seven figure logarithms, did all their work by hand, and were only too apt to make mistakes."[13] Many were youths: "About one-third of the staff are astronomers, and the rest computers, many of them young girls."[14] The performance level of these young computers varied considerably: "The chief trouble to the computers has been the intermixture of plus and minus signs. . . . One of the quickest boys averaged 2,000 operations . . . per week, for numbers of three digits, those done wrong being discounted."[15] As the computations became more sophisticated, adults came to predominate. By World War II, the U.S. Army "had started at [the Moore] school a program to train in ballistic computation women who had science degrees."[16] The common denominator, of course, is that all these computers were, as illustrated in figure 8.1, people.

Inevitably, in an industrialized age, thoughts of making life easier for human computers turned to thoughts of simply mechanizing them. Babbage recalled how the idea of building an Analytical Engine first came to him:

$$= \cfrac{\frac{4}{3}}{1 - \cfrac{\frac{6}{5}x}{1 + \cfrac{\frac{2}{5\cdot7}x}{1 - \cfrac{\frac{5\cdot8}{7\cdot9}x}{1 - \text{etc.}}}}}$$

Figure 8.1. By the early twentieth century, "computing halls" had become an integral part of any Big Science endeavor. Scientists stylized their formulations to match the capabilities of their hired computers, compressing them into the easily memorized step-by-step form that thought prefers.

The formulations of Newton were particularly well-suited to human information processing. Passed down through the centuries, they were the ones used in ballistics calculations during World War II. When the designer of the ENIAC needed to know what his circuits were supposed to do, he went down to the ballistics computing hall and copied what the human computers were doing there. Thus the *Principia Mathematica* became the design specification for the ENIAC and most every electronic computer since. Equational formulation courtesy of the Trustees of the Boston Public Library. Photo courtesy of the Smithsonian Institution.

One evening I was sitting in the rooms of the Analytical Society, at Cambridge, my head leaning forward on the Table in a kind of dreamy mood, with a Table of logarithms lying open before me. Another member, coming into the room, and seeing me half asleep, called out, "Well, Babbage, what are you dreaming about?" to which I replied, "I am thinking that all these Tables (pointing to the logarithms) might be calculated by machinery."[17]

He was not the first to think of computing as an assembly-line process. The originator of the French logarithm project had read Adam Smith's famous description of how dividing the manufacture of pins down into nineteen sequential tasks greatly increased the output. On the basis of this description, he "conceived all of a sudden of applying the same method to the immense work with which I had been burdened, and to manufacture logarithms as one manufactures pins."[18]

Babbage was familiar both with the work of the French hairdressers and with the design of the Jacquard loom, which read through a sequence of punched cards to find instructions for carrying out its weavings. It was in this industrial context that Lady Lovelace said of Babbage's machine: "We may say most aptly that the Analytical Engine weaves algebraical patterns just as the Jacquard-loom weaves flowers and leaves."[19] Babbage had been hopeful of rapid success when, in 1830, he wrote to Nathaniel Bowditch in Boston: "The construction of a large machine is now going on under my direction for the government and will probably be completed in about three years."[20] In reality Babbage never produced a working machine. It was a Swedish inventor, George Scheutz, who first published a machine-generated book of tables and asserted "how vain it would now be to attempt reprints of any of the existing tables . . . in any other way than by machinery."[21]

Meanwhile, as the Analytical Engine with its fabulously complicated mechanical rods and gear trains was facing endless delays, industrial "progress" was creating the need for a new kind of table, an artillery range table. Better metallurgy enabled more powerful guns that could no longer be adequately aimed by eye. Accurate tables were needed that told the gunner how high to angle the gun to hit a target. Reduced to its essentials, a ballistics computation works out the path of a single moving object, an artillery shell, under the influence of gravity, not unlike a planetary orbit. John Couch Adams supplied the basic formulations based on his immensely prestigious and influential work on Neptune. The computing task for an entire table, however, was enormous, because an artillery shell encounters resistance from the air. The computing hall at the U.S. Ballistic Research Laboratory employed nearly two hundred full-time computers during World War II. It was within this environment of human ballistics table computation that the ENIAC electronic computer was designed and built. The task of computing range tables was reassigned from human minds to electronic circuits just as, in an earlier age, muscle tasks were reassigned to animals.

It was via the development of the ENIAC to produce ballistics tables that the sequential thought processes of René Descartes made the segue from the human computing era to the electronic computing era. These thought processes and formulations dictated the design of the hardware. A comparison of Babbage's Analytical Engine to the ENIAC shows how dominating these ideas were. Save for the fact that one was mechanical and the other electronic, they are nearly twins. Yet as Presper Eckert, one of the designers of ENIAC, noted about himself and his codesigner John Mauchly, "Neither I nor John had any knowledge of Babbage's idea and had never heard of Lady Lovelace."[22] They did not need to. The necessary knowledge had been transmitted culturally. To determine what their device was supposed to do, Eckert and Mauchly had gone down to the Ballistic Research Lab's computing hall and watched what the computers there did. Thus, the design of the ENIAC traces back not so much through Charles Babbage as through John Couch Adams, who was the source of the sequential formulations that those computers were carrying out.

That Adams's methods were well suited to machines was already well known to Babbage. In his personal copy of Adams's paper on the Neptune computations, Babbage had proudly marked each of the steps that could have been carried out on his Analytical Engine.[23] Adams, in turn, was the Victorian Age's most prominent link back to his hero, Isaac Newton: "His mind naturally bore a great resemblance to Newton's in many respects."[24] Given the *Principia*, the discovery of Neptune was inevitable. Given the methods used in the discovery of Neptune, the ENIAC ballistics computer was inevitable. Given ENIAC, today's sequential (and anthropomorphic) computer-chip architectures were inevitable.

They were inevitable because it was not just ballisticians who looked back fondly "to the time when Newton applied his transcendent genius . . . into one of the sublimest products of the human mind."[25] John von Neumann, the most influential computer architect of the twentieth century, felt a similar reverence for what he called "the classic of theoretical physics in our time, Newton's *Principia*."[26] The tendency to cling to Newton during the formative days of electronic computing was understandable. It was overwhelmingly difficult to get electronic circuits to do even the most familiar forms of computing. A single vacuum tube or transistor by itself cannot perform any of the kinds of operations a person does. It typically required four tubes just to store a single binary bit of information and four of these binary bits to store a single decimal digit, much less do anything with it. Suddenly, engineers who were used to designing with a dozen tubes or less were faced with the need to use thousands of them. Mimicking a human ballistic computer was a formidable task.

> If a machine is to perform the functions of a human computer, it must possess—
> A. An arithmetic unit, capable of performing the normal operations of arithmetic. . . .
> B. A memory, that . . . will retain numbers which are needed in the calculation and also the instructions. . . .
> C. A built-in power of judgment. . . .
> D. An input–output mechanism.[27]

Fortunately for the circuit designers, the human computers could not keep very many numbers active at any one moment in time. Even three or four, a typical complement for an early electronic computer, meant many hundreds of tubes just to store them. Adding in all the other circuits needed "to imitate the human method of calculating"[28] brought the total number of tubes in ENIAC to eighteen thousand.

Only in one respect did the architecture of the electronic computers deviate meaningfully from the Cartesian dogma of how thought should work. Descartes had distinguished the *formulation*—what we now call the *program*—from the *data*. The formulation stayed in mind, while the data went out onto paper as necessary. The first electronic devices also distinguished program from data, but the separation turned out to have no advantages because both program steps and data were now treated as numbers. Storing them both together allowed short programs to have extra amounts of data, and vice versa. In addition, and ultimately far more important, it allowed the computer routinely to change its program as well as its data, something a human computer was loath to do.

This new ability of an electronic formulation to evolve itself over time was little used in the first fifty years of computing because the emphasis has been on keeping all the maths the same. Machines like ENIAC were trying their utmost to be indistinguishable from a human computer and to do things in exactly the same way they had been done all along. In von Neumann's words,

> the mathematical or mathematical–physical process of understanding the problem [and casting it] into equations and conditions . . . has nothing to do with computing or with machines: It is equally necessary in any effort in mathematics or applied mathematics. . . . It would be equally necessary if the problems were computed "by hand."[29]

The whole computational methodology of the Industrial Age, the "four hundred years of scientific wisdom," thus made the transition to electronics largely unchanged. The techniques for designing the iron railroad bridges of the 1870s, for example, came to be the techniques for designing the supersonic aircraft of the 1970s and the automobiles of the 1980s. The typical railroad bridge of Babbage's time was made up of iron girders assembled in triangular patterns with nothing but air in between. The bridge as a whole could be treated as divided into triangular elements with forces moving only along the edges and never through the middle. By the 1930s, the focus of transportation engineers had shifted from trains to planes, but the structural issues remained identical. An airframe of the period was made up of triangular ribs just like a railroad bridge. The airplane makers became serious users of the computational techniques invented originally for bridges.

Because the formulation was inherently sequential and repetitive, it was an excellent fit for the human computers of the 1930s. It also left them with some scope for individual decision making to speed up the process. As electronic circuits became increasingly competitive in the early 1950s, the computer was exhorted to "realize that he is in no way the slave of the method but rather that he is its master, that his work will reflect his own personality. He must not allow himself to become a human computing machine."[30]

Meanwhile, as the computers were perfecting their techniques of analyzing these triangular rib structures, the design of the airframes themselves changed. Aluminum sheets replaced the cloth that had covered the fuselages and wings of early planes. These aluminum sheets became the structural elements, and the struts underneath gradually withered away. The computational struts, however,

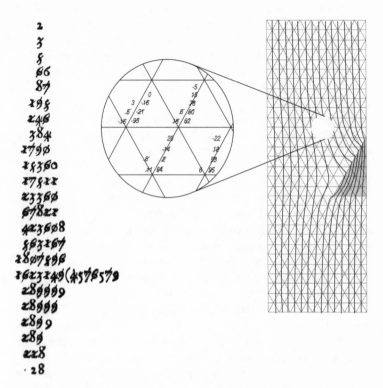

Clavius, *Epitome Arithmeticae Practicae*, 1588

Southwell, *Relaxation Methods in Theoretical Physics*, 1949

Figure 8.2. Numbers and equations became popular because they offered the kind of one-step-at-a-time computational environment that human thought prefers. Each step refines and then overwrites the results of the previous step, keeping the amount of active data very small. The basic number-crossout methods espoused for long division in the time of Shakespeare were the same as those used to compute stresses and force fields in the years leading up to World War II. Image from *Epitome Arithmeticae Practicae* courtesy of the Trustees of the Boston Public Library. Diagram from *Relaxation Methods in Theoretical Physics* courtesy of Oxford University Press.

remained in place. The change in the way airplanes were made did *not* result in a change in the way computers calculated their stresses. Designers simply treated the airplanes "as if" they were still made of triangular struts. Now formally known as "finite-element" analysis, this "as if cloth stretched over triangular struts" technique is still used to study the stresses in the most modern supersonic aircraft, as illustrated in figure 8.3.

Why have the old computational thought processes of the sailing and railroad ages endured into the Space Age? For one thing, early technical considerations reinforced the anthropomorphic design of electronic computers. The best way to keep circuit costs down was to operate on only one piece of data at a time, as human computers always had. The compactness of algebraic formulations, so much appreciated by the elderly Cornish clergymen, was a boon for the electronics as well. Early memory systems were themselves sequential— they stored data as sequences of ripples in a pool of mercury—giving additional impetus to sequential programming techniques.

None of these technical considerations endured, but sequential architecture did. To break through sequentialism and the numbers-and-equations vocabulary, as Kepler finally broke through the circle of geometry, requires breaking through the whole self-reinforcing infrastructure of sequential thought. It is a great irony that the reasons for sequential thought all exist and codepend on each other in parallel. The phenomenon of sequentialism emerges from the parallel interplay of many elements. Sequential, discursive thought may be incapable of understanding why it exists.

Electronic computers became sequential partly because that is the way their most influential architects preferred to carry out their own thinking. As von Neumann's collaborator Stanislaw Ulam observed, "Johnny gave the impression of operating sequentially by formal deductions."[31] He experimented briefly with parallelism, but when he could not get the circuitry to behave, he set the method aside and did not return to it.[32] It is possible that von Neumann, like Descartes, was innately sequential in his thought, but it is just as likely he learned it in school. Humanists looked to math as the "way to settle in the mind a habit of reasoning closely in train." Contemporary scientists like Ulam still look to mathematics as "one of the few ways to perfect the brain."[33]

Sequentialism and numericism are themselves linked. Descartes insisted that "all the thoughts that can come into the human mind must be arranged in an order like the natural order of numbers."[34]

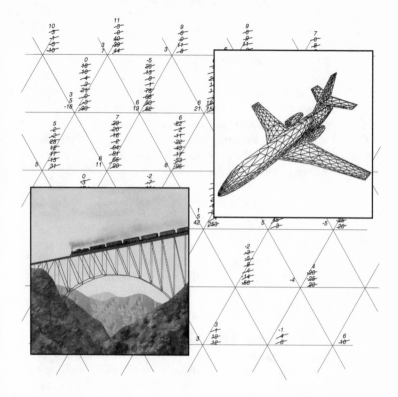

Figure 8.3. Railroad engineers were among the earliest users of computing for structural analysis. They used iterative techniques to work out the stresses along the triangular girder structures of their bridges. Because the first airplanes used a similar skeleton of structural ribs under their fabric coverings, aircraft engineers soon adopted these same techniques. As metal replaced fabric and the skeleton was eliminated from airframes, however, engineers simply maintained this "as if triangles" fiction in their finite element analysis programs. Thus sequential electronic computers were able to keep the mathematical techniques of the steam age alive into the era of the supersonic jet airplane. Airplane diagram courtesy of Thinking Machines Corporation. Background image courtesy of Oxford University Press.

Once established within human thought, sequentialism then reached out to color our view of nature itself. To Ralph Waldo Emerson, the laws of nature "answer to those of mind as image in the mirror."[35] George Boole, whose system of logic underpins all electronic computers, also saw "a close analogy between the operations of the mind in general reasoning and its operation in the particular science of Algebra."[36] Instead of recognizing the way human-optimized maths distort our view of the world, the astronomer and ballistician Forrest Moulton actually proclaimed them as our defense against such distortion. For other observers, however, the conflation has remained clear:

> By reducing the laws of nature to mathematical formulas, we largely remove our predictions and their verifications from the distorting influences of our prejudices.[37]

> A defining feature of deductive argument was exported to the external world—a prominent page of the recipe was mixed in with the stew. Nature, it was concluded, obeys the logic of the deductive method.[38]

Equations are attractive because they are both terse and general. Unlike diagrams, equations could be applied to whole ranges of behavior. To Babbage's delight, "infinitely varied phenomena emerge as the necessary consequences."[39] This seeming generality awakened the Laplacian fantasy of a single, albeit yet-to-be-discovered, equation that somehow governed everything since the Creation and would continue to do so forever. All that lay between science and the discovery of this equation was the capacity to crunch the data:

> An Intellect that at any given instant knew all the forces that animate nature and the mutual positions of the beings who compose it, were this Intellect but vast enough to submit his data to analysis, could condense into a single formula the movement of the greatest body in the universe and that of the lightest atom; to such an Intellect nothing would be uncertain, for the future, even as the past, would be ever before his eyes.[40]

What computer science has added to the tradition of Western thought is a concrete idea of how these immutable laws might play out and still allow for miracles. Rather than just being a Watchmaker who wound up the world and then stood aside to watch it tick, Charles

Babbage's God was a Software Engineer who programmed the world and then stood aside to watch it launch.[41] A child of his time, Babbage could not conceive of God "perpetually interfering" to keep the world on its appointed course. He was sure that "the Creator who selected the present law must have foreseen the consequences of all other laws."[42]

If a species became extinct, or a new one arrived on the scene, the change was a result of a plan that had been "impressed on matter at the dawn of its existence."[43] So, too, with miracles. Babbage described how his own Analytical Engine could be set up to carry out the same law for vast periods of time, then stop and do something completely different for a single cycle before returning to the original law. Onlookers might well exclaim that they had witnessed a miracle, but it would be no miracle at all because it had been in the code all along.

It was within this pervasive belief structure of unchanging natural laws playing out one step at a time that the first electronic computers were designed during World War II. Fortunately, this same war also inspired the first concrete steps toward the computation of social patterns of behavior and, with it, a whole new unit of the Book of Nature.

$\mathcal{T}$HE ADVENT OF NEW SCIENCES AND NEW MATHS

In August of 1938, when the British scientific community came together for their annual meeting, the news of the day was all about Czechoslovakia. Hitler and Germany were demanding redress of grievances among the German-speaking population of the Sudeten. There was sympathy within England for the view that the German-speaking minority was being discriminated against by the government in Prague. It was the job of the diplomats, however, not the scientists, to seek an answer to the potential crisis, because it was common knowledge that it was impossible to "trace the future history" of human events in any mathematical way.[1]

It had once been equally common knowledge among scientists that *none* of the events here on earth, including even the motion of falling bodies, were the appropriate subjects of predictive thought. According to Aristotle, the world beneath the level of the moon was qualitatively different from what lay beyond. The geometric methods of the day were appropriate for studying the perfect eternal motions of the heavens, but they were no match for the transient, corrupted, and violent motions of bodies down here on earth.

Galileo, who disagreed, had some choice words on this subject. He asked why the earth should be so different from, and so much sloppier than, the heavens. Was he to believe that "After the marvelous construction of the vast heavenly sphere, the divine Creator pushed the refuse that remained into the center and hid it there"?[2] Why should circular motion only occur in the heavens and straight-line motion only occur on the earth? Galileo brazenly asserted that God had, in fact, brought the planets up to speed by dropping them and then, when they had accelerated to the necessary speed, deflecting them into the circular orbits in which they continued to revolve. Having asserted a commonality between the behavior of the heavens and behavior here on earth, Galileo then proceeded to apply the maths of the former to the problems of the latter. His success was limited both because the old maths of geometry were ill suited to the new problems of dynamics and because few of the schoolmen of the day took his efforts seriously.

By the time of the British Association meeting in 1938, no scientist would have questioned the use of numbers and equations to describe the behavior of Galileo's physical objects. They did, however, question the use of these maths to chart the future history of the Czechoslovakian crisis, even when a Fellow of the Royal Society and its leading authority on scientific computing, Lewis Fry Richardson, proposed it. In an abstract presented at the meeting, Richardson introduced a set of differential equations to describe the behavior of arms races. Had Richardson been as imperious and publicity seeking as Galileo, the proposal might have stirred more interest and debate. He was, however, far more humble and self-effacing. He presented his equations, the result of almost twenty years of work, absorbed some ridicule, and returned to Scotland. His equations were software telescopes nobody wanted to look through.

Richardson is known today as the founder of the field of computational weather prediction as well as for his theoretical contributions to the field of fluid dynamics. In the 1920s, when he published his *Weather Prediction by Numerical Method*, the application of equations to the weather was audacious, but it was not heretical. His contemporaries agreed that if weather could be modeled at all, numbers and equations were the right tools for the job. After serving as an ambulance driver in France during World War I, Richardson returned to his job at the British Meteorological Office, but he resigned for reasons of conscience when it became part of the Air Ministry. A Quaker and therefore a conscientious objector during the war, he did not receive the university appointment that his extraordinary scientific accomplishments normally might have produced. Instead, he took up a long-standing interest in the field of psychology, earning a degree in the subject to go with his doctorate in physics. Even as a college student, he had felt that a famous German scientist had erred in becoming a doctor first and a physicist second: "Helmholtz had eaten of life in the wrong order. . . . I would like to spend the first half of my life under the strict discipline of physics, and afterwards to apply that training to researches on living things."[3]

Thus, the twentieth century's most creative practitioner of numerical computing turned his attention to psychology and its role in the phenomena of war and peace. Needless to say, there was nothing whatsoever for him to build on. Johannes Kepler had had his Tycho Brahe to provide data. For Richardson there were no reliable data, either about wars themselves or about the arms expenditures that seemed to precede them. He had to create the field of peace research from scratch. The absence of data was not new to him, however. He had had to forage for data about local weather as well, even poring over records of old balloon races to try to understand local wind patterns. Now he consulted scores of history books for records of wars. Ultimately, he identified just over a hundred wars in the period from 1820 to 1949.[4]

Because his original definition of wars as conflicts with more than a certain number of fatalities felt arbitrary, Richardson widened his scope to include "deadly conflicts" of all kinds, including individual murders. Using a technique common in physics, he categorized these deadly conflicts by the logarithm of the number of deaths they involved. A murder was a deadly conflict of magnitude zero since the logarithm of one is zero. According to the best data available to him, World War I and World War II were both fatal quarrels of magnitude seven, as was the nineteenth-century Taiping Rebellion in China. A nuclear holocaust that wiped out human life on earth completely would be a fatal quarrel of magnitude ten going on eleven.

To fill in the gap between single homicides—for which good data were widely available—and full-fledged wars, Richardson sought out statistics both from the Chicago gang wars of the period and from Manchurian gangster raids during the Japanese occupation. Until the Royal Society finally offered him a mechanical calculator, he had to do all his analyses by hand. His description of his work with the data, which he called his potted history book, recalls the image of Kepler rearranging his data in a posy first this way and then that, looking for a pattern.

Richardson saw arms races as precursors to wars and his interest was in controlling war, not just tallying it, so he focused his analysis on arms expenditures. His data for the pattern of arms expenditures prior to World War I encouraged him to do the same analysis for the arms buildup that he saw all around him in the 1930s. Although he recognized that leaders were free to act in singular ways, his data suggested that they did not. The actual behavior was all too consistent. He offered the words of the defense minister of the quasi-hypothetical country of Jedesland as standing tolerably well for all:

> The intentions of our country are entirely pacific. We have given ample evidence of this by the treaties which we have recently concluded with our neighbors. Yet, when we consider the state of unrest in the world at large and the menaces by which we are surrounded, we would be failing in our duty as a Government if we did not take adequate steps to increase the defences of our beloved land.

"We have now," Richardson said, "to translate that into mathematics."[5] As a physicist, he felt free to aggregate behavior in order not to become bogged down in detail, just as he had done in his studies of the weather:

> Foreign affairs as they appear day by day in the newspaper: the text of the despatch, the facial expression of the ambassador as he comes away from the important interview, the movement of warships, these may be likened to the eddying view of the wind. Whereas the theory here presented may be likened to an account of the general circulation of the earth's atmosphere.[6]

He also felt free to assume that the behavior of a nation was simply the sum of the behavior of its individual citizens, that "a nation is any set of people who are held together by a common loyalty, so that they act together in foreign politics."[7] With these assumptions, he translated the rhetoric of the defense ministry into a pair of differential equations:

$$\frac{dx}{dt} = ky - \alpha x + g \qquad\qquad \frac{dy}{dt} = lx - \beta y + h$$

The behaviors of the two nations, symbolized by x and y, are inextricably "coupled" in the sense that the current behavior of each nation appears on the right-hand side of the equation that predicts the future behavior of the other nation. If one nation increases its armaments, that fact alone is enough to drive the rate of arms expenditures of the other nation to a higher level. The second important point about the equations is that "history matters." If one nation harbors a grievance, symbolized by the final terms in the equations, that grievance alone increases the country's rate of arms expenditure independent of the other nation's more current behavior.

Clearly, in the absence of both grievances and opposing arms expenditures, the system of equations remains at a pacific equilibrium. This equilibrium is what Richardson saw along the borders between the United States and Canada and between Sweden and Norway. None of these countries were engaged in defending their common border, and none had any lingering reasons to start doing so. It was also possible, according to the equations, for existing tensions to relax and for each nation to behave in ways that motivated the other to decrease its expenditures or at least hold them constant. As events in the world indicated, however, most solutions did not stabilize. Nations tended to become locked into patterns of behavior that motivated the other side to increase its rate of spending on armaments.

Prior to the British Association meeting in 1938, Richardson had tried three times to place his work for publication and had been three times turned down.[8] Psychology journals found his work tainted by mathematics; physics journals found it tainted by psychology. Only the journal *Nature,* committed to publishing in all areas of science, accepted his brief notes.[9] After his uneven treatment at the British Association meeting in August 1938, he gathered his materials for publication in December of that year. In the interim, of course, Neville Chamberlain had met with Adolf Hitler in Munich in September, abandoned his country's commitments to Czechoslovakia, and returned to London to proclaim "peace in our time." As illustrated in figure 9.1, Richardson looked behind Chamberlain's words to what his equations told him.

According to Chamberlain's words, the world was relaxing as a result of Munich. By Richardson's analysis, it was doing no such thing: "According to the debate in the London Parliament there was to be a maintenance or speeding up of British rearmament. . . . Consider especially Germany, which has got rid of a grievance, and yet is going to

$$\frac{dx}{dt} = ky - \alpha x + g$$

$$\frac{dy}{dt} = lx - \beta y + h$$

"Peace in our time."

Figure 9.1. Social and biological behavior have traditionally been considered to be outside the realm of mathematical vocabulary, just as physics was considered to be outside the reach of mathematics until the time of Galileo. Thus, when, in August 1938, the Scottish physicist and student of psychology Lewis Richardson proposed a set of equations to predict the course of arms races, his scientific colleagues were scornful. Just one month later, when the British Prime Minister Neville Chamberlain returned from Munich and proclaimed "peace in our time," Richardson was able to use his formulations to foretell a very different outcome, a pioneering use of computation in the social and behavioral sciences. Photo courtesy of UPI/Bettmann.

extend fortifications; and the United States of America, which was not directly threatened, but has responded by deciding to increase its Atlantic fleet from fourteen warships to approximately sixty."[10]

Richardson's equations, of course, charted the future history of Europe far more accurately than did the prime minister's words. With the predicted war indeed under way, Richardson turned his attention to postwar realities. Already in 1944, he was pointing to the inherent instability of the stated goals of the United Nations: "The Germans and Japanese are to be defeated and disarmed, and thereafter watched for so long a time as may be necessary by an armed force controlled by the United Nations, who are firmly resolved to remain united."[11] By the 1950s, when he died, Richardson was analyzing with alarm the third global arms race of his lifetime. The participants were the same members of the United Nations who had so firmly resolved to remain united. His final observations in *Nature* magazine noted that his equations did allow for an arms race to end without a war but that he did not expect it to happen.[12]

As a trained psychologist, Richardson was particularly interested in what changed people's minds about subjects such as war and what the rate of change was. On the one hand, war moods seemed to change radically in the first few days of a conflict. Citizens who were urging peace one week were pushing to the front of the enlistment lines the next. No such instant change seemed to mark the end of a war. Instead, war weariness set in gradually. He wondered if "something might perhaps be done by propaganda to diminish the defence coefficients and thereby give ballast to foreign politics,"[13] specifically mentioning in this context that the International Advertising Convention had just been held in Glasgow.[14]

In sum, Richardson's efforts, like Galileo's of an earlier era, were halting, tentative, and totally outside the bounds of accepted investigation. In addition, Richardson's were not wholly accurate. His equations did not, for example, predict the subsequent dynamics of the Arab–Israeli arms race very well,[15] nor did they project the collapse of the East–West arms race in the late 1980s. It is easy in hindsight to join his contemporary critics and pronounce his efforts a failure. On the other hand, the single most important European event in the months following the 1938 meeting of the British Association was the abandonment of Czechoslovakia. Of all the scientists assembled at that meeting, only Richardson had anything substantive to say on the subject. The paper by his far more famous contemporary John Maynard

Keynes, in contrast, chose to focus on government subsidies for ware-houses.

Richardson's efforts illustrate the burden that scientists take on when they venture outside established computational bounds. The whole supporting infrastructure vanishes: There are no data, there are no forums for scholarly interchange, there is no support, there are no prior results that are known to be wrong and in urgent need of cor-rection. Richardson's efforts were constrained both by the magnitude of the task and by the limits of the tools at his disposal. Decades of effort gathering statistics about deadly quarrels yielded only a few ten-uous megabytes from which to work. Although still respected today, the data are way too skimpy for the task at hand.

Furthermore, like Galileo, Richardson was trying to use incumbent maths to do a job they were simply not designed to do. From his suc-cesses in physics and meteorology, Richardson had developed an abid-ing confidence in the vocabulary of partial differential equations and pace. Thus, for example, he talked in terms of the "speeding up of British rearmament." The mathematical biologist Anatol Rapaport, writing in the 1960s, first noted that it was the fundamental limitations of obsolete vocabulary that had stymied both Galileo and Richardson:

> Let us turn the tables on classic analysis and ask, "To what extent is classic analysis (admirably suited to classical physics) applicable to theories of human behavior?" Is it possible that it lacks necessary con-cepts, in the sense that ancient mathematics lacks certain concepts necessary for physical theory? If so, then no amount of development of the techniques of classic analysis will break the barrier which sep-arates its range of applicability from that of human behavior.[16]

The philosopher of science Norwood Hanson has paid especial tribute to Galileo for being able to see beyond the limits of established vocabulary and hence to stimulate others: "Thinking new thoughts in a conceptual framework not designed to express them requires unprecedented physical insights. In the history of physics few could sense the importance of things not yet expressible in current idioms. The task of the few has been to find means of saying what is for others unsayable."[17] Rapaport suggested that the new mathematics of game theory would turn out to be the one needed to do the job Richardson tried to do with partial differential equations. He felt that some of the issues addressed by game theory "may be as essential to a mathematical theory of human behavior as the dynamic notions of functions and rate of change (absent in ancient mathematics) were for physics." If this turned out to be true, then Richardson's equations of arms races, like Galileo's diagrams of acceleration, would turn out to have "only historical value."[18]

We now know what was not clear in the 1960s: that the new electronic circuits of the computer industry would grow to become the dominating factor in the viability of new maths. Game theory has not ridden the crest of this new technology wave. Other new maths have made far greater progress because they tied themselves more directly to the progress in circuit technology. The first of these new maths was invented at the end of World War II and came to be known as "Monte Carlo" because it involved finding answers by adding up large numbers of random events. At Los Alamos, Ulam arrived at one early version of the method while he was "convalescing from an illness and playing solitaires. . . . I wondered whether a more practical method than 'abstract thinking' might not be to lay it out say one hundred times and simply observe and count the number of successful plays."[19]

His experience echoed that of the injured Civil War officer who showed that π could be computed by dropping pins and tallying how many landed across the cracks in the hospital floorboards. Over an extended convalescence, he obtained a value of 3.16.[20] Both he and Ulam were engaging in forms of math that, under normal circumstances, no humans in their right mind would have chosen to employ. The Monte Carlo approach ultimately boils down to playing out the possibilities over and over again to see what the pattern of results is. It quickly became the primary tool for predicting the behavior of neutrons within nuclear devices.[21] Rather than trying to track the diffusion of atomic particles through radioactive material equationally, scientists such as Nick Metropolis used computers to create "a genealogical history of an individual neutron"[22] over and over and over again.

A more explicit challenge to the hegemony of numbers and equations within physics came in the 1970s with the following question: "How does God solve differential equations?"[23] If, as the prevailing wisdom had it, natural phenomena play out according to partial differential equations, then the phenomena must be, in some meta-sense, cognizant of those equations in order to obey their constraints. Posed in this way, of course, the hypothesis becomes ridiculous. God obviously does not solve partial differential equations any more than a planet traces out its orbit by, in Kepler's phrase, "obtaining the values right from the Prutenic or Alphonsine tables."[24] Were there other approaches?

In the early 1980s, physicists such as Stephen Wolfram and the team of Uriel Frisch, Brosl Hasslacher, and Yves Pomeau made an audacious prediction. They said that once electronic computers became powerful enough, they would be able to save the appearances of even very complex behavior like fluid flow without any numbers and equations at all. Instead, they would use "cellular automata," tiny computational objects that move on a very simple playing field akin to a checkerboard. Unlike complex differential equations, these cellular automata operate by trivially simple rules. A typical rule is that a cellular automaton moving in a direction keeps moving in that direction until it hits another one. Other rules determine, in equally simple-minded ways, what happens when two cellular automata collide. Obviously, a small number of such cellular automata could never exhibit the complex swirling behavior of a fluid. The hypothesis was based on having millions of them bumping and jostling all at once. From trillions of individually trivial interactions, the theory went, complex behavior would emerge, as illustrated in figure 9.2.

Finally, supercomputers became powerful enough to run the tests, and indeed the complex behavior of fluids emerged. The successes of the post-equational formulation promptly reopened the old Renaissance issues of truth: that in Galileo's words, "it should be granted that a system that agrees very closely with appearances may be true."[25] Contemporary critics of the cellular automata methodology currently acknowledge, in essence, that "what could be more useful for research, better suited for teaching . . . they have been thought up by extraordinarily ingenious men"[26] and that as long as it is only used *ex suppositione*, the formulation "holds no danger and it suffices for the mathematician."[27] The practitioners of these new forms of digital physics, meanwhile, assert that their formulations are reflective of nature itself, that they are true.

The case for cellular automata as reflective of nature itself is grounded in the molecular nature of matter. A flowing fluid is actually a huge volume of individual molecules all bumping and jostling against each other in ways that have nothing to do with partial differential equations. Cellular automata represent simplified packets, or bundles, of molecules. Although far bigger than individual molecules, they retain the simple bumping and jostling behavior. Like the molecules, their capacity for complex behavior lies in the interactions, not in the individual automata:

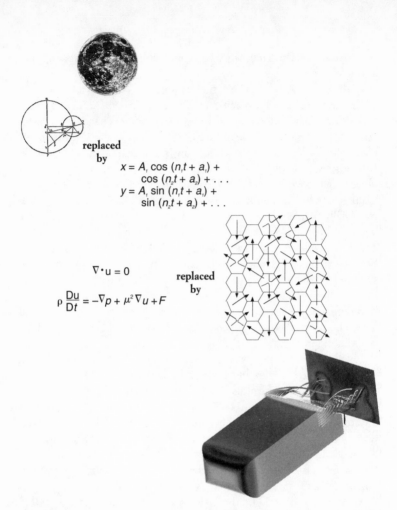

$$x = A_1 \cos (n_1 t + a_1) +$$
$$\cos (n_2 t + a_2) + \ldots$$
$$y = A_1 \sin (n_1 t + a_1) +$$
$$\sin (n_2 t + a_2) + \ldots$$

replaced by

$$\nabla \cdot u = 0$$
$$\rho \frac{Du}{Dt} = -\nabla p + \mu^2 \nabla u + F$$

replaced by

Figure 9.2. Just as scientists once used the vocabulary of algebra to reexpress the old idea of epicycles, they are now using the vocabularies of the new intermaths to reexpress long-standing ideas of fluid behavior, such as the wake behind a simplified auto body. While difficult for us to grasp and impossible to ever carry out "by hand," these intermath formulations are a much better fit to the strengths and weaknesses of the electronic circuits that actually do all the computing work in a modern society. They are already spawning new fields such as digital physics that will change not only the way we express physical behavior, but also the way we ultimately understand the behavior itself. Geometric design courtesy of the Trustees of the Boston Public Library. Fluid flow simulation courtesy of Exa Corporation.

It is common in nature to find systems whose overall behavior is extremely complex, yet whose fundamental component parts are each very simple. The complexity is generated by the cooperative effect of many simple identical components. Much has been discovered about the nature of the components in physical and biological systems; little is known about the mechanisms by which these components act together to give the overall complexity observed.[28]

The patterns of automobile traffic provide an everyday example. Traditionally, scientists have treated traffic "flow" as a continuous fluid because that is what it looks like from the tops of skyscrapers. In reality, of course, traffic is made up of discrete vehicles reacting to other vehicles in their immediate vicinity. Cellular automata are a more faithful rendition of traffic realities than fluid-flow equations because they allow for the fact that "drivers, unlike molecules, make individual decisions."[29]

The role of partial differential equations, meanwhile, has become recognized as inherently problematic in the context of electronic circuits. The equations are appealingly elegant when they enter the electronic context, but what happens next makes a mockery of that elegance. The process, in the words of the physicist Brosl Hasslacher, entails "an inelegant disassembly of our beautiful and compact, continuous and smooth description of the system. . . . Here lies the paradox. By the time the [equational vocabulary] has been reduced (inside the computer) to a form that can be worked on, [even] the original idea of number has been taken away."[30]

The same illusions obtain on the way out. As Langer reminds us, patterns need to be communicated visually: "An idea that contains too many minute yet closely related parts, too many relations within relations, cannot be 'projected' into discursive form."[31] The sequential numerical outputs of the equations require transformation into pixels, again masking the underlying realities inside the machine: "The partial differential equation and the movie coming out are elegant and attractive, but the process in between—the process that actually happens inside the computer—is a tangle."[32]

Thus, during the past fifty years, two dynamics have been playing out side by side. On the one hand, sequential electronic circuits have been elevating the four-hundred-year-old Part Two of the Book of Nature to its final heights of performance. The original ballistics tables of the 1940s had required computing just 3,300 trajectories. John von Neumann estimated that a simple fluid flow computation would be the equivalent of 330,000 such trajectories.[33] Today's national computing centers have the capacity to do computations as big as 330,000,000 trajectories. Since rates-of-change have been the primary focus of Part Two, it has been these increases in the pace of computing that have garnered all the headlines. Mere performance, however, does not break new ground. The true revolution has been taking place elsewhere.

As our sequential hardware circuits have been faithfully fulfilling Gordon Moore's Law and increasing their pace of performance each year, it has been iconoclastic scientists such as Lewis Richardson and Stephen Wolfram who have been quietly opening Part Three of the Book of Nature. Richardson used the traditional equational maths to engage whole new fields of enquiry in the social sciences, just as Galileo first engaged the field of physics using geometric maths. Meanwhile, Wolfram has validated bold new maths in established fields such as fluid dynamics, just as the algebraic contemporaries of Descartes once did. These are the scientists who have set the stage for a change more fundamental than any since the Renaissance. The long-term role of the new vocabularies lies in the new scientific territories, just as it did four hundred years ago. Cellular automata and other parallel intermaths are epochal because of their potential in the biological and sociological areas where the physics-based equations of Lewis Richardson came up short. As Hasslacher has noted:

> the real future of the methodology lies in applications where traditional methods have not been successful at all: phenomena for which no fundamental partial differential equations have been discovered, only patchword descriptions. . . . I have in mind large-scale economic models, sociological schemes, molecular cell dynamics, and the like.[34]

During the Renaissance numbers and equations received a big boost because they were a more natural fit to what human minds were inherently good at and what printing presses were inherently good at. Today the new intermaths have the same unfair advantage. They are a far more natural fit to the sorts of minute parallel operations that electronic circuits have been best at all along and to the pixels that are now the medium of scientific expression. All that remained was for parallel computer architects to break the sequence as Kepler broke the circle.

10

L ISTENING TO NEURON

Descartes aside, the people who have defined the processes of scientific thought and prediction have tended to be people who were more interested in the results themselves than in the thought processes behind them. Ptolemy, Kepler, Galileo, Newton, Lewis Richardson, John von Neumann: None had any desire to be known as a pedagogue or "computer scientist." They were simply investigators who were willing to follow the physicist James Clark Maxwell "and to be for a season a calculating machine if he can only at last make his ideas clearer."[1] As they saw opportunities to make the processes more efficient, they did so, but only as means to an end. Joseph Napier, on the software side with his logarithms, and Charles Babbage, on the hardware side with his Analytical Engine, are among the few scientists to have entered the history books purely for their contributions to computer science itself.

What happens, however, when being a computer for a season, or even a hundred seasons, is not enough? That was the question faced in the 1970s by artificial-intelligence researchers such as Danny Hillis. He and his colleagues wanted to manipulate information that was stored in complex patterns such as "semantic networks." These networks are very different from the tables of numbers in a ballistics computation or even a weather simulation. Individual pieces of data in a network are connected in very complicated ways rather than in neat rows and columns.

Such a network can be used, for example, to analyze what it means for an astronomer to marry a star, as illustrated in figure 10.1. It would, draw on its knowledge of "astronomers" and "stars" and confirm that they were related concepts. It would then test these initial connections against its understanding of "marriage" and, when faced with a contradiction, would dig deeper into its knowledge of stars. Ultimately, it would produce a self-consistent understanding of the sentence, just as we do.

Unfortunately, the task of managing a meaningful semantic network was far beyond the capabilities of even the largest computers in the 1970s:

> We know just enough about each of these [pattern recognition and semantic] tasks so that we might plausibly undertake to program a computer to generate one-sentence descriptions of simple pictures, but . . . what the human mind does almost effortlessly would take the fastest existing computers many days.[2]

The solution, as is well understood today, was to have the electronic circuits do more than one operation at a time. In this realm, however, there was no multi-century track record of success as there was with sequentialism. The architects of von Neumann's generation had shrewdly realized that if they could just build circuits that behaved the same way human computers behaved, those circuits would carry out already-formulated ballistics computations and many others besides. In designing the Connection Machine® system, one of the first massively parallel computers, Hillis had to rely heavily on the indirect evidence of the brain itself for the conviction that parallel processes could potentially add up to something useful:

> Why do we even believe that it is possible to perform these calculations with such a high degree of concurrency? . . . First, we have the existence of the human brain, which manages to achieve the performance we are after with a large number of apparently slow switching components.[3]

We do not experience this parallel level of brain functioning because it happens at a tacit level. Humans never give their brain an

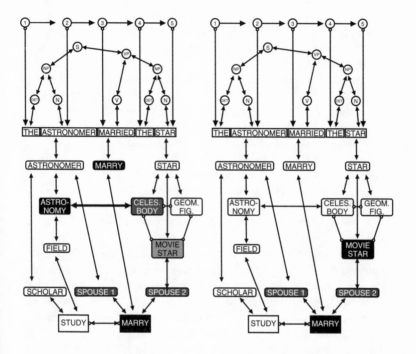

Figure 10.1. The numerical information used by Industrial Age maths typically lined up in neat rows and columns. A sequential computer, whether human or electronic, could move up and down these matrices very efficiently. The word meanings of a language, however, do not line up in any such neat rows and columns. Word meanings interconnect in a much more complex pattern known as a semantic network. Even a single sentence such as "The astronomer married the star" involves a complex and dynamic semantic net. This network must, for example, take account of three alternative meanings of the word "star." (The small circles on the lines connecting the three alternatives indicate that only one meaning may ultimately be true at a time.) At first the very strong linkage between "astronomer" and "celestial body" biases the interpretation of "star" in that direction. Only after many processing cycles does the network resettle on the Hollywood meaning of "star." The need to process complex patterns of ambiguous data such as semantic networks helped stimulate the development of parallel computer architectures. Courtesy of Thinking Machines Corporation.

explicit set of instructions for recognizing their mother's face. Nor do professors typically give their students instructions on how to solve math problems in parallel. The precedents for formulating in parallel, therefore, were still immature at the time the Connection Machine was being designed.

Aristotle had denied that humans could even hear and see at the same time. The one place he embraced simultaneity was in the behavior of the winds, where a quartering wind could be interpreted as the result of two primary winds blowing at once and combining. St. Augustine would have made a much better parallel architect than Aristotle, because he was willing to think in radical ways. He imagined that, for God, time itself was parallel. To Augustine, all of God's years existed at once; only on earth did the years go by one at a time sequentially: "Thy years neither go nor come; whereas these years of ours do both go and come, that in their order they may all come. Thy years stand all at once."[4]

Galileo was able to imagine all the stars in the universe rolling down ramps at once, although there was no way for him to follow up on this inherently parallel idea. Therefore, having apologized to his reader for even wandering off onto this speculation, he went back to his original "line of thought." Today we call Galileo's approach "data parallel," meaning that the parallelism exists at the level of the phenomenon itself, and hence of the data that describe it, rather than in the way humans have chosen to formulate it. The rich potential of data parallelism, even in the traditional fields of the physical sciences, can most easily be seen by returning to the endlessly fertile mind of Lewis Richardson.

When World War I began, Richardson was still working at the British Meteorological Office. The Office's standard way of predicting the weather was to consult a vast picture file of past weather patterns and find the one that looked most like the current situation. The assumption was then made that the current weather would play out the same way the pattern had before. Richardson found this method crude compared to what the astronomers had accomplished with equations over the years: "One may reflect [that] the Nautical Almanac, that marvel of accurate forecasting, is not based on the principle that astronomical history repeats itself in the aggregate."[5]

As an ambulance driver during the war, he, like Ulam in the hospital, had had abundant time to think about how to apply the vocabulary of the astronomers to computing the course of the weather. As a computational fiction, he created a checkerboard of points that

aligned with actual weather stations in Europe. He imagined computational weather moving into and out of each of his square lattice
areas according to the differential equations that described the flow
of fluids. Working in foxholes and abandoned barns, it took him six
weeks to do the computations that advanced one lattice point by
three hours. Speed hacking reduced the time to below a hundred
hours, but that was as far as he could shrink it. He therefore took the
logical next step and proposed to do the work in parallel, as illustrated in figure 10.2:

> 64,000 computers would be needed to race the weather for the
> whole globe. . . . Imagine a large hall like a theatre, except that the
> circles and galleries go right round through the space usually occu-
> pied by the stage. The walls of this chamber are painted to form a
> map of the globe. The ceiling represents the north polar regions.
> England is in the gallery, the tropics in the upper circle, Australia on
> the dress circle and the antarctic in the pit. A myriad computers are
> at work upon the weather of the part of the map where each sits, but
> each computer attends only to one equation or part of an equation.
> The work of each region is coordinated by an official of higher rank.
> Numerous little "night signs" display the instantaneous values so
> that neighboring computers can read them.[6]

With this formulation, Richardson showed that parallelism could be
applied quite neatly to the traditional formulations of science. Babbage had worried that it was impossible to keep such activities coordinated: "If ten thousand men were hired to act simultaneously, it
would be exceedingly difficult to discover whether each exerted his
whole force."[7] Richardson solved that problem by putting a conductor
in the center of the hall "to maintain a uniform rate of progress. . . . He
turns a beam of rosy light upon any region that is running ahead of the
rest, and a beam of blue light upon those who are behindhand."[8]
Because the laws of fluid behavior are universal, they are the same in
Australia as they are in Scandinavia. The computers for each part of
the world were carrying out exactly the same programs and hence
could keep in step.

The advent of electronic circuits interrupted this early foray into
parallelism. When von Neumann took up the task of predicting the
weather, he felt that even with one electronic computer, "one has reason to hope that Richardson's dream of advancing the computation
faster than the weather may soon be realized."[9] The way his sequential

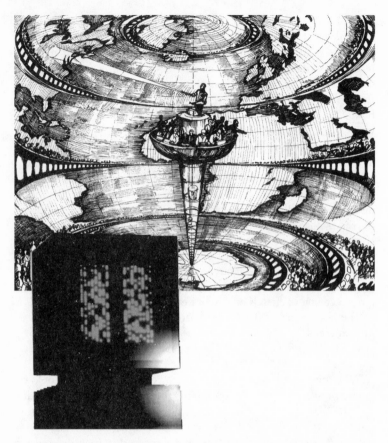

Figure 10.2. All of the important elements of a modern parallel computer were present in the computing hall designed by Lewis Richardson shortly after World War I. Sixty-four thousand professional computers were to be seated around a large globe-shaped hall, each computing the weather for their particular section of the globe. Individual computers wrote their results on little night signs so they could be read and used by neighboring computers. A director in the middle of the hall kept everyone computing in lock step. Illustration of Lewis Richardson computing hall courtesy of Alf Lannerbäck. Image of CM-2a courtesy of Thinking Machines Corporation.

computer attacked the problem was, in effect, to move from seat to seat to seat in the computing hall, Santa Claus fashion, and carry out the computations for each seat in turn. After completing the computation for a particular seat, the computer would, in essence, write data on the little night sign above that seat and then move on to the next. At each seat, as it needed data, the sequential computer would read from the neighboring night signs the data that it had written itself when it had been at that seat.

It is only in this very narrow way that scientists typically use the ability of an electronic computer to modify its own program. The scientist, in effect, writes the program for a single seat in the computation, then encloses it in a programming "loop." The purpose of the loop is to modify the program slightly so that it works correctly at each seat in turn. Specifically, it must address the right data at each seat. The actual equations of the formulation do not change, because the formulation is, in the Newtonian tradition, universal. Thus, a single computer moving from seat to seat around the globe not only is able to carry the same equations along with it, it is required to. Only the addresses of the data undergo modification.

This use of an unchanging core program to operate on different pieces of data represents the first and most obvious way to exploit parallelism: replication. A copy of the program is simply replicated across many individual processors. The power of parallelism does not, however, end at this point. Two much more subtle forms of parallel behavior are *competition* and *emergence*. When many things are happening at once, it is not necessary for them all to be correct. Some can be dead wrong as long as the wrong ones are weeded out along the way. In a competitive environment, weeding out can and does take place. Thus, it is possible in a parallel environment, for example, for multiple interpretations of the sentence "the astronomer married the star" to be brought forth in parallel. The fact that some of them are wrong does not matter as long as the right one survives the competition, as it does in the human mind.

When many things are happening at once, it is also possible for the interactions among them to play a major role in the result. Instead of the whole being synonymous with the sum of the pieces, the whole becomes something more than and different from the sum of the pieces. It is not always correct to assume with Spinoza that "if a number of individuals so unite in one action that they are all simultaneously the cause of one effect, I consider them all, so far, as one individual thing."[10] Richardson made exactly this mistake when he asserted that "a nation is any set of people who are held together by a common loyalty, so they act together."[11]

A rare example of emergent behavior in the early Western intellectual tradition can be found in the doctrine of the Holy Trinity. The Father, Son, and Holy Spirit are three individual elements, but from the Three emerges the One. They were, in Galileo's words, "efficient causes [that] coexist temporarily with their effects."[12] Jane Jacobs's more pedestrian street behavior is also emergent. Street sociology is necessarily parallel because it emerges from the interaction among participants rather than from the participants individually:

> Under the seeming disorder of the old city, wherever the old city is working successfully, is a marvelous order . . . an intricate ballet in which the individual dancers and ensembles all have distinctive parts which miraculously reinforce each other and compose an orderly whole.[13]

Richardson resorted to parallelism, not because he saw weather patterns as inherently emergent, but simply because his computers were too slow to race the weather individually. When these tasks were reassigned to electronic circuits, this particular impetus for parallelism went into abeyance. The burgeoning performance of single computers made parallelism seem unnecessary. Furthermore, until the 1970s, the circuitry that did the processing and the circuitry that did the remembering used different technologies. Maintaining data in the processing section was still expensive, so it was returned to memory immediately. Doing so meshed perfectly with the prevailing formulations, of course, because human computers could not keep multiple results in mind either.

It was only later, in the 1970s, that computer architecture developed a disconnect. By then, processing circuits and memory circuits had become totally indistinguishable, both being made out of the same silicon. As it became cheaper, the circuitry devoted to memory subsequently expanded a thousandfold. The result was an array of poorly utilized silicon, because "the number of interesting events per second per acre of silicon is very low. Most of the chip area is memory and only a few memory locations are accessed at a time."[14] The hardware technology, the silicon, was arguing for the maximum number of processors, preferably millions, spread throughout the memory to keep it all busy all the time. The whole corpus of Western scientific thought, however, continued to argue for the fewest possible processors, preferably one.

The tradeoffs can be seen in the respective architectures of three supercomputers designed in the 1970s: the Cray 1, the ICL DAP, and the CM–1 Connection Machine. The Cray 1 was the ultimate von Neumann, or Cartesian, computer, carrying out tens of millions of operations per second inside a single, highly engineered processor. It made extensive use of the trick that Descartes had discovered in his own mind: If a sequence of operations could be homogenized and lined up, it was possible to whir through them all at accelerated speeds, starting into the next while still working on the last, "moving continuously in such a way that while it is intuitively perceiving each fact it simultaneously passes to the next."[15] The Cray 1 thus presented itself to scientists at two levels. Without any change to their way of thinking, the scientists could run their "four hundred years of scientific inquiry and wisdom" faster than ever before. With a modest change to their formulations, in order to line the data up in the requisite "vectorized" manner, they could run their programs *much* faster than ever before.

Meanwhile, the ICL DAP, with four thousand very small individual processors, was aggressively following up the opportunities for replication that are evident in the Richardson computing hall design. A variety of scientific formulations were decomposed at the data level for simultaneous execution by the DAP's parallel processors.[16] Each of these processors could communicate data to its neighbors in a manner not unlike Richardson's little night signs. The first Connection Machine, with 64,000 processors, was superficially similar to the DAP. It did not, however, attempt in the beginning to connect to the existing corpus of scientific inquiry, although the possibility that it could some day do so was acknowledged: "The machine is designed for symbol manipulation, not number crunching. . . . Similar architectures may have application in numeric processing, but we do not at this time plan to investigate these possibilities."[17]

The design of the Connection Machine was pushed by the realities of circuit technology and the needs of the cognitive sciences rather than pulled by the formulations inherited from the Industrial Age. Because the bottleneck in the von Neumann architecture lay in the constant shuttling of data between processor and memory, the Connection Machine in effect sprinkled its processors throughout the memory. Each one was tiny and feeble, but Hillis, like Galileo, was confident that the power of the individual processor was not critical because "any resistance, so long as it is not infinite, may be overcome by a multitude of minute forces."[18] Using the human brain for design inspiration, the Connection Machine went far beyond other architectures in the way it allowed individual processors to communicate with each other. Processors could connect to others clear across the machine as well as those that were right next door. This rich interconnection, together with the very large number of processors and the artificial-intelligence orientation of its architects, made the Connection Machine a major stimulus for all three modes of parallelism: replication, competition, and emergence.

The Cray 1 and the Connection Machine 1 cost roughly the same amount of money and contained roughly the same total amount of circuitry, approximately a square meter each. The difference in their performance was a function of the task being carried out. The more traditional the formulation, the greater the Cray 1 speed advantage. Provided all the data could fit into its memory, the Cray 1 operated ten times or more as fast as a CM–1. At the other end of the spectrum, operating on vast numbers of small numbers and especially on single bits of information, the Connection Machine was ten times faster or more.

The first uses of the Connection Machine did in fact come from artificial-intelligence researchers, because these areas had seen the least success with sequential machines. The processing of images was an early application because images are made up of thousands, or millions, of pieces of pixel data. Successive satellite images of clouds, for example, can be used by weather bureaus to judge wind speeds. Between satellite passes, individual clouds move a bit and change shape a bit. The job of the computer is to recognize the cloud pattern in its new shape and position. In arctic regions, the same process is used with ice floes to judge ocean currents. The best formulations for these kinds of tasks are not always simple replications. Sometimes competition can be used very effectively. In other cases, the desired behavior must emerge from many parallel processes operating at a lower level. The first Connection Machine provided impetus for the development of these inherently parallel methods.

At the same time that cognitive scientists were demonstrating the power of parallel competition and emergence, physical scientists were continuing to exploit parallel replication. A traditional program that had been designed to move from seat to seat in a computing hall may quite easily be modified to put a replicated copy in each seat. Thus, it became feasible to modify, or "parallelize," existing sequential programs to take advantage of the higher absolute performance and larger memories of a parallel machine. A new version of the FORTRAN programming language made it possible to write a single version of a program that would run in both environments.

Slowly but inexorably, computational scientists broke the sequence just as Kepler broke the circle. It is now clear that the "four hundred years of scientific inquiry and wisdom" could have been computed largely in parallel all along if only a suitable parallel computing resource had been at hand. As the old sequential formulations of physics and engineering are recast into parallel form, they may well fade from memory just as the geometric formulations of astronomy did. In the future, "DO loops" may become as obscure as epicycles. Meanwhile, the new parallel ideas of competition and emergence, as expressed in the new intermaths, have grown dramatically in importance. Thus it was that when it proved impossible to fold a protein by equational methods, the biologist Richard Friesner and his colleagues looked to the new methods:

> We present a method for determining the tertiary structure of α-proteins through computer simulation. . . . The optimization consists of a Monte Carlo simulated annealing procedure combined with a genetic algorithm.[19]

There are many important forms of behavior that depend on competition and emergence and cannot be understood by merely replicating numbers and equations across many processors. As summarized by Holland, they are the subject matter of Part Three of the Book of Nature.

> Many of our most troubling long-range problems—trade balances, sustainability, AIDS, genetic defects, mental health, computer viruses—center on certain systems of extraordinary complexity. The systems that host these problems—economies, ecologies, immune systems, embryos, nervous systems, computer networks—appear to be as diverse as the problems. Despite appearances, however, the systems do share significant characteristics, so much so that we group them under a single classification at the Santa Fe Institute, calling them complex adaptive systems (CAS). This is more than terminology. It signals our intuition that there are general principles that govern all CAS behavior, principles that point to ways of solving the attendant problems.[20]

Today scientists focus increasingly on questions of social and biological pattern and use pixels and computer networks as their communications technology. To compute the patterns of entities such as environments, economies, and embryos, leading practitioners are adopting bit-level intermaths based on readily computed genetic matings and parallel evolution. In so doing they are showing both that there is a pattern to life and that there is a life to patterns. Courtesy of Thinking Machines Corporation.

0

PART THREE
OF THE
BOOK OF
NATURE

℘ATTERN

noun   verb   noun   noun

The New Intermaths
of the
Information Age

The chairs in the classroom are neither in the rows and columns of the traditional math class nor in the circle often favored in the English department. Instead, Mr. Rose has placed eight seats across the front, four in the back, and the rest in the longest row through the middle. Thus configured, the class as a whole will compute.

Each of the eight front-row students receives a simple geometric feature card with an object such as a line or a cross or a circle on it. Each of the four back-row students has received a card with a single capital letter on it. The instructions for the computation are simple. Students in the back row are each to choose, at random, about half the students in the middle row as their inputs. Whenever a majority of this subset raise their hands, the student in the back row should in turn hold up the letter card. Those in the middle row have a similar assignment. They individually choose, at random, four of the front-row students and raise their hands if two or more of these front-row students have their hands in the air. The front-row students themselves are to raise their hands if, and only if, they see something that includes the geometric feature that is on their card. That is the entire "program."

The teacher starts the computation by showing a letter of the alphabet to the front-row students only. Those whose feature appears within it raise their hands. After some initial hesitation, a few of the middle-row students in turn raise their hands and, perhaps, one or more of the back-row students hold up their letter cards. The instructor has one final role: to praise a back-row student for holding up a letter card that matches the one shown to the front-row students and to rebuke a back-row student mildly for holding up a letter card that does not match. Then, the process repeats with a new letter being shown to the front-row students.

At first, the results of the computation are woeful. Sometimes, no letters are held up, sometimes two or more at once. Sometimes, there is a match, other times not. Within ten minutes, however, the errors have disappeared. Each time the teacher shows a letter to the front row, that same letter, and only that same letter, rises in the back row, although none of the students in the back row can see the input letter itself. The class has now programmed itself to do pattern recognition on a subset of the alphabet. Then, one or two at a time, students in the first two rows are allowed to step out of the room. This pruning is analogous to deleting a few randomly chosen lines of code from a conventional program. Such deletions to traditional formulations are invariably fatal. Performance of the letter-recognizing program, however, is unaffected at first. Only as more and more students leave do errors creep back in.

What has taken place is a mathematical computation quite unlike what is traditionally taught in a classroom. The normal practice is for the teacher to pose a problem and for each student to undertake its solution individually. Raising one's hand signifies, "I have the answer" and, perhaps, "the rest of you can stop trying now." If no hands go up, the teacher proactively reprograms, providing a review of the kinds of explicit steps that are likely to yield the desired answer. In Mr. Rose's classroom, no such program instructions were ever issued. The class did not even know explicitly that it was "doing character recognition." Individual students, therefore, were incapable of doing the task on their own. Right and wrong, the class computed as a whole. Without any specific instructions, an ability to recognize characters simply emerged.

Problems of pattern understanding are pervasive in our world today. We are no longer content to know where an artillery shell will land; we also want to know how the economy and the AIDS virus will behave. We may use the fiction that an economy also has a trajectory and that it can perhaps be brought in for a "soft landing." We may also pretend that it has a physical structure and that it may not achieve a soft landing because it has "overheated." To the extent that these mechanistic abstractions are appropriate, we can use the maths of place and of pace to describe and predict the behavior. To the extent that they are inappropriate, we need new maths.

The computation carried out in Mr. Rose's classroom is one such new math. The excitement about these new intermaths lies in their similarity to the patterns of behavior we wish to understand and predict. The behavior of an organism adapts, and so do the new maths. The behavior of a street society is emergent; so are the maths. The behavior of an economy is inherently parallel; so are the new maths. Thus, when the Santa Fe Institute held a contest to predict the behavior of the Swiss franc based on a historical data set, the contest was won by a computation exactly of the form carried out in Mr. Rose's classroom. Because it was carried out electronically, the Swiss franc computation had more participants, or "nodes," in its front, middle, and back rows. It trained for millions of iterations instead of just a handful, and it had somewhat more sophisticated ways of interconnecting its nodes, but other than that it was the same process.

A program that recognizes data that fit a pattern can also recognize data that do not. After training itself on data from normal business transactions, this same mathematical approach is being used by credit card companies to spot potentially fraudulent credit card transactions and the merchants who generate an unusual volume of them. In a completely different setting, oil companies use these same techniques, which are called "artificial neural networks," or "neural nets" for short, to sort out the data they obtain from field surveys and to predict geologic patterns in oil fields. A field may have a dozen or more existing wells. The company knows the exact geology at each of these well holes; it needs to guess the patterns of the rock layers in between them. Depending on these guesses, it may invest the money to drill additional wells. In each of these settings, the computer is simply doing what the rural network did:

> In farm-yard, in tap-room, at market, the details were discussed over and over again; they were gathered together for remembrance in village workshop; carters, smiths, farmers, wheel-makers, in thousands handed on each his own little bit of understanding . . . the details

were but dimly understood; the whole body of knowledge was a mystery, a piece of folk knowledge, residing in the folk collectively but never wholly in any individual.[1]

Instead of carters, smiths, farmers, and wheel makers, we now have electronic processors and memory banks. Instead of farmyards and tap rooms, we now have networks. The details are discussed over and over again, but in microseconds rather than centuries. Computers are extremely good at these kinds of formulations. Unlike numbers and equations, neural nets are a very natural fit to the inherent strengths and weaknesses of electronic circuits.

None of these computations produce perfect answers, or perfect wagons, right away. They are not like traditional maths, which make a beeline for the result. Like Johannes Kepler, these methods forage. In the classroom instance, the participants foraged for five or ten minutes before settling in on the answer. The changes in the course of those repeated trials comes in the interrelationships of the students in the back and middle rows. Those in the back row have a hard time keeping track of all the hands in the middle row. Because they prefer praise to rebuke, they home in on the middle-row students who seem to be involved in their successes and lose interest in those who seem to be associated with their rebukes. These slight adjustments are all that are needed to produce a crisp and decisive, albeit limited, character-recognition system.

With the answer residing "in the folk collectively but never wholly in one individual," larger problems require somewhat larger networks. Reaching the level of a world-class computation, such as pronouncing all of written English, would require several math classes worth of students to cooperate, perhaps in an auditorium. Twenty-seven students (one for each letter of the alphabet plus space) might sit in the front row. In the back would be about two dozen students, each with a sound box that creates one of the articulatory features, or phonemes, of spoken English. Across the middle row are as many as eighty students. Finally, a large group of students holding individual letters of nursery rhymes (M-A-R-Y- -H-A-D- -A- -L-I-T-T-L-E . . .) parade across the stage and circle around the back so that seven are on stage at any moment. The job of the system is to pronounce correctly the letter that is in the middle of the stage at that moment.

The rules for the students are slightly more sophisticated than before. At each step, individual front-row students raise their hands in each of seven cycles, corresponding to the three letters ahead of the current one, the current character itself, and the three that follow. On the basis of hands raised in the front row, students in the middle row raise their hands, but they are now free to raise them partway if they choose. The students in the back row activate and make the sounds of the English language on the basis of what they see in the middle row. They then receive feedback on how close they came to doing the right thing. This time, however, they each have the ability to complain to the middle-row students when things go badly, motivating these middle-row students to change their interrelationships to the front row as well.

Training this large array of students to handle all the vagaries of the English language would work, but like designing wagons, it would take years and perhaps centuries. At the end of each training cycle, each student in the middle row is bombarded with feedback from every single student in the back row. These students are individually free to alter their responses to each student in the front row, but it is not entirely clear which ones to alter and by how much. Will not a change that improves the current instance likely cause other pronunciations to suffer? Indeed, it will, but by endlessly nipping here and tucking there, the overall performance inexorably improves without any individual participant knowing exactly why.

Prior to the advent of electronic circuits, there was no point in studying these kinds of maths. They are much too tedious and much too boring to carry out by hand. It is the modern parallel computer or network of computers that shrinks the centuries to seconds and makes these maths viable. Because the real learning goes on in the linkages—the electronic taprooms that link up the nodes—a massively parallel computer such as a 16,000-processor Connection Machine may assign a separate processor to manage each individual linkage between each pair of nodes. In the beginning, these connections are all medium strong, meaning in effect that all middle-row students raise their hands about halfway regardless of which front-row students have their hands raised. Each back-row student in turn activates halfway, and the electronic auditorium drones with continuous and meaningless babbling. After each cycle, however, each output node (or back-row student) is told how closely it came to the correct response. The magnitude of this error is then propagated back to the front. Links respond by increasing or decreasing their strengths a little bit even though they have no way of knowing for sure that the change will be helpful. Some of these changes indeed make things worse for a while.

Patterns of pronunciation are hard to compute because an individual character is pronounced in different ways depending on what comes before and after it. There is only one character that is always pronounced the same way, regardless of what precedes and follows it: the space character. This is the first character the neural network learns to pronounce correctly. The network learns to respond with silence whenever the space character takes center stage; the continuous babble of the earlier stages becomes individual bursts of babble separated by brief silences corresponding to the spaces between words. The sounds of the consonants emerge next, because they are comparatively insensitive to their context, and the network soon learns the particular cases that affect their pronunciation. Only at the very end of the training period do all the nuances of the vowels finally come clear. In the course of a few hours on a large parallel machine, the network has learned the patterns of the English language as competently as the best available product based on traditional methods. With the 1980s-vintage minicomputer on which this work was first done—a minicomputer comparable in performance to a modern home computer—the job of training took a few days instead of a few hours.[2]

What the neural network cannot do, however, is explain exactly how it does what it does in terms that make sense to humans. Nor can it invent pronunciation itself. It has to be told what the right answer is. All it can do is assert that when the thousands of linkages are set to the weightings it has learned, good pronunciation results. It can assert, but not prove, that it will continue to do an equally good job pronouncing text it has never seen before. Like the message of a specialist to the general public, the message of an intermath formulation to a human collaborator is, "Trust me. I know what I am doing." The requirement to be given the right answer as feedback may also seem like a big disadvantage, but that was only true when data were scarce. Now the world is awash in training data.

The success of a neural network on a problem like pronunciation, a problem that had proved very difficult with traditional maths, was not entirely serendipitous. The functioning of the system is related to the behavior of language. Pronunciation itself has developed and adapted over many centuries. Awkward pronunciations have continually evolved to make them easier on the vocal cords. To predict the next sound in spoken text, it is sometimes enough merely to determine which phoneme will require the least effort for the human vocal-cord muscles to reach. Neural networks and other intermaths are particularly good at spotting and mimicking these kinds of biological and social optimizations, just as numbers and equations have been particularly good at mimicking smoothly varying physical behavior. In its realm, the neural net seems to have the same aura of magic that Heinrich Hertz once attributed to equations when applied to physical science: "These mathematical formulae have an independent existence and an intelligence of their own. . . . We seem to get more out of them than was originally put into them."[3] In the case of neural networks, all we put in is the training data.

The ability to learn from training data has made neural nets competitive with equations in a variety of tasks. When terrorists blew up Pan Am Flight 103 over Lockerbie, Scotland, for example, they forced airports all over the world to deal with a new pattern-recognition problem. Because plastic explosives hidden in luggage can be stretched into almost any imaginable shape, new methods of detection had to be found. The most reliable is based on the fact that plastic explosives typically have a lot of nitrogen in them, and nitrogen responds to a beam of neutrons. Scientists tested both equational formulations and neural networks on the patterns created by the neutron beam. The neural network was chosen for airport deployment because "clearly the detection rates are similar and the false alarm rate for the NN [neural net] is considerably better."[4]

Neural networks illustrate four of the important characteristics of the new intermaths. First, they are inherently *parallel* in that many individually trivial procedures are carried out simultaneously. In the pronunciation example, thousands of individual linkages between nodes are modified at once. The computation is replicated, but it is also *competitive*. Each node competes for influence over other nodes. Those whose voices prove valuable win this competition and receive a larger share of attention. No single node is ever allowed to take over completely, however; loud and soft voices are always blended. Third, the formulations are *sprawling*. They involve thousands of component parts instead of a dozen or so, as a typical diagram or equation does. With so many individually trivial pieces, it is possible to change them without invalidating the whole. Finally, and most important, the behavior of a neural network computation is *emergent*. None of the participants are consciously engaged in the task of pronouncing or looking for plastic explosives, yet these are the results that emerge from their collective actions. The behavior of the whole network is different from and far more sophisticated than the behavior of individual participants. The added value comes from the interrelationships among nodes, not from within the nodes themselves.

Compared to other intermaths, neural networks use a comparatively small number of active elements and a very dense network of intercommunications links. The cellular automata intermath that came into scientific use in the 1980s to simulate fluid flow has the opposite balance point. Each cellular automaton site may connect to only half a dozen others, but the total number in a computation can rise to the hundreds of thousands. The memory cells of a modern computer and the pixels of a computer screen are the right places for these computations to play out. Even so, the most famous cellular automata computation was initially carried out by hand.

The Game of Life, invented by John Conway, was first published in 1970 in the form of English-language text, not as a computer program at all.[5] Unlike the automata of a fluid-flow simulation, Conway's automata do not move. They live and die on checkerboard squares with eight neighboring squares (including diagonals) according to just two rules. First, automata with fewer than two neighbors, or more than three, die. Second, empty squares with exactly three neighboring automata spawn a new one.

Because it was assumed that the game would be carried out by hand, the original directions exhibit all the confusion that attends an inherently parallel process being carried out by an inherently sequential resource. Counters of a different color must be temporarily placed atop counters that are perishing until the cross-effects are worked out. As with Galileo's geometric proof, "while" is the word that tries to communicate a parallel reality in a sequential, discursive way:

> Because births and deaths occur simultaneously, newborn counters play a role in causing other deaths or births. It is essential, therefore, to be able to distinguish them from live counters of the previous generation while you check the pattern.[6]

As the game moved to a more capacious electronic checkerboard, it proved able to generate a wide variety of behaviors, which came to be recognized as blinkers, gliders, glider guns, Cheshire cats, harvesters, barber poles, and so on. The variety of behavior that emerges unbidden from such simple rules has made the Game of Life a staple of modern computer graphics.

There are two important differences between the pronunciation computation and the Life computation. First, they use different intermaths. The pronunciation example uses neural networks; Conway's Life uses cellular automata. Second, they use their maths in different modes of discovery. The pronunciation computation constrains its development to match real-world phenomena, whereas Life does not.

Life is an exercise in pure math; the pronunciation system is an exercise in applied math.

The geometry of place and the algebra of pace also have rich heritages of both pure and applied usage. The applied mathematician weeds out equations for which there is no corresponding behavior in the real world; the pure mathematician, on the other hand, is willing to follow diagrams or equations or Cheshire cats whither they lead, independent of any immediate relationship to the world itself. Sometimes the excursions of the pure mathematician turn out later to be valuable in explaining behavior. Imaginary numbers, for example, were investigated solely because the vocabulary of algebra, which includes both negative numbers and roots of numbers, allowed it. Their very name belies the initial understanding that they were pure hacks, products of the mathematical language itself. Only much later did they prove valuable in an applied sense, successfully mimicking certain elements of physics. The Game of Life is similarly unconstrained except by the rules of the math. Its charm, like the charm of pure geometry and pure algebra, is that it produces beautiful results without being constrained to do so.

Applied intermaths, on the other hand, respond to the constraints implicit in their training data. They adapt and evolve automatically in ways that bring them inexorably closer to the patterns in the data. They no longer need a scientist to decide if they save the appearances or not.

$\mathcal{T}$HE PATTERNS WITHIN LIFE

ntermath formulations process their own feedback. Unlike geometry or algebra, they have the capacity to learn and to do a progressively better and better job of saving whatever appearances they are presented with. Without data to train on, however, the capacity to learn is useless. It is here that the new Thoreauean data-gathering capabilities of electronic circuits are so revolutionary.

Access to data is very powerful. The reason, for example, that Thoreau became able to tell the calendar date of the year from the flowers and trees of Walden was that he had accumulated the necessary data.[1] He had personally tramped through the woods and seen how each plant behaved from season to season. Similarly, it has traditionally been the human scientist who has looked through the telescope first and seen the position of a planet, or into the bubble chamber first and seen the path of a subatomic particle. When Johannes Kepler published Tycho Brahe's astronomical observations, he was publishing data that had all passed through human minds first. Furthermore, and it seems almost ludicrous to note it, the paper pages of the published copies of Kepler's book have had no ability to react to the data stored on them. Those pages have had that data in their possession for more than three million hours now, with no effect. They have learned nothing because pages of paper lack the ability to learn from the data they happen to be storing.

Today, it is increasingly rare for a human to get first look at data about the world. Even our telescopes are often operated remotely, with computer sensors sitting in the chilly mountaintop observatories and the resulting pixels of data transmitted back to cozy campus computer screens. Financial transaction data and satellite information are routinely handled by electronic circuits first and human beings later, if at all. Instead of computers seeing only the pieces of data that scientists choose to share, it is increasingly the other way around. The cockpit of an advanced fighter airplane illustrates the new pecking order. The airplane's sensors see other aircraft way before the pilot does. They feed the information to the airplane's computer circuits, which process it. By the time the existence of the other aircraft is finally displayed to the pilot, the computer's guess of its make and model may be displayed right alongside. The computer can do this because it has first access to the data.

Intermaths take advantage of this increasingly rich diet of data for their feedback and learning. They may start out in a random and useless state, but as they come to understand what is expected of them, they gradually become more and more terrific. Adjusting weightings within a neural network is just one way for competence to emerge in response to training data. A second way is by genetic interbreeding. In one such experiment, the computer architect Danny Hillis used a Connection Machine parallel computer to breed a world-class sorting program.

The sorting-program breeder fully exploits the truly fundamental advance of the von Neumann computer: the ability to change the program itself as readily as the data. Any operation that can be performed on data by electronic circuits can also be performed on instructions. This radical capability lay dormant for the first fifty years of electronic computing. (Humans do not have it, because we cannot efficiently delete what we have previously learned.) Its use in the realm of numbers and equations has been meager, limited largely to compilers and to moving the focus of a fixed set of instructions from one piece of data to the next, like a person moving from seat to seat in a Richardson computing hall. In the Hillis sorting program, however, the wholesale modification of the formulations themselves is the essence of the method.

The traditional first step in a computation is to load a prewritten program into memory: essentially, to teach the circuitry the ropes from outside. Normally, "such formulation is itself a problem, but it is one with which the computer (as such) has no concern: accepting the formulation, his task is to [carry it out]."[2] The sorting-program computation skipped this step and used random instructions in each of 16,000 memories instead. Each of these 16,000 sets of random instructions was then given some numbers and asked to sort them, rather like plopping number blocks into the cribs of day-old babies and telling them to kick them into numerical order. Needless to say, none of them succeeded. From amidst 16,000 alternatives, however, some did a little bit of useful work, just as some of the 16,000 babies would be bound to kick a block or two, even though they had no idea they were supposed to do so. Genetic maths, however, are incorrigible optimists. To them, a glass with one or two drops in it is part full, never part empty. Each of the 16,000 programs was evaluated to determine which were the least hopeless. In this evaluation, the programs that performed least badly were the heroes.

Compared to the first philosophical observations of the pre-Socratic Greeks, the sorting protoprograms were still at an unbelievably primitive level. In between each of its repetitive attempts to sort numbers, however, the system performed a mating and breeding process. Programs from among the 16,000 paired off. The first part of one program was combined with the second part of the other, making a new program with characteristics inherited from each of its parents. This new program then replaced an existing one. In choosing programs to become parents, a genetic program slightly favors those that were "more heroically successful" the last time they were tried. In selecting programs to replace, such a system slightly picks on those that were "less successful" in the previous trial.

The only result of the first interbreeding was that 16,000 hapless sorting programs became infinitesimally less hapless, but that was all it took to ensure ultimate triumph. In a community where all the children are above average, the definition of average keeps ratcheting up and up and up. Gradually, for example, the programs with one or two useful opening instructions spread those instructions to the rest, so that every program started to at least do something. The next big event occurred when, purely by chance, a program swapped the positions of two numbers and thus made the whole set of test numbers slightly more ordered. Such a program went to the head of the breeding line.

Whatever its little trick was, it was remembered and inexorably bred into the wider population.

At this point, the Hillis process became doubly interesting. The sorting programs were tested by giving them a sample data set and seeing if it was sorted. Gradually, the programs learned to sort this particular data set, although not others. To keep the programs challenged, the test data also evolved. Training data that caused the programs to fail were preferred over data that the programs were successful at. Thus, just when the programs seemed to be homing in on success, the problem changed, forcing them to become more and more general-purpose.

The sorting of numbers is a particularly interesting test for intermaths because it has been closely studied for many years. Until the late 1960s, the best known program needed sixty-two steps to sort sixteen numbers. At that time, a method was invented to do the job in sixty steps. After a few hours of breeding time, the Hillis approach produced a program that sorted the numbers in sixty-one steps.[3]

Examples like Rose's classroom neural network and Hillis's created-out-of-whole-bits sorting program may make intermaths seem easy. If a pattern exists, the maths just forage around in the data until they find it. The difficulty is that in any problem of fit or optimization, there are many potential directions to take, each of which is initially plausible but only some of which lead to the truly best answer. Once a genetic program or neural net comes close to the right answer, it can be counted on to home right in. If these techniques get close to another superficially promising alternative, however, they can home in there instead and get stuck.

Users of these new maths often employ mountaineering analogies to describe this problem. The computation is thought of as starting out at the base of a mountain with a goal of arriving at the peak. The simplest formulation for getting there is to "always go up." Climbers who do so, however, can find themselves stuck at the top of a foothill. The only way to reach the true peak would be to come back down off the foothill peak, which violates the instruction always to go up. The mountaineering analogy is also used in the other direction, with a group starting at the top and being told "always to go down." The group can find itself stuck in a small hollow, or "local minimum," far above the actual base of the mountain. The solution to this problem of local minima is illustrated by a third new intermath: simulated annealing.

A common use of annealing is to help pack more transistors onto an integrated circuit, an increasingly important optimization in the Information Age. The microprocessor circuits that provide the processing power for workstations and personal computers start out as abstract diagrams, independent of how their transistors and connecting wires will actually be placed on a piece of silicon. When the circuit is first placed, therefore, it tends to be a nightmare of wires. More than 99 percent of the total area can be used up for the interconnections, leaving less than 1 percent for the transistors where the actual circuit operations are carried out. In such a form, the circuit as a whole is much too big to be manufactured efficiently. If individual transistors could be moved around, however, so they would be on average closer to the ones they needed to interconnect to, then the circuit as a whole could shrink, because the total amount of interconnection would be less, while the total number of transistors remained the same, as illustrated in figure 12.1.

Simulated annealing is so named because its operation is similar to the behavior of a slowly cooling metal. When a metal is very hot, individual atoms move around with abandon. As the metal cools, the atoms lose energy and move over shorter and shorter distances. If the annealing process is done correctly, the atoms gradually settle themselves into a closely packed crystalline structure in the final product. Simulated annealing of a circuit works the same way. Pairs of individual transistors are chosen at random and swapped temporarily. If the swap reduces the total amount of wiring in the circuit, the swap is generally accepted and made permanent. If it makes matters worse, it is generally rejected. At the start of the process, the circuit is considered to be "hot" in the sense that very distant pairs of transistors can be selected for swapping. Individual transistors can move clear across the circuit. As the process cools down, only pairs of transistors that are already in the same region of the chip are selected for possible swapping. In the final stages of the process, akin to the stage when atoms of a metal are jiggling into their final tightly packed crystals, only transistors that are already next to each other are tested for swapping. When nothing further is to be gained by swapping already-adjacent transistors, the process is complete.[4]

Such an approach, although very powerful, is unfortunately capable of making a rush for a false peak, or local minimum (the two phrases are used interchangeably), and missing much better solutions. The system avoids this fate by sometimes rejecting promising matches and

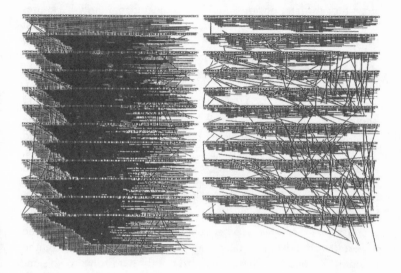

Figure 12.1. Complex pattern computations rarely have a unique "right" answer. Instead, they have a range of possible outcomes; the computer's job is to find one of the better ones. For example, there are many ways to improve the internal layout of a microprocessor chip, which typically starts out as an inefficient tangle of wires. By randomly swapping the positions of individual pairs of transistors over and over again, a simulated annealing intermath gradually produces a much more efficient layout with much shorter wires. If the same computation were carried out on the same circuit tomorrow, a different final answer would emerge. It might be slightly better or it might be slightly worse, but the annealing techniques themselves provide assurances that a dramatically better result is not lurking totally undiscovered. Courtesy of Thinking Machines Corporation.

sometimes accepting some extra wiring. Particularly at the early stages, when the process is still hot, random matching allows the system to range widely over the possibilities. All intermaths must have this willingness to take an occasional step back to enable them to take two steps forward later on. In so doing, they may temporarily back away from the ultimate right answer. Kepler did this, too. He immediately thought of his fat-bellied sausage as being ellipse-like, but then he wandered away to inspect all the other possibilities first. Only when he had ruled each of them out did he come back and conclude that therefore it was an ellipse. He later spent a decade arriving at his third law, a result that modern observers replicate in less than a day, because they know in advance that an equation is what they are looking for.

Simulated annealing keeps its options open by starting out hot. The purely genetic approaches such as those used in the sorting program keep their options open by genetic recombination. They also allow individual bits to mutate randomly, but the true power of the genetic approach comes from recombination, not mutation. Tracing back through the genealogy of a successful program shows how genetics takes advantage of good building blocks. At the earliest stages, the candidate programs that are most often selected for interbreeding are ones that have stumbled on a way to solve some small piece of the problem, although they bungle the rest of it completely. As the computer scientist John Koza has shown, the process advances when programs that succeed at different parts of the problem happen to interbreed. When the parts they both pass to their offspring include the successful bits, the offspring will outperform either parent alone and hence become more prevalent in future generations. At the penultimate stage, programs emerge that can solve one-half of the problem, but not the other half. When two such programs with complementary abilities mate, they produce offspring that solve the whole problem.[5]

In normal practice, such genetic programs are under no compulsion to be concise. When one of Koza's genetic programs evolved Kepler's third law, it produced it in a somewhat verbose and redundant form, as illustrated in figure 12.2. As Koza has pointed out, the fact that Kepler said it in half as many bytes no longer matters as much as it used to. Just as printing destroyed the economic advantage of diagrams, silicon memory is destroying the economic advantage of compressed formulations. The incumbent aesthetic of Laplace is being challenged by a new aesthetic of data.

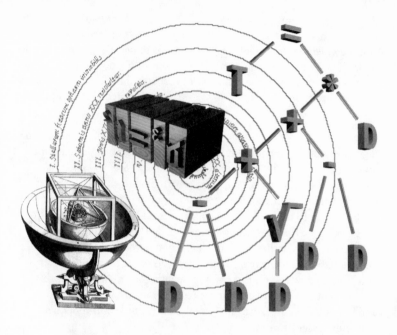

Place**Pace****Pattern**

Figure 12.2. Genetic intermaths breed their own solutions to problems based on repetitive testing against training data. In one example, the computer scientist John Koza gave a computer the same training data that Tycho Brahe once gave Johannes Kepler. The computer then spliced and respliced its initial guesses over and over again. Pieces that were successful with parts of the data gradually spread to the population as a whole. The final breeding cycles brought together the right combination of successful pieces to solve the whole problem

Since intermaths typically operate at the level of bits, it is usually very difficult for us to understand their results. Koza's result is decipherable because the program was constrained to using the vocabulary of arithmetic. It is tempting to believe that the computer's version, with its unnecessary "D minus D" clauses, is not as valuable as our more compact version. Not so. These additional clauses, while not needed for this problem, have the potential to evolve and become useful for something else. Biological evolution and bit evolution both depend on having capacity in reserve. Drawing of Kepler's nested figures courtesy of the Boston Athenaeum.

An Intellect . . . but vast enough to submit his data to analysis, could condense into a single formula the movement of the greatest body in the universe and that of the lightest atom.[6]

Large parallel computers, with large amounts of memory, may allow us to develop an entirely new sort of physics where, instead of reducing the facts to equations, we can just store in the computer the facts.[7]

Traditionally, we have not even accorded the raw-data approach the dignity of being considered science at all. For example, there has been long-standing debate over the authorship of the so-called law of refraction. Both Descartes and Willebrord Snell formulated the equation, which relates the angle at which a light ray approaches a refracting boundary to the angle at which it emerges. Nowhere do the history books concede that the relationship is really Ptolemy's law. More than a thousand years earlier, Ptolemy had listed out all the light ray angles he cared about and next to them listed the resulting angles of refraction.[8] Writing at the end of the nineteenth century, Ernst Mach was still ridiculing this tabular form of presentation, not because it gave the wrong answer but because "no human mind could comprehend all the individual cases of refraction."[9]

This prejudice against formulation directly at the level of the data remains strong. The ancient Babylonian method of describing the current behavior of Jupiter by listing out its behavior seventy-one years earlier, a good approximation, is considered "prescientific" by today's historians of science.[10] Lewis Richardson's work on numerical weather prediction was first stimulated by the same aesthetic preferences. Weather prediction in his day drew on a large database of previously seen weather patterns together with information about how they had played out. The prediction process started by looking through the files to find the best match to the current weather pattern. The new prediction was based on assuming similar outcomes. Richardson preferred the equational method, by which the moon's behavior was predicted:

The index [of weather maps] enables the forecaster to find a number of previous maps which resemble the present one. . . .[This] past history of the atmosphere is used, so to speak, as a full-scale working model of its present self. . . . At present three days ahead is about the limit for forecasts in the British Isles. This alone is sufficient reason for presenting, in this book, a scheme of weather prediction, which resembles the process by which the Nautical Almanac is produced, in so far as it is founded upon the differential equations, and not upon the partial recurrence of phenomena in their ensemble.[11]

It did not occur to Richardson that the very process of reducing the behavior to equations could itself introduce error. Like his predecessor Laplace, he saw brevity as the soul of scientific truth, and he saw the equations as being a universal answer, whereas the file of historical images could never be truly complete.

Recent experiments, however, have shown that it is not necessary to store a complete set of facts in order to reason usefully from them. Very good results can be obtained by simple lookup even within a partial set of reference data.

Memory-based reasoning experiments by the cognitive scientists David Waltz and Craig Stanfill have shown, for example, that it is not necessary to load a whole dictionary in order to get good pronunciation results based on simply looking up the answer. Even a small subset of data is very powerful. In one such test, 4,000 words, averaging eight characters per word, were selected at random from a dictionary. Each of the 32,000 letters in this sample, along with the context of the characters before and after and the correct pronunciation in the particular context, was loaded into the processors of a 32,000-processor parallel computer. As new words were presented to the system for pronunciation, the computer looked not for an exact match to the pattern of surrounding characters but for the closest matches, and it pronounced accordingly. The results were comparable to the neural network's performance.[12]

Memory-based reasoning requires more memory than a neural network. One advantage is that there is no training. The memory-based reasoning system performs at its maximum effectiveness right from the start, whereas the neural network needs time to train. The memory-based reasoning approach is also imperturbable in the face of strange, new data. New words with very unfamiliar pronunciation, perhaps imported from a foreign language, may simply be added as specific knowledge. A neural network must retrain, potentially introducing temporary errors in pronunciations it used to know, until it finishes factoring the new data into its weightings. A further advantage is that a memory-based reasoning system knows when it does not know. It behaves like the chess-playing friend of Charles Babbage, who himself employed just this technique:

If I played any of the ordinary openings, such as are found in the books, I was sure to be beaten. The only way in which I had a chance of winning, was by making early in the game a move so bad that it had not been mentioned in any treatise. Brande possessed, and had read, almost every book upon the subject.[13]

The friend may have been stumped when presented with Babbage's novel data, but at least he knew he was stumped. A neural network, on the other hand, does not distinguish a totally unforeseen situation from one it has handled successfully thousands of times. It responds with the same level of confidence to either.

As parallel computer memories continue to grow in size, the memory-based reasoning approach may also have renewed relevance to its former role in predicting the way weather patterns unfold. Two patterns that are initially very similar sometimes play out in totally different ways. This sensitivity to initial conditions is often referred to as the "butterfly effect." If a butterfly flaps its wings in China, the result could theoretically be enough to trigger a storm elsewhere on the planet. Typically, it does not. Similar patterns usually unfold in similar ways. Building up a database of weather patterns that have proved to be sensitive to initial conditions may help forecasting programs to realize when it is simply not possible to give a reliable forecast.

The common denominator of all of these intermaths is their capacity to feast on cheap training data. Indeed, some of the early intermath successes are doubly remarkable because they happened when data were still scarce and expensive and computing power was still sequential. Scarce data and sequential execution are what numbers and equations are optimized for. The new maths come into their own when data become cheap and abundant. A perfect example of the new role of data is already occurring at the supermarket. Market researchers used to stand outside and gather data on consumer preferences by the low-bandwidth process of interviewing. Now, checkout scanners automatically collect millions of times as much data as the old market surveys ever did. The equational techniques that companies once used to seek trends in survey responses have been overwhelmed. Consumer products companies have turned to intermaths to find the patterns in consumer buying behavior.

Soon satellite data will dwarf consumer transaction data, and even the most powerful intermaths will seemingly be overwhelmed as well. The reason they will ultimately prevail is that they are a fundamentally close fit to what electronic circuits are inherently good at doing, and the manufacturers of computer chips will ultimately adapt their designs accordingly. Current microprocessors have complex and expensive wiring patterns because the circuits are still, for cultural compatibility reasons, being designed to carry out the complex numerical manipulations inherited from the Industrial Age. These manipulations require information to come together from all over the chip. They also put a premium on reliability, because some bits of information are far more important than others. A single error in the sign bit of a number or its exponent can cause an entire computation to crash with a division by zero or a square root of a negative number. Meanwhile, the bits at the other end of the number are meaningless because a numerical computation typically carries five times as many bits in its numbers as it will actually use in the result.

Intermaths can relieve the circuit designer of much of this stress. Cells in a cellular automata computation, for example, typically communicate only with their nearby neighbors. A chip that implements this approach directly can dispense with the long, expensive, hard-to-optimize wires that a numerocentric circuit must include. Nor does the chip necessarily have to be so fanatical about detecting errors. In the "bit democracy" of intermaths, each bit matters the same trivial amount, potentially reducing the impact of bit-level hardware errors. In the case of a genetic algorithm, a bit-level error could as easily be a useful mutation as an unuseful one. As Hasslacher has noted, hardware based on intermaths can be much bigger and much cheaper than traditional circuitry: "These approaches have the potential to stimulate a new form of computer hardware, incomparably more compact and more powerful than anything available today."[14]

The contemporary human brain will continue to be blessed with, or stuck with, a rich array of long-distance connections. Because this was the way the brain already worked, it made sense for cultural evolution to develop ways of using these connections to the full. Electronic circuits, however, open up the possibility of benefiting from simplicity instead. Intermaths and silicon are coadaptive, each offering what the other needs. As more appropriate circuits become available, the intermaths can become even more general and more powerful. It is these more-generalized formulations that will provide the fertile environment for bit evolution.

13

THE LIFE WITHIN PATTERNS

The first uses of intermaths during the 1980s and 1990s have inevitably focused on specific applications. Simulated annealing routines helped the designers of the Connection Machine fit sixteen parallel processors onto each integrated circuit chip. Neural networks began recognizing printed characters in both roman and kanji text. Neural nets have also aided in the analysis of electrocardiograms and in predicting when metal castings would develop internal flaws as they cooled.[1] A variety of intermath techniques are even in use in making financial investment decisions.

The financial investment applications are illustrative. Collaborators such as Swiss Bank Corporation and the Prediction Company use the existing supply of market and financial data to train their systems. Periodically, opportunities open up for profitable, low-risk trades.[2] These opportunities may only last a few minutes. Techniques such as neural networks can potentially spot these patterns first, although their use involves a Faustian bargain. The system may declare that a buying or selling opportunity exists, but it will not necessarily supply proof in any human-absorbable form. The decision to trade becomes a leap of computational faith. For this reason, the use of intermaths for financial trading has remained largely the purview of experienced users of the technology. For example, David Shaw, the designer of the NonVon parallel computer in the early 1980s and the person who asked how God solves differential equations, now runs the D. E. Shaw investment firm. The scientists Norman Packard and Doyne Farmer run the Prediction Company. The adoption of intermaths requires two simultaneous training processes. The computers must train themselves to find the patterns. At the same time, they must train the scientists to have faith in their ability to do so. Both training processes take time.

Systems that are highly adapted to a single specific environment, however, are not the ones that do the best and respond in the most creative ways when things change. The tragedy for the wheelwrights of rural England was that, although they could feel their world changing, there was ultimately nothing they could do about it. Their way of learning was exquisitely sensitive to small changes in their environment but unable to adapt quickly to big ones. Studies of changing ecologies confirm what common sense suggests: The organisms that are most tightly adapted to a specific environment can be the ones most at risk of extinction when that environment changes. The warbler and the vireo, for example, compete successfully for the specialized foods available in the deep woods, but they do not know how to fly across open lands if they need to find a new pocket of deep woods. Robins and grackles, meanwhile, are comfortable ranging across a variety of habitats in search of food. When the deep forest is disturbed, it is the robin and the grackle that have the behavioral wherewithal to adjust, more so than the warbler and the vireo.[3]

Organisms that are somewhat sloppier in their adaptations, that carry traits of no direct value in their current environment, often use exactly those traits as a source of creativity to survive and flourish in a new situation. Any such sloppiness had long since been wrung out of the wagon shops. What remained was nothing but the pure, and vulnerable, "picked experience of ages." The Hillis genetic sorting algorithm, also the product of a single-minded drive for efficiency, most directly echoes the poignant vulnerability of the wagon shop and the vireo. The final algorithm had shed all of its interim messiness and become highly regular. The genetic version of Kepler's third law shows a less advanced result, because it was required only to get the right answer, not to get it in the minimum possible number of steps. This version, although sloppier, has greater potential to change and adapt because it is less compressed.

To get beyond the simple repetitive worlds of numerical sorting and planetary orbits, therefore, computers must travel lighter, use fewer prior assumptions, and not try to become perfect at any individual task. To invent their way out of corners when life changes, they must maintain competition among their internal rules, never allowing the "picked experience of ages" to take over completely and kill off alternatives that may be needed later on. Such very general behavior is the province of intermaths known as "classifier systems." As pioneered by the computer scientist John Holland, they are sophisticated genetic formulations designed to operate in a world of perpetual novelty.[4] Because they are inherently more primitive than such methods as neural networks, classifier systems start out in an even more helpless state. Because they are more primitive, however, they are also more general and have the potential, given sufficient training, to be far more creative and to become far more alive.

Operating a classifier system can be a little like running one's life from a telephone answering machine. The outside world is free to place data on the machine's message list. At a minimum, these messages have a source ("Hi. It's George.") and an action ("Remember to get milk.") A classifier system also puts its own messages onto the list. Such internally generated messages might include extracts from messages that come in from outside. Thus, the system, in response to hearing George's message, might place a new message on the machine that says "go shopping at 2:00 and . . . ," followed by the last part of George's message, which says "remember to get milk." Alternatively, it may be that the owner does not know anyone named George. Because a message from "George" has no credibility in these circumstances, it is simply deleted and ignored.

What is desired for this system is that it spontaneously teach itself both to detect patterns and to act in accordance with them, perhaps, for example, replenishing the milk supply at the proper times. To do that, it needs to get some feedback. When someone opens the refrigerator and says, "Oh wow. Somebody remembered to get milk," that positive reinforcement needs to go on the message list. So does negative feedback, like "Who bought all this milk? There's no room for juice." A satellite camera inside the refrigerator would be a useful source of feedback and training data.

The system also needs a way to influence the milk supply. It might, for example, process a message to "send milk" on the message list by having that message transmitted over the Internet to a delivery service. One strategy would be to do so repeatedly until the system hears complaints about too much milk and then to stop until it hears complaints about too little. The system, however, also has a second, much more sophisticated tool with which to manage the milk supply. It might create, through its message list, a bit-level analog to a human "mental model" of how milk consumption happens and use it to try to predict when there will be complaints about too much or too little milk. It could then inexorably tune and refine that model on the basis of whether its earlier predictions were borne out.

The way such adaptive modeling can work out in practice is suggested by a model of consumer behavior developed by the economist Brian Arthur at the Santa Fe Institute.[5] It is based on a local pub that is comfortably full with sixty patrons but has a loyal following of a hundred customers. All the customers like to go there, but not when it is too full to be comfortable. These hundred customers, or "agents" as economists prefer to call them, are left by Arthur's computer simulation to breed their own little methods of deciding whether or not to patronize the bar on a given evening. And they do. Each develops a unique personal set of decision processes in its own way and learns from the outcome which ones to trust. Over time, the average patronage of the bar settles in right around sixty.

An initial reaction of people not familiar with adaptive intermaths is often to assume that some one of the agents must have taken charge.[6] It would be a simple matter for a leader to assign each patron three nights out of five and ensure that exactly sixty people show up each night. In fact, there is no leader. The makeup of the sixty patrons does not repeat, but it does average out at sixty. This assumption of a leader used to be made about the behavior of bird flocks, too. Flocks can be seen to change direction very sharply and coherently in response to a threat. The assumption that all the birds were keying off a leader went largely unchallenged until the late 1980s and indeed was used by social scientists as an analogy for industrial behavior in general, because "if the flock of birds have a leader, who usually heads the array, and a fixed order of procedure, which indicates some division of labor, I would say that this is more like a decision unit. A flock is more like a firm."[7] Then, in the late 1980s, an intermath simulation showed that bird flocks need not have a leader at all.[8] If each bird simply keys off its nearby neighbors, coherent behavior emerges all on its own. It is this kind of coherent group behavior that also emerges from the pub simulation, although individual patrons are actually evolving their own individual decision processes.

Part Three of the Book of Nature is at work at two levels in these examples, because the new, decentralized version of the bird flock in turn reflects the latest organizational development theories about "reengineering" and "empowerment." It is likely that late-1990s management consultants will once again assert that "a flock is like a firm," but this time because the reengineered flock acts coherently in the absence of a leader, not because it acts coherently owing to a fixed order of procedure as bird flocks ostensibly did back in the 1960s. Such consultant advice moves the subject matter of economics itself in a direction that more closely fits the new mathematical vocabulary, precisely the adaptive process that makes a unit of the Book of Nature itself coherent.

It is the coherent distributed behavior of the bird flock or the pub clientele that a classifier system must develop, but in a more generalized way. Starting from nothing but an empty telephone answering machine, however, it seems impossible to evolve behavior as complex as managing a family milk supply, and it is. Left to its own devices, the machine will never even learn how to invent a message that says "buy milk," much less a message that says "if someone complains about being out of milk, queue a message to buy milk." Nor is it likely to invent the idea of a mental model and then proceed to create one out of messages.

On the other hand, a newborn baby would never successfully develop if it had to learn how to handle the milk supply successfully or to kick a pile of number blocks into numerical order before it was allowed to hear any other inputs or feedback from the world around it. The real world is awash in data of all kinds. It is in this sense that the telephone answering machine analogy is wholly misleading. A typical answering machine is a small-data device. It receives a very high-level symbolic message every few minutes or every few hours and has room for only a few dozen messages. A modern network of computers can keep tens of thousands, perhaps millions, of little classifier messages in play simultaneously. It has access to an abundance of information, including the equivalent of a satellite passing over the refrigerator every hour or so and sending in pixels of information about each shelf. All the information necessary to build a predictive model and all the vocabulary for expressing it are out there for the asking. The problem is to sift through it all, and here one of the paradoxes of learning and evolution weighs in on the side of the new intermaths: "It is often easier to learn a complex set of interrelationships among events than to learn a single relationship between two events."[9]

In everyday life, the consumption of milk may go way up some days or stop completely. But when it changes in these ways, it is rarely the only behavior in the environment that changes. Perhaps there was a big party, and consumption of other kinds of fluids soared. Perhaps

people were away, and no food was consumed either. A classifier system that receives both satellite scans of the refrigerator shelves and
complaints about the milk supply does not need to know the whole
culture of milk usage or even what milk is. It only needs to notice that
the pixels of certain parts of the refrigerator image tend to look a certain way the day before complaints start being queued. A classifier system takes this simple-mindedness down to its primal, bit-level roots
and then counts on modern computing and data abundance to boot-
strap back up.

> Classifier systems combined with the genetic algorithm for example
> can gather information, improve their actions as they receive feed-
> back from their environment, make sudden discoveries, and "learn
> to learn" at a meta-level.[10]

At its lowest level, a classifier system absorbs and exploits data
about the behavior of the world around it from a base of extremely
simple bit-level messages placed on a large list. The messages may
come from the outside, or they may be generated within the system
itself. As developed by Holland, each message, or "rule," has two
parts. The first is its identifier, the second a call to action. The call to
action activates other rules on the next cycle. The call to action of a
very short rule might be as follows:

$$1\ 0\ 0\ \#\ 1\ \#\ 0\ 0$$

All rules in the system whose identifier section matches this call to
action are placed on the message list, where they will potentially take
effect the next round. To be a match, an identifier must match each 1
with a 1 and each 0 with a 0. The # is a wild card, meaning that either
a 0 or a 1 will match. Thus, the preceding call to action will cause rules
with any of the four following identifiers, among others, to activate:

$$1\ 0\ 0\ 0\ 1\ 0\ 0\ 0$$
$$1\ 0\ 0\ 0\ 1\ 1\ 0\ 0$$
$$1\ 0\ 0\ 1\ 1\ 0\ 0\ 0$$
$$1\ 0\ 0\ 1\ 1\ 1\ 0\ 0$$

Actually, identifiers may have wild cards as well, so rules with identifiers like the following would also activate:

$$\#\ 0\ 0\ 1\ 1\ 1\ 0\ \#$$
$$\#\ 0\ 0\ \#\ \#\ 0\ \#$$
$$\#\ \#\ \#\ \#\ \#\ \#\ \#$$

The latter, with all wild cards as an identifier, is a potential trouble-maker, of course. It would be activated every time and stay active for-ever. Worse yet, a rule with all wild cards as both its identifier and its call to action would activate every rule in the system, including itself, and hence keep doing so forever.

To be useful, a classifier system must constrain its own behavior to the parts that are useful, while retaining the ability to create new behavior when nothing in its existing repertoire turns out to be useful. The first step in constraining behavior is selectively to ignore some of the rules, even though they have been called to action and placed on the message list. Rules that are very general, in the sense of having many wild cards, are given a lower chance of being activated than other, more specific rules on the list. This approach is analogous to that of the teacher who is quick to call on students who raise their hands rarely but filters out the student whose hand is in the air all the time. A second step in constraining behavior is to favor rules that were called to action by many previous rules over those that were called by just one or two. In both cases, the classifier system is using the power of competition.

The third step in constraining behavior is more subtle, because it favors rules that have worked well in the past. In essence, all the rules that happen to be active when the outside world says "Oh, wow. Somebody remembered to get milk," or when some other prediction is borne out, are given a greater strength as a result. All those that are active when a negative result occurs, on the other hand, are reduced in strength. Even after a rule goes on the message list, it competes for activation with all the other activated rules on the basis of its speci-ficity, its previous track record, and the size of its constituency, that is, the number of previously active rules that activated it.

Even weak and very general rules will be carried out once in a while. If they prove useful, and they often do, they will gain enough strength to counterbalance their generality and thus become regular partici-pants. Such rules become valuable because they are the defaults that guide behavior when the system does not know anything more specific to do. Cynical tennis players use a default rule (when in doubt, call it out) to help decide whether an opponent's shot needs to be returned. They may also have much more specific rules to handle specific situa-tions: If playing on grass and a puff of chalk comes up, then the ball has hit the chalk line and is in play.

More specific rules typically come from the system's continuous mating of existing general rules. The mating process, common to many intermaths, takes a portion of one rule and brings it together with a portion of another rule. Rules with higher strengths have a higher probability of participating in matings and thus propagating their components. It is in this way that a slightly more specific version of a default rule might come into being. If the more specific rule turns out to be useful, it will gain in strength to the point that it will be activated ahead of a similar default rule.

The final subtle component of a classifier system is called a *bucket brigade;* its job is to spread out the credit for success and thus to encourage teamwork among rules. Whenever a rule receives a payoff, it shares that payoff with the rule or rules that activated it. These rules become stronger and hence more likely to be activated in the future. As always, a rule may be called to action but not activated. The stronger it is, the more likely that it will be activated when it is called to action. In a further refinement of the bucket brigade, rules that are actually activated when they are called to action share some of their strength with the rules that called them, even if they themselves do not receive a direct payoff. Gradually, in this way, the early rules that set up the ultimately successful rules gain strength.

The bucket-brigade process is similar to the way a mouse is thought to learn a maze.[11] The first turn it learns for sure is the final turn to the exit because the payoff is strong and immediate. Then it learns the penultimate turn and so on back to the beginning. The process of learning is backward to the order of the knowledge that is being sought. Success requires that the process and the content interact. In the beginning, everything for the mouse is guesswork and blunder, just as it was for Lewis Richardson as he first tried to understand arms races:

> Before we can attempt to measure anything we must have a preliminary ideal of what we wish to measure. But it would be most unwise to give that ideal a rigid definition at the outset, because the experience gained during the process of measurement should be allowed to react upon and refine the ideal.[12]

Only as he gathered data did Richardson (and the mouse) learn what kind of data was needed. Given a set of training data, Richardson formulated a theory to explain it. His first version of the theory, published in 1919, was based on data from the years before World War I. His next version, described at the British Association meeting the month before Chamberlain met with Hitler, was based on data about the new arms race that was just then unfolding. His final versions, developed in the 1950s, incorporated data from a third arms race. Each time, Richardson modified both his theory and the format of his data as he sought to save the appearances more and more accurately.

One element Richardson did not create from scratch was the vocabulary used in his theory. From the beginning, he expressed his theory in the high-level symbolic vocabulary of differential equations. He brought this vocabulary across from his work in weather prediction, where it in turn had been an import from the related field of fluid flow. He saw enough similarities between the way weather behaved and the way societies behaved to motivate using the vocabulary of one to study the other: "Foreign affairs as they appear day by day in the newspaper: . . . these may be likened to the eddying view of the wind."[13]

Today, there are two practical differences between compressed equations like Richardson's and sprawling intermaths like Holland's. On the one hand, the bit-level formulations can, as we now know, adapt and evolve on their own, whereas the compacted equational ones cannot. On the other hand, equational formulations are running on millions of computers every day, and intermath ones are not. It is a chicken-and-egg situation, with training required in both directions at once. We must give the intermath formulations a chance to do the training necessary to compete successfully with the compressed equational formulations that are there now. At the same time, they must train *us* to have faith that tiny computational elements like classifiers can come to do useful work and hence are worth spending spare computing cycles on.

Our lack of faith in the collective power of small agents may be the harder of these two training hurdles to surmount. As products of the culture of sequential thought, we prefer our big results to come from big causes. Since early in the century, we have been comfortable, for example, with the image of a giant iceberg taking down the equally giant *Titanic*. Here is a villain worthy of its deed; the huge ship and the huge iceberg go well together in a picture. Reports that the collision itself was minor and that rumblings worked their way through the hull after the impact have been discounted because they did not fit with our causal preconceptions. Also rarely mentioned is the fact that the *Titanic* was built from a cheap grade of steel known to be brittle in the cold. A sister ship built from the same steel broke up when cracks at the molecular level started to propagate through its hull plates. It remains hard for our minds to let go of the symmetry of one iceberg, one *Titanic*. A similar and more current challenge to our preconceptions is the recent proposal to equip airplane wings with thousands of tiny microflaps, each controlled by its own little neural network and each responding adaptively to its own local air behavior, somewhat as local sections of the skin of a dolphin respond to the water around them.[14]

Sometimes, as Galileo speculated, armies of ants really can carry ships ashore. Sometimes armies of brittle molecules really can carry ships to a watery grave. And sometimes armies of microflaps really can steer and optimize airplane flight. In each case, the bigger the army and the smaller the individual soldiers, the better for electronic circuits. The challenge is for *us* to accept this reality, not the circuits. As Alfred North Whitehead pointed out, a healthy society must be able to shed its old abstractions in order to advance:

> You cannot think without abstractions; accordingly, it is of the utmost importance to be vigilant in critically revising your modes of abstraction. It is here that philosophy finds its healthy niche as essential to the healthy progress of society. It is the critique of abstractions. A civilization which cannot burst through its current abstractions is doomed to sterility after a very limited burst of progress.[15]

Civilization's most recent burst of scientific progress, the one that started during the Renaissance, is fast reaching its denouement. Already, intrepid economists, sociologists, biologists, ecologists, and cognitive scientists are constructing new abstractions for the future. The new intermaths are a natural fit for these subject areas. As high school students become as fluent in neural networks and classifiers as they are in intersecting lines and integrals, they too will recognize the opportunities to apply them to urgent real-world problems. At first the results will be poor, of course; however, there is an endless supply of data to train on, endless unused computer time when the training can take place, and increasing communications capacity to support the sharing of good building blocks as they are found.

More important, there are urgent new problems to be solved. Numbers and equations did not solve the seventeenth-century problems of global navigation right away either. At first, the errors were of twenty miles and more. The pressure to do better forced the equational maths to become better. In similar fashion, the problems of managing economies and ecologies, and of gaining perspective on our own form of intelligence, are stimulating the new intermaths. These applications are the source of the evolutionary pressure that will bring the intermaths out of the laboratory and into the mainstream, where they will increasingly challenge numbers and equations in fields like economics, where there is too much novelty and therefore too much data.

14

COMPUTING THE PATTERNS OF SOCIETIES AND ECONOMIES

When the Turks overran Constantinople in 1453 and drove many Greek scholars westward, Europe was still, as it had been for almost a thousand years, an isolated region. It imported very few ideas from the rest of the world and sent very few of its own back out. With the wave of Greek scholars came an infusion of Greek learning, including the algebraic ideas that stimulated Regiomontanus. With the advance of the Turkish armies into Europe came also the Moslem religion. Even before Constantinople, the Turks had defeated a combined force of Serbs, Bulgarians, Albanians, and Bosnians at the Battle of Kosovo. A century later, as Copernicus was developing the last great work of the geometric computing era, the Turkish advance was finally being stopped just outside the gates of Vienna, although attacks continued for decades, one of them predicted by the horoscope Johannes Kepler prepared for his prince.

Under the new Turkish rule in the Balkans, any citizen could convert to the Moslem religion. Particularly in Bosnian and Albanian lands, many did, thereby becoming part of the favored class. In addition, the new Moslem rulers extracted, as tribute, a quarter of the Christian male teenage population. These youths were sent east to be educated at palace schools; many rose to positions of high authority in the government. Others became part of the elite Janissary military forces. From the perspective of the 1960s, a historian suggested that this tribute policy could "be regarded either as a terrible misfortune inflicted upon the Christian families or as a magnificent opportunity for an able child to escape the raw and brutal life of his village."[1] It is the task of social scientists to try to understand how people will actually behave and react to such changing circumstances in their lives and cultures. In the centuries since, these twin ideas, the terrible misfortunes of ethnic disruption and the magnificent opportunities of new economic activity, have ebbed and flowed and rubbed up against each other, challenging sociologists and economists to predict their parallel impacts.

> We are all familiar with the Wallerstein thesis that world capitalism since its inception in Europe in the 16th century, has spread like a tidal wave.... However, it leaves out of account another parallel process that consisted of the differentiating, carving out and fragmentation of the same world in terms of "nation-states."[2]

The flow of new religious and mathematical ideas into Europe at this time was not accompanied by any biological changes; there were no corresponding waves of physical immigration and new genetic material. Those who converted from Christianity to the Moslem religion, like those who converted from geometry to algebra, were the same peoples who had lived in the area for centuries. The changes were purely at the level of cultural evolution.

For the final years of the European Middle Ages, predicting the course of this cultural evolution would have been easy in any mathematical vocabulary because nothing much changed. The "raw and brutal" villages of Europe were barely able to maintain the small stock of culture they already had. When average life expectancy was one score and ten, it was difficult to teach the next generation even the most rudimentary skills and beliefs. There was little room for new ideas to develop. Innovations such as the Gothic arch were few and far between. In the Europe of the Middle Ages, there was no advantage in having an advantage. There was little point in trying to steal a march on the Pope.

A modern multicentury computer simulation of such a society illuminates some of its underlying dynamics. In this random-event-based simulation, individuals and their offspring continue in their current stations in life unless they become so much better at some other task that they take it over from somebody else. New ideas and inventions, the building blocks that are necessary for someone suddenly to become better at a task, are modest in scale. They occur randomly and not very often. No single, new idea by itself is big enough to upset the status quo. When the rate of new ideas is low, as it was in Europe in the Middle Ages, it requires an exceptional run of luck, a succession of innovations rather than just one, for individuals to move up out of their inherited station in life. Even when they did, society as a whole settled back into the same stable pattern as before. Thus, a Fugger family in medieval Augsburg might experience a great run of luck in their copper mines and use it to become powerful merchants, at the expense of others, but society itself did not change as a result.

All it takes to change the tenor of life in this computer simulation, however, is a slight increase in the rate at which new ideas are generated. Suddenly, a threshold is reached at which there is indeed an advantage to having an advantage. Combined with a slight increase in average life expectancy, the flow of new ideas into a culture such as Europe's made the Fugger family motto—"I want to gain while I can"—meaningful across the board. As illustrated in figure 14.1, activity rises from its original guildlike quiescence to a permanently higher pitch.[3]

In Europe, this quickening of innovative activity was accompanied by a desire to study it and understand it. The Renaissance's new method of algebraic prediction, which was instrumental in creating the quickening, was in turn called on to help explain the social consequences. The groundwork for the new social science of economics was laid down by a keen student of astronomy and passionate follower of Isaac Newton, the Scottish philosopher Adam Smith. Before writing *The Wealth of Nations*, he had already written a history of astronomy from ancient Greek times up through the innovations of Newton. He knew his epicycles as well as his fluxions.

Inevitably, Smith made the new mechanistic vocabulary of Newton an important ingredient of his theories. Before Smith, the mercantilist philosophers had taken a much more static and geometric approach to the questions of wealth. Using the vocabulary of place, they had measured the wealth of a nation by how much bullion was physically within its borders. Smith, in contrast, saw a "great wheel of circula-

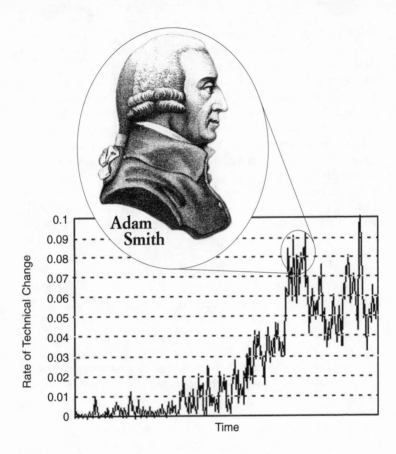

Figure 14.1. Intermath formulations provide insight not just into the way behavior changes but also into the way it might have been created in the first place. For example, an intermath model of economic behavior shows the way that modern economies can come about after many centuries of low activity. The evolutionary economists Gerald Silverberg and Bart Verspagen refer to the early phases of this multi-century model as the medieval guild period, when economic functions were highly concentrated (in guild monopolies) and the rate of innovation was very low. As the concentration broke down, the level of innovation and overall economic activity suddenly moved to a new level. Not surprisingly, the field of economics itself was born at the same time that western society made this shift. Adam Smith was a product of his age. Time series diagram courtesy of Springer-Verlag.

tion," where phenomena such as comparative advantage were equational in nature, "either perfectly equal or continually tending to equality." Like a Newtonian planet, economic activity could change its pace. In analyzing the wealth and revenue of the realm since the time of Henry VIII, Smith found that "their pace seems rather to have been gradually accelerated than retarded. They seem, not only to have been going on, but to have been going on faster and faster."[4]

Just as the followers of Newton were coming to see the universe as a vast machine, created by a God who was a watchmaker at heart, Smith saw the economy of England as a vast machine because "systems in many respects resemble machines. . . . A system is an imaginary machine invented to connect together in the fancy those different movements and effects which are already in reality performed."[5] Over time, the analogy became self-fulfilling. The new methods of scientific prediction stimulated the development of more and more powerful machines, which in turn imposed their sequential cadence on the society that invented them. As Thorstein Veblen observed at the end of the nineteenth century, "what the discipline of the machine industry inculcates . . . in the habits of life and thought of the workman, is regularity of sequence and mechanical precision."[6] The sequential maths were helping to create a production-line world, which was imitated in new sequential habits of society, making the sequential maths themselves that much more appropriate as tools to predict that behavior. The universities passed this sequential–mechanical mind-set on to future generations, just as the poet William Blake said they would:

> I turn my eyes to the Schools & Universities of Europe
> And there behold the Loom of Locke, whose Woof rages dire,
> Wash'd by the Water-Wheels of Newton.[7]

A second source for the new mode of economic thinking was Plato's idealism and its focus on the similarity of individual objects rather than their differences. What was important to Plato was the way, for example, in which all chairs were the same: the "essential chairness" that they all shared. The little quirks that distinguished one chair from another were not important. Sociologically, it was this new belief in equality of birth that finally broke down the feudal privileges of inherited place in life. The Jeffersonian ideal of equal creation translated readily into an economic system in which all participants, like all atoms, were seen as responding to similar circumstances in similar ways. These notions of individual responsibility, emphasizing success in the economic sphere as an indicator of God's favor, were further reinforced from the Protestant pulpit each Sunday.

Ethnicists find that, compared to other cultures, "those of us in Western societies are accustomed to thinking about behavior in individual, cost–benefit terms."[8] To the extent that individual members of Western societies indeed acted interchangeably and individually, they became even more like Adam Smith's mechanistic system and even more amenable to useful prediction in mechanistic terms. During World War II, economists at the University of Leeds and the London School of Economics were able to design serious models of the economy out of pipes and tanks and water pumps. At a time when economic modeling was only beginning to migrate to electronic circuits, the Leeds model deliberately took a different path, as illustrated in figure 14.2. It was designed to be "a calculating machine" just as the new electronic computers were, but since it was "intended for exposition rather than accurate calculation, a second requirement [was] that the whole of the operations should be clearly visible and comprehensible to an onlooker. For this reason hydraulic methods have been used in preference to electronic ones which might have given greater accuracy."[9] It went without saying that the onlooker to whom the behavior needed to be comprehensible was a human onlooker.

The Leeds economic model was a sequence of tanks, pipes, and pumps through which colored water flowed. The degree to which the mechanistic language of flow and pace had come to inform economic vocabulary becomes patent from the descriptions of the model's operation. It is often unclear from these descriptions exactly which is being addressed: the "macro-economic theory in terms of money flows" as it is taught in the classroom; the "liquid stocks" maintained to "fill" customer orders, which are stored out in the actual factory warehouses of the society; or the movement of colored water in the tubes and tanks of the model. Thus, "the production flow goes into the tank containing stocks, from which is drawn the consumption flow, controlled and measured by a second valve similar to the first."[10] And, "in equilibrium the level of water inside the float will be the same as that in the M_1 tank, and the position of the valve is that of zero induced investment."[11] A more sophisticated version of the model added a government component, with some of the income flow being taken off the top and sent to the public sector of the model. The final step of the model's evolution was to connect two such models and attach "the imports flow of one model into the exports tube of the other"[12] through a currency exchanging servomechanism.

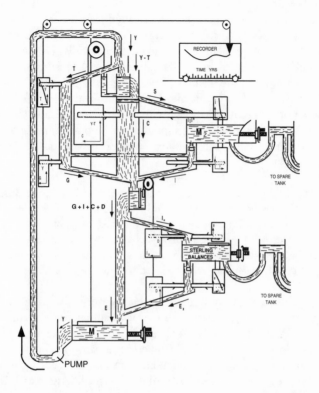

Figure 14.2. The maths of the Industrial Age were often used to express fundamentally mechanistic fictions. Thus the patterns of behavior in a national economy could be expressed interchangeably by sets of equations and by sets of pipes, as they were in a model designed by Leeds University and the London School of Economics in the 1940s. The slow-moving flows in individual pipes add together in the same predictable way that numbers do. Thus the large pipe in the center of the model represents "G+I+C+D" with "E_1" being added in at the bottom. The whole model reflects Adam Smith's original conception of an economy as a "great engine of circulation." Courtesy of Blackwell Publishers.

Although such a model would have been impossible to fabricate in Adam Smith's time, with its hulking steam-powered pumps, he would have understood it instantly because it expressed his conception of "the channel of circulation" so directly and vividly. He would also have taken for granted, as did the fabricators at Leeds, that the flows of various parts of the realm, such as those of England and Scotland, could combine and intermingle without turbulence. Smith's Scottish compatriot Lewis Richardson, from his studies of deadly conflicts, knew that such intermingling should never be taken for granted. He knew that there were other, ethnic factors constantly at work in the world, and that

> although it is hundreds of years since the time of Robert the Bruce, the relations between Scotland and England might still be describable in partisan language thus: "A noble army of Scots fully equipped with the latest means of defence might still be encamped on the north side of the Cheviots facing a dastardly horde of English cruelly armed with their wicked weapons of destruction."[13]

For whatever reason, the relationship between England and Scotland did not and does not work that way, although the relationship between England and Ireland still can. It is one reminder among many that life does not, in fact, flow as smoothly as slow-moving water and that more sophisticated prediction methods may be needed. Thus, the influential economics textbook of Alfred Marshall, written early in the twentieth century, opens with the observation that the Mecca of the economist lies in biology rather than in dynamics. Such a Mecca was, however, out of Marshall's pedagogical reach. He was forced to recognize, as did the builders of the fluid model of the economy, that a biological approach was impossible to construct or to communicate to beginning students:

> The Mecca of the economist lies in economic biology rather than in economic dynamics. But biological conceptions are more complex than those of mechanics; a volume on Foundations must therefore give a relatively large place to mechanical analogies; and frequent use is made of the term "equilibrium."[14]

Marshall, like Descartes, was willing to distort and stylize his subject matter into a form that matched the strengths and weaknesses of the human mind, capitulating to the fact that it is "necessary for man with his limited powers to go step by step; breaking up a complex question, studying it one bit at a time, and at last combining partial solutions into a more or less complete solution of the whole riddle."[15] Marshall did not, however, join Descartes in an embrace of the numbers-and-equations vocabulary that had proved so effective in the physical sciences. Marshall found them to be distorting in ways that the vocabulary of words and sentences was not:

> I had a growing feeling in the later years of my work that a good mathematical theorem for dealing with economic hypotheses was very unlikely to be good economics: and I went more and more on the rules—(1) Use mathematics as a shorthand language, rather than as an engine of enquiry. (2) Keep them until you have done. (3) Translate into English. (4) Then illustrate by examples that are important in real life. (5) Burn the mathematics. (6) If you can't succeed in (4), burn (3). This last I often did.[16]

For Marshall, the tacit process of translating ideas from numbers and equations into text within his own mind was a more powerful and illuminating process than the translation of numbers and equations into new numbers and equations on the blackboard. It is, after all, possible to make valuable statements in the language of text that cannot be said in numbers and equations. Economists since Smith have, for example, quoted Jonathan Swift's comment about the destructive effect of customs duties: "In the arithmetic of the customs two and two, instead of making four, make some times only one."[17] This aphorism cleverly appears to use the language of numbers and equations, but it does not, and the fact that it does not is illuminating. The statement "2 + 2 = 1" is one of many that are expressly forbidden in the language of numbers and equations. If an outcome analogous to a "1" emerges from a process that brings together two phenomena that are each analogous to a "2," there is no simple way in algebra to say that. That is why the statement was "translated into English," where the word *and* is available to bring concepts together in sophisticated ways that the symbol "+" never can.

It is not a trivial point. The vocabulary of numbers and equations, whether in physics or economics or ethnicity, is predicated on the belief that numbers meaningfully express the reality under study. To use numbers to describe human economic behavior, one must believe, with Schumpeter, that important economic behavior really is "made numerical by life itself." Jane Jacobs, on the other hand, did not need to resort to equations to develop a sophisticated theory of the way cities work. The ethnicist Benedict Anderson is also suspicious concerning social behavior described as inherently numerical. The process of coercing life into numerical form can miss its essence or, worse, corrupt it:

> Take, for example, the 1911 Federated Malay States Census. . . . It is extremely unlikely that, in 1911, more than a tiny fraction of those categorized and subcategorized would have recognized themselves under such labels. . . . The fiction of the census is that everyone is in it, and that everyone has one—and only one—extremely clear place. No fractions.[18]

> Everyone, everything, had (as it were) a serial number. This style of imagining did not come out of thin air. It was the product of the technologies of navigation, astronomy, horology, surveying, photography, and print, to say nothing of the deep driving power of capitalism.[19]

Like Marshall, John Maynard Keynes doubted that numbers and equations could "carry us any further than ordinary discourse can."[20] It is ironic, therefore, that Keynes became the source for some of the most equational economic formulations of the twentieth century: "Keynesian theory evolved from disconnected, qualitative talk about economic activity into a system of equations [because it] lent itself so readily to the formulation of explicit econometric models."[21] That had not been Keynes's intention.

Keynes was conscious of the simultaneous and mutual interactions among the elements of an economy. He found a colleague's proposal for a thirty-nine-equation model of the American economy to miss the point because its author pretended he was "dealing with non-simultaneous events and time lags. What happens if the phenomenon under investigation itself reacts on the factors by which we are explaining it?"[22] Keynes also recognized the danger in his critiquing such an equational model: that instead of curing the problems in the model by moving away from equations, his colleague might try instead to cure them by adding more such equations and "that his reaction will be to engage another ten computers and drown his sorrows in arithmetic."[23] If all one has is numbers, the whole world can look like equations, just as if all one has is circles, the whole universe looks like epicycles.

Keynes's own approach was more subtle and non-Cartesian. He disagreed with Descartes's assumption that the mind could do only one thing at a time. Keynes saw the human mind, or at least his own human mind, as able to keep track of simultaneous effects in ways that algebra did not. He saw his mind as a parallel resource and hence superior to a machine:

> After we have reached a provisional conclusion by isolating the complicating factors one by one, we then have to go back on ourselves and allow, as well as we can, for the probable interactions of the factors amongst themselves. This is the nature of economic thinking. . . . It is a great fault of symbolic pseudo-mathematical methods of formalising a system of economic analysis, such as we shall set down in section VI of this chapter, that they expressly assume strict independence between the factors involved and lose all their cogency and authority if this hypothesis is disallowed; whereas, in ordinary discourse, . . . we can keep "at the back of our heads" the necessary reserves and qualifications and the adjustments which we shall have to make later on, in a way in which we cannot keep complicated partial differentials "at the back" of several pages of algebra which assume that they all vanish.[24]

Neither Keynes nor Marshall was willing to go all the way back to the primitivism of Kepler, however, and arrange the data in mental posies, first one way and then another. They had more compressed methodologies in mind. Ultimately, Keynes went ahead with the numbers-and-equations approach just as Lewis Richardson was doing in his peace studies. It was not Richardson, however, who carried the equational vocabulary into university social science departments. Right in the opening chapter of his book *Foundations of Economic Analysis*, the economist Paul Samuelson savaged Marshall's "literary" technique of processing preliminary equations back through his mind and rendering them into text:

> The laborious literary working over of essentially simple mathematical concepts such as is characteristic of much of modern economic theory is not only unrewarding from the standpoint of advancing the science, but involves as well mental gymnastics of a particularly depraved type.[25]

The resulting equational formulations of the postwar economists turned out to be, of course, a perfect fit to the new von Neumann electronic computers being developed separately by the physicists and engineers at that time. When the business-trained policy makers of the Kennedy Administration sought guidance in the fields of third-world development and demographics, they found the two to be a perfect match. The economist Brian Arthur, writing in the 1970s, described how the prevailing cultures of business, economics, and electronic computing came together at this time:

> Economic development is complicated and imperfectly understood. . . . A flexible, rounded view would draw from many sources. Formal modeling, on the other hand, requires a particular perspective to be selected. . . . Selection was narrowed by a simple fact: computers require [sic] equations. The neoclassical tradition stood ready to provide them. . . . These became, and have remained, the core of economic–demographic models.[26]

Just like the nineteenth-century models of the moon's behavior, the models of the economy soon grew from a few dozen equations to thousands. While they were doing so in the second half of the twentieth century, however, the world changed. The Industrial Age became the Information Age. Life speeded up and became much more uncertain. As it did so, ethnic tensions, some of which had lain dormant for centuries, flared anew. Each of these changes has motivated social scientists to reexamine their Darwinian evolutionary roots and to question the universal fitness of the numbers and equations borrowed from physics.

Equational techniques of looking for patterns in data are designed to build up from too little data rather than to render down from too much. Given a direct marketplace hypothesis like "people buy more fans on hot days," equational techniques can work their way through a few billion pieces of sales data and confirm it. Independent discovery of relationships, such as that late-afternoon purchasers of disposable diapers are very likely to want a six-pack as well, are well beyond the range of equational techniques. It is the new, nonnumeric intermaths that have become the tools of choice in computational marketing systems that now analyze market behavior for private industry.

At the same time that the increased data of the Information Age is overwhelming traditional equational techniques, the increased pace of life is overwhelming each of us. We no longer have time to work out the optimal and "rational" Cartesian responses that economists have traditionally depended on in their equation-based models. Equations have always described this sort of optimal behavior nicely. The equational approach is also relatively simple, and when it arrives at the desired answer, there is no motivation to dig any deeper. Karl Popper described this process of science going down just deep enough to get the job done:

> Science does not rest upon rock bottom. The bold structure of its theories rises, as it were, above a swamp. It is like a building erected on piles. The piles are driven down from above into the swamp, but not down to any natural or "given" base; and if we cease our attempt to drive the piles into a deeper layer, it is not because we have reached firm ground. We simply stop when we are satisfied that the piles are firm enough to carry the structure, at least for the time being.[27]

The rational expectations model has, for example, carried the structure of economics without having to explain conscious action, which "is a task for psychology but not for economics."[28] In its most direct form, the rational expectations assumption asserts that "all human behavior can be viewed as involving participants who maximize their utility from a stable set of preferences and accumulate an optimal amount of information."[29] Where do those preferences come from? The equational pilings do not necessarily go down that deep; the preferences themselves are taken to be *terra firma*.

> Since economists generally have had little to contribute, especially in recent times, to the understanding of how preferences are formed, preferences are assumed not to change substantially over time.[30]

The resulting "rational agents" with their stable preferences and well-considered actions behave, by definition, like the molecules of water in the hydraulic model of an economy. Both individually and as a group the molecules know where they are supposed to go, and they go there. If there were a period in the adolescence of a water molecule when it had not yet learned to behave consistently and optimally, it has long since outgrown it. That may have been the way life was in the Agricultural and Industrial Ages. It is not how life is in the Information Age.

15

COMPUTING THE NEW REALITIES OF THE INFORMATION AGE

To understand how the new cadence of life interacts with our choice of thought processes, settle for a day into the research facilities of a traditional library, perhaps the Athenaeum on Beacon Hill in Boston. This particular library actively collected science texts until late in the nineteenth century; hence its collection mirrors almost exactly the scientific knowledge a Charles Babbage had available to him as he worked for fifty years on his Analytical Engine. The chairs are upholstered, the cards in the card catalog are in long hand, the call numbers are unique to this library, the label on the astronomy shelf still reads "The Globes," and many of the volumes are in Latin, but the collection is essentially complete.

It is in this environment that traditional Cartesian thought prospers. Copernicus, like Babbage, spent his entire life on a single project. Only at the very end of his life did he write it all down. Newton was among the first to feel the prod of scientific competition. After developing the calculus and applying it to the behavior of the planets in the fullness of time, he finally awoke to the fact that others, most gallingly Robert Hooke, were coming to the same conclusions. To establish his priority,

Newton had to interrupt his theorizing and publish the *Principia*.

For Copernicus, for Descartes, and for Newton, the cadence of thought and the cadence of life and cultural evolution were nicely in balance. It sometimes took effort to obtain a copy of a recently published book, but it could invariably be done. Serious libraries, soon to include several in America, routinely accumulated all the knowledge that was in print. (The Yale College library received its *Principia* directly from Sir Isaac.) Although it was no longer possible for a single individual to keep up with all fields, it was comfortably possible to stay current in one's own. Cartesian thought was invented in and for this world, a world where it was possible to gather all the relevant information and reflect on it, then come to a reasoned conclusion. Because everyone had access to the same finite amount of information and had time to think it through, everyone could be expected to come to similar, and rational, conclusions.

Now, exit down the library steps, strap on the inline skates, and roll off into a qualitatively different milieu. Totally. Six-second sound bytes. Hundred-hour wars. Fax machines on the ski lifts. Conferences that must be attended because those who wait for new theories to show up in next month's journal articles are hopelessly behind. E-mail discussion groups that must be monitored because those who wait for new theories to be discussed at next week's conference are hopelessly behind. Truth du jour. Ready, fire, aim. Details at eleven.

Once before, the world seemed to have slipped out from under human control. The ultimate conclusion of Copernicus's lifetime of study was that the earth, and hence humankind, was *not* at the center of the universe after all. It was as this reality was gradually sinking in that Descartes promulgated the new ways of thought and put the human mind back in the driver's seat. Implicit in his method is the confidence, even today, that life marches to our drumbeat.

> In social as in physical systems there are generally limits on the simultaneous interaction of large numbers of subsystems. In the social case, there are limits related to the fact that a human being is more nearly a serial than a parallel information processing system. He can carry on only one conversation at a time.[1]

We now know that time and tide await no uniconversationalists and that we must keep multiple windows open at once and chase after life as best we can. Neither individuals nor companies have the luxury of figuring out the optimal next step. Each interacts with its environment on an increasingly ad hoc basis and hopes it all works out. The task of raising children is just one example. Parents must individually make guesses about what the future will hold and try to raise their children accordingly. The choices are not necessarily as grim as those faced by the Balkan parents of a teenage son in the years after the Turkish conquest, but they are not nearly as clear-cut either. Medieval parents knew for sure what life in the village held in store for future generations, because it never changed. Even in the early twentieth century, parents could still encourage their children to use their grandparents as role models for what their lives in turn would be like.[2]

Today's parents, like today's business managers, face only shifting shades of gray. The shape of the future is totally uncertain. Different siblings have different psychological makeups. Each psyche must ultimately fit together with those of the surrounding groups and cultures. Those groups and cultures in turn are also adapting to each other in complex ways. The cross-currents of urban populations are typical of a new multiethnic, multicultural world and not unlike the shifting cross-currents of business organizations and their markets:

> The first path of Puerto Rican interaction with North American culture is toward those groups to whom they stand in closest proximity, not only spatially but also because of parallel cultural experience. For Puerto Ricans in New York, this means, first of all, Black Americans and other migrants from the Caribbean and Latin America. With such groups, a strong process of cultural convergence and fusion occurs, what one commentator, J. M. Blaut, has called the "partial growing together of the cultures of ghettoized communities." This "growing together" is often mistaken for assimilation, but the difference is clear in that the convergence is not directed toward incorporation into the dominant culture. For that reason, the "pluralism" that results does not involve the dissolution of national backgrounds and cultural histories but their continued affirmation and enforcement even as they are transformed.[3]

Businesses face the same blurry boundaries. Companies that are competitors in one market collaborate as partners in others and experience a partial growing together of their own. Even if one buys out the other, however, there is rarely total assimilation. The individual corporate cultures continue to be affirmed and enforced just as individual ethnic cultures are. Instead of groups all converging on the same optimal goal, or populations all melting together into the same dominant and homogeneous culture, there is sustained diversity. Sustained diversity is the seed corn of evolution: "The idea of Population diversity or variety demarcates Darwin's theory from the essentialist mechanics of Newton."[4] For Newton as for Plato, diversity was a bother, something to be swept under the carpet. Enter the modern entrepreneur:

> It is to destroy the tendency towards classical and neoclassical equilibrium and to create a new disequilibrium—to engage in the process of "creative destruction"—that is the role assigned to the innovators in the capitalist economy.[5]

Innovative entrepreneurialism provides one of the key ways that an individual's unique psychological makeup influences the wider society and economy. Entrepreneurs may be cult leaders, entertainers, or business executives, or they may be all three at once. They innovate not just to get rich, but to satisfy an internal psychic need: "For its innovators, be they charismatic prophets, saints, or more humble souls, the new pattern of behavior or belief has an immediate relation to their own psychological resources."[6]

In this ever-changing world, coherence and order are more likely to emerge from the lowest levels of activity than to be imposed from the top down. Compare the flow of fluid in the Leeds economic model to the flow of food into the nest of an ant colony, as illustrated in figure 15.1. In the Leeds model, the channels of flow are fixed in advance. Molecules of fluid must occasionally decide which way to go at an intersection, but they are not free to create their own paths. Ant colonies, on the other hand, are forced to invent their own paths or they starve.[7]

Ants forage for food in an initially random manner. Individual ants look for food, and if they find it, they work their way back to the nest with it, at the same time leaving a chemical trail that other ants can smell. As additional ants stumble onto the trail laid down by the first, they too find food and carry it back, adding more chemical to the trail. Gradually, the trail attracts a wider and wider following. As the food runs out, ants return to their random searching. No more chemical is laid down along the trail. It fades away to be replaced by a new one as the next food source is stumbled on. Within computer simulations, this overall behavior of an ant colony emerges from simple rules of individual behavior. All the process requires is enough individual "agents" and enough randomness. If all the ants start out searching in the same place, they overlook a lot of food sources. Worse, if they all

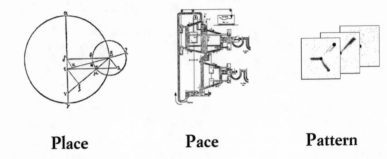

Place　　　　　　　**Pace**　　　　　　　**Pattern**

Figure 15.1. When science began, both its formulations and the parameters within those formulations (what today we call the "program" and the "data" respectively) were fixed for all time. Thus each planet had its own diagram of fixed eccentrics and/or epicycles. Each of these circles revolved at its own fixed and constant rate. There are no "variables" in geometric diagrams.

The equational maths of the Industrial Age allowed the data parameters to become variable for the first time. Thus the amount of water flowing through the pipes of an economic model could change in ways that the rate of an epicyclic rotation could not. The pipes/equations themselves, however, remained fixed for all time.

Intermaths allow both the data *and* the program to evolve. Thus, in a model of an ant colony, the amount of food being transported along an active path can rise as more and more ants join in and use it. In addition, the paths themselves can change. As food supplies are exhausted and new ones found, old paths go away and new ones are created. In the most advanced uses of intermaths, the whole formulation itself changes and adapts as it learns better ways to operate. Frozen onto the pages of a book, all three approaches become equally static. Within the circuitry of a modern electronic computer, however, their fundamental differences are dramatic. Geometric diagram courtesy of the Trustees of the Boston Public Library. Pipe model courtesy of Blackwell Publishers. The ant simulation is from *Turtles, Termites, and Traffic Jams* by Mitchel Resnick, courtesy of MIT Press.

behave "rationally" and wait for the location of food to be known before they venture forth, then no food is ever found.

Adam Smith himself was among the first to notice social and economic behavior that emerged inexplicably from individual actions of a completely different sort. As he looked at individual butchers, brewers, and bakers, he saw business people motivated by their own self-interest, with no benevolent desires to help their customers out by charging low prices. Yet the economy as a whole showed considerable pricing restraint. Because there was no way for the mathematics of Newton to express this inherently parallel phenomenon, he and subsequent generations of economists have invoked an "invisible hand," an emergent *deus ex machina* to account for it. Smith's analysis of the division of labor was even more sophisticated, as many observers have noted. He saw that the bigger the market for a product, the more opportunity manufacturers had to divide up the production tasks and thus reduce their costs, which in turn would expand the market, and so on. Thus, division of labor and market growth each caused the other.

It is the entrepreneurial element of discovery that is hard to predict in traditional equational ways. At any particular moment in time, the Leeds model and the ant model may look similar. Each has a number of well-established channels over which a lot of material is flowing. The difference is that the channels in the ant model dry up and are spontaneously replaced. The traditional equational vocabulary does not capture this aspect of the behavior:

For theoretical purposes an economic system consists of a designated set of unknowns which are constrained as a condition of equilibrium to satisfy an equal number of consistent and independent equations.[8]

By its very nature entrepreneurial behavior cannot be predicted using deterministic models. Entrepreneurship . . . is essentially a spontaneous and evolutionary process.[9]

Human societies and economies, of course, are much more complex than the typical ant colony because they have more layers and because they have more sophisticated behavior at each layer. The fundamentals appear similar, however. Out of individual behavior emerges a group behavior that cannot be understood or predicted by looking at the behavior of the individuals alone. Out of the behavior of many groups comes still higher level behavior, again inexplicable in terms of the individual groups looked at in isolation:

The ability to reduce everything to simple fundamental laws does not imply the ability to start from these laws and reconstruct the universe.... At each level of complexity entirely new properties appear.... Psychology is not applied biology, nor is biology applied chemistry.... In general, the relationship between the system and its parts is intellectually a one-way street.[10]

When all computers were people, we had no choice but to try to reason our way from one level to the next. Now we are much better off putting the lower levels of behavior into our electronic circuits and seeing what emerges. Such a process is not as unconstrained as it may sound. In an economic world where seemingly everything changes, the source of constancy increasingly appears to be human *habits*, which are the manifestations of our inability to forget. It may no longer be "rational," for example, to encourage children to emulate their grandparents, who lived in a completely different world, but parents and grandparents do it. As the economists Nelson and Winter have pointed out, old habits and ways of doing things die hard. Within organizations and companies, they die even harder. The world is changing rapidly, but people are up against the stops. We are held back by thought:

The relatively invariant unit is the social institution. We may define institutions in broad terms. They refer to the commonly held patterns of behaviour and habits of thought, of a routinized and durable nature, that are associated with people interacting in groups or larger collectives. Institutions enable ordered thought and action by imposing form and consistency on the activities of human beings.[11]

It is this "permanent coexistence of history-dependent routines and routine-breaking uncertainty-ridden novelties"[12] that must be modeled in order to understand the behavior of an information society. The traditional assumption was that the more efficient firms in an economy drove out the less efficient, because the market stood still long enough for optimization to have its day. Now that products have lives of months instead of decades, however, firms can win by happening to be in the right place at the right time. As the economist Paul Romer has explained, economic growth is more like a parallel gold rush than a sequential orbit:

People understand that the development of technology is something that is subject to a lot of randomness, that if you try to make a discovery, you might succeed and you might not. But then they slip into saying that if the individual cannot control technology then technology is like manna from heaven, something completely outside our control. Now that logical step is clearly wrong. Think about prospecting for gold. For you as an individual, the chances of finding gold might be so small that it would seem like pure serendipity if you actually did. But if you have 10,000 people out looking for gold across a wide geographical area, the chances of finding gold greatly improve. For society as a whole, it is very clear that discovery—whether of gold or of new technology—is a function of how much effort we put into it.[13]

Equally competent individuals and firms can use different strategies and thus be effective for different reasons. Changes elsewhere in the economy, such as a tripling of the price of oil, can have a buoying effect on firms that happen to use it sparingly and a devastating effect on others. The firm that is in the right place at the right time prospers, at least temporarily. Every participant makes mistakes. An individual or a firm is never sure what it should do next, because the world around it is changing too fast. The firm invests in creating new ideas in the research and development department. To some extent, the direction of that research is shaped by the perceived needs of the marketplace. It is also, however, shaped by the ingrained habitual behavior of the firm itself.

Alternatively, a firm may not search out new ideas at all. It may leave that activity to others and quickly clone the ones that look most promising, recognizing that it can afford to copy two ideas for every one it might create from scratch. A firm that copies may also be an inherently more resilient firm, forced to know how to do many things fairly well rather than doing a few things exquisitely because it is in love with them. Thus, even if multiple firms all focus on the same narrow task, each will go about it in its own unique way, colored by past experiences.

The higher level economic behavior that emerges from all the triumph and heartbreak at the individual and firm level is, like the higher level results of Romer's gold rush, both robust and adaptable. The economy as a whole is able to deal effectively with major surprises, not simply because of great forethought but also because of the reservoir of dormant skills. Individual firms may not anticipate events like oil price shocks, but some of them happen to have spare skills that come into their own under these circumstances and prove to be useful. These firms sprint ahead and fill in the gaps.

Positive feedback is an additional attribute of the new information society. Contrary to the traditional doctrine of diminishing returns, "the more we know, the easier it is to know more; the more we make, the easier it is to make more; the richer we are, the easier it is to get richer."[14] The old idea of "equilibrium" was built atop the assumption of diminishing returns. Farmers, as Smith and David Ricardo pointed out, farmed the best land first, so each increment of production became harder and less profitable than the last. With information products such as software and entertainment, however, the hardest sale is often the first one. Often, nobody wants to go to a movie that nobody has ever heard of. Once a product or a celebrity becomes known, and known as being known, commanding a high price becomes easier and easier. The financial returns increase instead of diminishing.

> The parts of the economy that are resource-based (agriculture, bulk-goods production, mining) are still for the most part subject to diminishing returns. Here conventional economics rightly holds sway. The parts of the economy that are knowledge-based, on the other hand, are largely subject to increasing returns.[15]

When there are diminishing returns, it is possible to use equations to look out ahead and predict where the process will converge, or reach equilibrium. Positive feedback situations eventually peak, too, but they can end up in any of several places. It is not possible to know in advance which one it will be. However, once a process starts going in a direction, it tends to keep going in that direction. History matters. Often the product that succeeds is not the "best" one but rather the one that happened to be first, benefiting from what biologists call the "founder effect."[16] Economists call these historical influences "path dependencies." Neither individuals nor firms are free to act "rationally" in the sense of doing what is optimal at the moment. They are constrained by what others have already done.

The impact of history can be seen in a study of the spreadsheet market during the 1980s,[17] when Lotus 1-2-3, SuperCalc, and Framework competed. Lotus gained the biggest share, partly because of product features, but partly because it also had more companies offering add-in modules, training courses, or both. More people bought 1-2-3 because more people were already familiar with it. The authors of the study ran almost five hundred simulations of this market development, varying a range of product and market parameters. Most veered off to a prediction of one of the three vendors taking the whole market.

Only a dozen or so accurately saved the appearances of the marketplace, with most of the sales going to Lotus but some persistently to SuperCalc and Framework as well. Traditional Cartesian thought instinctively looks for the underlying reasons that these dozen models were "inherently right all along." The alternative is simply to recognize that certain formulations do correspond to reality and that, because history matters, they are probably good ones to listen to going forward. It would also be prudent, however, to keep some of the others going as well, because they might turn out to have increased predictive power in the future and the computing power required to do so is now cheap.

To the extent that electronic computers get first look at the actual market data, none of this process need be "tractable," or even visible, to us. It is not necessary to satisfy the criteria of the Leeds model: that the internal behavior of the predictive model be comprehensible to a human observer. The computer simply learns on its own which formulations are working, gives them higher weightings, perhaps cross-breeds them, and communicates the resulting predictions to us. It is exactly this course of development that is visible in the study that evolved during the 1980s of a decision process called the Prisoner's Dilemma.[18] In Prisoner's Dilemma, two suspects are interrogated separately. If one confesses and implicates the other, the implicating prisoner is treated favorably. Economists use multiplayer versions of this game, particularly when it is played repeatedly and each participant knows what the others have done previously, to study oligopolistic markets, in which both collusive price-fixing and ruinous price wars are possible outcomes. The deregulated airline industry is often used as an example.

Early in the 1980s, scientists were invited to submit strategies, in the form of computer programs, to such a repeated Prisoner's Dilemma game. The computational biologist Anatol Rapaport, who has dramatically furthered Lewis Richardson's original work in peace studies, submitted the program that did the best in the ensuing competition among strategies. Called Tit-for-Tat, its strategy was to do whatever the opponent had done last time. Two years later, when the contest was repeated, one entrant took advantage of the electronic contest milieu and submitted a program that adapted and learned from its adversaries during the contest itself. Although not superior to the Tit-for-Tat strategy overall, it was able to exploit specific weaknesses of specific competitors in a superior way. The final step in the evolution of the contest was to cancel the competition and simply breed strategies and test them within a classifier system environment.[19] In the beginning of this study process, formulations that were the fruits of human thought were essential. A decade later, the need for thought had completely withered away.

Clearly, there is powerful resonance between the new social and economic realities of emergence and adaptation and the emergent adaptive properties of the new intermaths, a resonance that the sequential maths of algebra and calculus (originally developed for physics) lack. After all, as the astrophysicist Paul Davies has pointed out, "when physicists talk about a theory of everything, they don't mean literally everything. They don't mean a theory that would explain how the stock market rises and falls."[20] Such a theory is now being explored by Holland and Arthur at the Santa Fe Institute, using adaptive agents. In the initial version of the system, agents trade in a single stock. They individually evolve their buying and selling rules genetically. At first, the pattern of trades is quite placid, but then an agent learns to take advantage of this predictability. Soon the others also learn to anticipate trends, and the behavior in the market becomes more agitated. Ultimately, bubbles and crashes emerge. Both are phenomena that are difficult to generate at all with classical equational models.[21]

A wholesale shift of economic practice out of the physics vocabulary of numbers and equations and into intermaths and classifier systems is unlikely, however, because it runs up against the mother of all path dependencies: our dependency on the psychic comforts of traditional thought. Right or wrong, we can take an answer developed in the traditional numbers-and-equations manner and trace it back and see exactly where it came from. Economists refer to such a retraceable step-by-step process as being "tractable." Tractable methods produce both a conclusion and a comforting audit trail of where that conclusion came from. The economist Milton Friedman, for example, proposed to treat billiard players "as if" their shots were lined up by means of Newton's equations.[22] (Galileo went further. He asserted that coopers really did use the theorems of geometry in shaping their barrels.[23]) Having made this one substitution, Friedman was then able to carry the argument forward in equational terms. A billiard table, of course, lends itself to that sort of substitution. Made from thick slabs of slate, it is famously impervious to the changing world around it. Even the billiard balls are totally autonomous. When we hear "eight ball, corner pocket," we do not need to know what other balls that ball has had contact with of late and how it might have been changed by that contact. Within the artificially static confines of a billiards table, there are no intractable concerns about, paraphrasing Keynes, whether the eight ball feels it is worthwhile reaching the corner pocket or whether the pocket wants it to.

When faced with a choice between tractability and realism, economists have often chosen tractability. The reason that many economic formulations have assumed perfect competition and denied path dependencies, for example, was not that perfect competition was what was observed, but rather because "from Ricardo until about 1975, what economists knew how to model was a perfectly competitive economy."[24] Theory and appearances are not always required to match:

I'm not talking about the reality now. I'm talking about the theory.[25]

To achieve tractability, an economist analyzing the behavior at the aforementioned pub, which holds sixty patrons comfortably but has a hundred regulars, might say that patrons behave "as if" a master patron had assigned each one of them certain nights when they could, indeed must, show up. Further predictions about the wider economy would then be tractable in the sense that they could be traced back to the "as if" assumption. The emergent model produces the same behavior, but it offers no explanatory solace. The same number of people show up each night, but their presence emerges from a bit-level learning process that cannot be "explained" by tracing it back. It has simply emerged, shedding its intermediate forms as it evolves. The real differences in the value of the two approaches may only come about, of course, when the bar is made to be realistically dynamic: adding a new wing, replacing two-across seating with three-across seating, closing for a month and reopening as a juice-and-java bar, opening new franchise locations across town, replacing the jukebox selector boxes with Internet ports in each booth, offering digitized jukebox selections over those Internet ports, and so on.

Unfortunately, the transition from the old mechanical view of societies and economies to the new evolutionary view cannot be done incrementally. Ideally, one would like to unplug the old fluids-inspired equations from the existing models and plug new equations of evolution in their place. Alas, there are no such direct equations of evolution. There is a "Navier–Stokes equation" to govern the Leeds model but no corresponding "Darwin equation." Nor can an equation be made evolutionary simply by adding a random factor on the end: "The Darwinian process of continued interplay of a random and a selective process is not intermediate between pure chance and pure determination, but in its consequences qualitatively utterly different from either."[26]

Because of these powerful path dependencies in the culture of economics itself, adaptive models of subjects such as ethnic strife may come before adaptive models of industries or market segments. Because sociologists historically have not been intense users of equational models, they need feel no threat from a "competence-destroying innovation" such as the new intermaths imply. On the other hand, there is no tradition of mathematically gifted students studying sociology in the first place, as there is with economics. Twice more, history matters. If economics does become a strong early adopter of the new intermaths, it is likely to be because of what evolutionary economists call an exaptation, i.e., a latent capability that is already in the system for some other reason. The economist Myra Strober notes, for example, that traditional economic formulations can be particularly hard to swallow for people who have had primary responsibility for raising children.[27] That kind of life experience has an impact on how one processes theories such as one advanced recently to explain sibling behavior within families. Although evolutionary, it relies on equational vocabulary:

> At the most direct level this paper explores the economics of the family, offering an evolutionary explanation for the degree of altruism to be expected between siblings. . . . This paper is concerned with large populations for which it is assumed that expected proportions are always realized. This makes it possible to treat the dynamical system as a deterministic system of difference equations.[28]

A person who has not raised children might be willing to accept these deterministic realization-of-expected-proportions assumptions that allow sibling behavior to be expressed in the language of difference equations, at least to see where the subsequent math may lead. Those whose backgrounds are different may reject them out of hand and look for approaches that more accurately save the more emergent appearances of their own direct experiences of family life.

Ultimately, the social sciences need a computational model of the individual human being that reflects how that human being actually behaves: "The ideal would be algorithmic behavior that could pass the Turing test. . . . Calibration ought not to be merely a matter of fitting parameters, but also one of building human-like qualitative behavior into the algorithm specification itself."[29] This problem of passing the Turing test lies within the province of the artificial-intelligence community, whence many of the intermaths themselves first came.

COMPUTING THE PATTERNS OF BODIES AND MINDS

By the early 1950s, computer engineers were well along in their initial goal of using electronic circuits to mimic the basic arithmetic behavior of human computers. A new computer language, FORTRAN, allowed scientists to give formulations to their computers in direct equational form as they had in centuries past and as the designers of econometric models would soon so enthusiastically do. What the new computers could not do, however, was to demonstrate the discretion and good sense of their predecessors, because these attributes had not been successfully carried across. The machines were still, as they were in Oliver Wendell Holmes's day, like "Babbage's calculating machine . . . that turns out results like a corn-sheller, and never grows any wiser or better, though it grind a thousand bushels of them."[1] Unable to learn from their work, electronic circuits were, in reality, only partially compatible with the "four hundred years of scientific inquiry and wisdom." They were still a long way from passing the test that Alan Turing proposed at the time.

In 1956, a small group of investigators came together at Dartmouth College to reason out and plan ways to get electronic circuits to reason out and plan their work. The group labeled this activity "artificial intelligence." In the same decade, the discovery of DNA and the genetic code was opening a second way to apply information-processing techniques to the sciences of life. These two new areas of interest, biology at the level of DNA and reasoning and learning at the level of mind, have burgeoned with the arrival of the new adaptive maths in the 1980s. Both topics are extremely complicated, however. If the medieval king Alfonso was upset by God's design of the heavens, he would have been apoplectic about the way biological organisms work. Even the simplest are byzantine—and parallel. As Kauffman has noted:

> Despite our fascination with sequential algorithms, organisms are more adequately characterized as complex parallel-processing dynamical systems. . . . Genes act in parallel, synthesizing their products, and mutually regulating one another's synthetic activities. Cell differentiation, the production of diverse cell types from the initial zygote, is an expression of parallel processing among the 100,000 genes in each cell lineage. . . . Other adaptive features of organisms, ranging from neural networks to the anti-idiotype network in the immune system, are quite clearly examples of parallel-processing networks.[2]

Kauffman has shown that this sprawling behavior of genes, far from being incorrigible, may have been essential to the development of life itself. More compact ways of performing these tasks would not have been better from the point of view of evolution. Compact formulations evolve poorly because any change is perforce a drastic change: "Minimal programs are not themselves evolvable."[3] Even more startling, complex webs of elements "exhibit unexpected and powerful collective spontaneous order."[4] Imagine a large school, perhaps in California, where every student has a two-line cellular telephone with certain other students' phone numbers memorized within it. These numbers are set randomly such that each student's own number is stored within two other students' phones. Now imagine that these students independently choose their own personal rules for deciding when to press the "dial memorized number" button on the basis of the status of the incoming lines. An example of such a rule is "place a call if, and only if, line one is free but there is a call on line two."

It would seem that the resulting pattern of calls would be totally unpredictable and would take a very long time before it repeated itself.

Kauffman's parallel computer simulations show that the behavior is
nowhere near so unpredictable. What emerges are "frozen cores,"
subsets of nodes (cliques of students) that lock into constant behavior
that is unaffected by what is going on around them. These frozen cores
drastically restrict the options of the remaining nodes in the network.
A network of ten thousand nodes ends up with only about a hundred
possible patterns of behavior, and it settles on its own into one of
them. The self-ordering of this random parallel network, what Kauffman calls "order for free," once again evokes the same sort of admira-
tion that equations did during the Industrial Age:

> One cannot escape the feeling that these mathematical formulae
> have an independent existence and an intelligence of their own, that
> they are wiser than we are, wiser even than their discoverers, that we
> get more out of them than was originally put into them.[5]

Kauffman interprets these binary elements as genes switching each
other on and off. The experiment suggests that a bewildering array of
cross-influencing genes could have come about more naturally and
easily than the kind of compact, compressed version that would have
been more to King Alfonso's taste, and ours.

However it came about, the sprawling nature of DNA poses its own
set of obstacles for biologists. Only a small portion of a gene sequence
contains instructions for making proteins. The rest is where activities
such as regulation take place. Biologists are using neural networks to
home in efficiently on the active protein-recipe sections. After training
on DNA sequences where the location of the protein-coding sections
had already been determined, a neural net has been able to find them
in new data with 90 percent accuracy.[6]

The problem that drug companies care about most is the one that
comes next in the chain of biological events. On the basis of genetic
coding within its DNA and RNA, a cell strings together a specific
series of peptides, which then folds itself up into a protein. Hemoglobin and insulin are two well-known examples of the proteins that
human life depends on. The role, if any, that a protein will play is
dependent not on the peptides specifically but rather on the shape that
the molecule takes when it is folded up. For example, hemoglobin has
a folded-up shape that offers attractive sites for four molecules of oxy-
gen to bind into and be carried through the bloodstream to the cells.

It is now possible for scientists to pre-specify folded-up protein
shapes that have a high probability of being effective drugs. They may,

for example, specify a protein shape that could block the undesirable actions of another protein by plugging into the same site it normally uses. It is also possible by genetic engineering to create almost any arbitrary string of peptides in the unfolded form. What scientists have been unable to do is to predict which string will fold up into which shape. In nature, identical strings reliably fold themselves up into identical protein shapes under the influence of internal atomic forces. Equations that describe these forces are well known, but to carry them out numerically for an entire protein could take years on the fastest available computers. Biologists have turned to intermaths to predict the folded shapes in hours and days instead of months and years.

Viewed from the perspective of the new maths, an unfolded string of peptides is a piece of information perched at the peak of an "energy mountain." Its height is a measure of the total amount of unrequited attraction that exists between portions of the protein. As the protein starts to fold, these tensions relax because molecules that want to be close to each other have, in fact, come closer. The protein descends the energy mountain. The danger, of course, is that the partially folded computational protein becomes stuck in a local minimum rather than working its way all the way down as it does in nature. Getting to the bottom of things computationally has required a range of the new maths, a set of powerful parallel computers, and a generous supply of knowledge and hints built up from the study of other proteins. By using all three, the team of Gunn, Monge, Friesner, and Marshall was able to fold a myoglobin molecule.

Their mix of intermaths included Monte Carlo, simulated annealing, and a genetic formulation.[7] Large numbers of unfolded myoglobin proteins were loaded into a sixteen-processor parallel computer and then repeatedly reshaped in random ways. If the new shape was physically impossible, it was rejected, but if it was plausible, it was investigated to see if it was a promising step toward full folding. Gradually, the system built up a set of increasingly plausible folding possibilities. These were in turn mated and bred by snipping off the end of a partially folded molecule and attaching new ends snipped from other molecules in the system. The most promising of these children were then added to the permanent pool of possibilities.

At each step, existing knowledge about protein behavior was used aggressively. Certain sequences were assumed, by analogy, to take on specific secondary shapes such as helixes because that is how they have been seen to behave in other proteins. (The discovery of these secondary patterns has itself been powerfully aided by neural network maths.[8]) Potential geometries along the peptide chain were also constrained to follow patterns known to occur in other proteins. After twenty-four hours, the system produced a set of candidate answers for how myoglobin would fold up. One of the candidates corresponded to the way myoglobin actually folds up in nature, an important advance over the results obtained by traditional maths.[9]

At a very high level, this process of predicting the folded geometry of a protein molecule echoes the way a classifier system works. A large number of raw alternatives is churned in quasi-random ways to see where this churning makes the results better. Over time, a body of knowledge about recurring patterns is built up. This stored-up knowledge is used aggressively to constrain the churning to directions that are known to have had a high payoff in the past. More general rules of manipulation are used early in the process, with increasingly specific rules being applied as needed.

We are still a long way, however, from the point at which the biologists can remove themselves from this particular computation and leave a classifier system to discover all the knowledge completely on its own. Protein folding is an unusually complicated task. It requires far too much computation within a single cycle and too many repetitions in order to build up the knowledge of how proteins tend to fold. In this case, it still makes more sense for scientist and computer to collaborate, with the scientist actively imparting knowledge to the computer rather than leaving it to learn all the basics from scratch. Classifier systems are best used in areas like the analysis of marketplace data that require comparatively less computation per individual example and for which there are huge numbers of training examples to work from. What is striking about this protein-folding computation, however, is that it would now be possible to back out the huge university computing center and carry out this experiment with the computational resources of a high school advanced-placement biology class. Each of the sixteen parallel processors used in the computation was more powerful than a modern home computer, so the whole computation might require a month instead of a day. Students would need to exchange genetic material in class each day, or by way of modem at night, but most of this computation proceeds within individual processors.

Folding proteins is not a traditional part of the high school biology curriculum, because the biology curriculum was largely established back when all computers were people and the task was impossible. Even today, the task is impossible for classes schooled only in the maths of the Industrial Age. Success requires both substantial student skill in the new intermaths and substantial teacher insight into the behavior of proteins.

The intermath skills can be applied more widely once they have been learned, however. They are, for example, becoming increasingly important in the study of the immune system, which adds the element of learning. The immune system does not store a response to all possible future situations; it adapts and learns as it encounters new threats:

> The basic task of the immune system is to distinguish between self and non-self, and to eliminate non-self. This is a problem of pattern learning and pattern recognition in the space of chemical patterns. This is a difficult task, and the immune system performs it with high fidelity, with an extraordinary capacity to make subtle distinctions between molecules that are quite similar.[10]

Because the new maths themselves incorporate learning, they offer a promising tool for simulating and predicting the behavior of systems like the immune system. Cellular automata were first used in these investigations in the 1970s.[11] Other intermaths are now being used as well.

> As with classifier systems and neural networks, there are several varieties of immune networks. . . . The dynamics of the real immune system are not well understood. The situation is similar to that of neural networks; we construct simplified heuristic immune dynamics based on a combination of chemical kinetics and experimental observations, attempting to recover some of the phenomena of real immune systems.[12]

Meanwhile, knowledge gained about the immune system is in turn being fed back into computer science, where the immune system itself is being used as a model to design more powerful and adaptive antivirus software.

To understand the processes of learning, both biologists and computer scientists turn to the work of the artificial-intelligence community. Today, after decades of trying to teach electronic circuits how to think in sequential Cartesian ways on sequential Cartesian architectures, this community has moved into the lead in embracing parallel intermaths as standard tools. As the artificial-life researcher Christopher Langton notes, it was thought that we could effectively ignore the architecture of the brain and get intelligent software running on our newly engineered [von Neumann] universal computers. . . . Our engineered computers involve a central controller working from a top–down set of rules. . . . There's something in the dynamics of parallel, distributed, highly nonlinear systems which lies at the roots of intelligence and consciousness—something that nature was able to discover and take advantage of.[13]

When Alan Turing originally challenged computer programmers to "make them play the imitation game," he was willing to settle for success at mimicking human behavior 70 percent of the time. The group that came together at Dartmouth College in the 1950s felt it would be possible to do much better: "Every aspect of learning or any other feature of intelligence can in principle be so precisely described that a machine can be made to simulate it."[14] Achieving this goal meant "precisely describing" thought as Descartes had once specified it and as the schools and universities have taught it over the centuries. The fact that an early artificial-intelligence program scored 84 out of 86 on a college freshman exam and that another successfully solved high school algebra problems showed how successfully Descartes had worked both sides of the street. He had channeled the standard curriculum into well-defined methods of dignified sequential thought and had influenced the hardware architecture in analogous directions. When the two were brought together in structured ways, the results could be quite satisfying.

Sometimes too satisfying. One of the first forms of structured academic thought attempted on electronic computers was formal logic. The goal was to use the program to learn how the human mind developed such proofs: "What we were interested in from the beginning was not simply getting it to prove theorems in logic. We were interested in having it do it in a humanoid way."[15] Tension arose when a new technique, called *resolution,* came into use. Resolution "condones single inferences which are often beyond the ability of the human to grasp (other than discursively)."[16] Should these proofs be allowed, or should proof steps be artificially constrained to what could be "apprehended as correct by a human being in a single intellectual step"?[17]

After these early efforts in formal reasoning, the focus of artificial intelligence moved to supplying programs with the base of factual knowledge needed to make appropriate decisions. Such systems came to be known as "expert systems." The way they were intended to work can be seen from one of the most successful such systems, called XCON. XCON was developed to configure computer systems for Digital Equipment Corporation. A computer family such as the PDP–11™ had hundreds of pieces of optional equipment from which customers could choose. Typical systems, however, consisted of a dozen or less of these options, and customers did not want to pay for all the cabinetry and infrastructure necessary to support the hundreds of options they were not buying. Customers wanted the options they had ordered packed into just enough cabinetry with just enough cabling, just enough power, and so on. Salespeople, meanwhile, knew that when the factory personnel discovered months later that needed pieces were missing, they would build them in for free to keep the production line moving. The result was a stream of factory orders that were systematically underconfigured.

Galileo would have been good at this problem of quickly checking and correcting configurations before accepting orders, because it involves keeping many constraints in mind simultaneously. Two options might be able to go next to each other in a cabinet, for example, if a third option were added but not if a fourth option had to be present as well. XCON had to go through its rules one at a time, ignoring ones that did not work in a particular situation and looking for ones that did. Just as the formulations for the motions of the moon ultimately grew to thousands of individual equations, XCON grew to thousands of individual rules.

XCON was successful because rules were the native language of computer configuration. Few real-world activities have such clear and accessible rules. Certainly, the rural wagon shops did not. The workers knew how to build a wagon, but they did not know it in a way that they could explain to a knowledge engineer: "The nature of the knowledge should be noted. It was set out in no book. It was not scientific."[18] The workers knew collectively, but not individually. The problem of getting knowledge from practitioners becomes acute in trades that are themselves on the verge of extinction and hence are no longer able to support a full web of group knowledge. General Electric's last universal expert in electric locomotive repairs and Campbell Soup's resident expert in bacteria-killing cookers became part of the folklore of artificial intelligence as these companies tried to upload their dying savvy into an expert system. Expert systems faltered at this knowledge-transferal step.[19] It has been estimated that a single domain of expertise can involve seventy thousand pieces of information, a lot to play back.[20]

In addition, there is all the generic background knowledge that humans acquire about the world. Perhaps if computers could be given this same base of human knowledge, more durable expertise could be built atop it. The artificial-intelligence researcher Douglas Lenat defined the problem when he noted the following, in the 1980s:

> I would like to present a surprisingly compact, powerful, elegant set of reasoning methods that form a set of first principles which explain creativity, humor, and common sense reasoning—a sort of Maxwell's Equations of thought . . . but sadly, I don't believe they exist.[21]

To remedy that situation, Lenat launched an effort to put the entire base of human knowledge, estimated to be ten million assertions, into a form that electronic computers could access. The first two assertions, "Napoleon died on St. Helena" and "Wellington was saddened," took months to communicate because the computer had no prior knowledge to build on. The project continues, building up a codification of human knowledge called CYC for its resemblance to a human encyclopedia.[22]

The anthropomorphic nature of this project is obvious when the undertaking is compared to the way a classifier system builds up its knowledge. Classifiers store what they choose to store, and they do so in a low-level manner. Over time, they decide what tiny pieces of stored information are related and start linking them together with mechanisms such as bucket brigades and rule hierarchies. The resulting store of knowledge is incomprehensible to humans because it is strictly of the computer, by the computer, and for the computer. CYC explicitly seeks to teach the electronic circuits human knowledge in human form.

What a hard slog for the circuits: Learning ten million facts that humans have accumulated over the centuries. Mastering formal logic and perhaps the tricks of the locomotive-maintenance trade. Empathizing with Wellington empathizing with Napoleon. It seems an arduous way for an electronic computer to become more knowledgeable and skillful. Cleopatra expressed similar misgivings in the George Bernard Shaw play when she approached an old musician for music lessons:

CLEOPATRA: I want to learn to play the harp with my own hands. Caesar loves music. Can you teach me?

MUSICIAN: Assuredly I and no one else can teach the queen. . . .

CLEOPATRA: Good: you shall teach me. How long will it take?

MUSICIAN: Not very long: only four years. Your Majesty must first become proficient in the philosophy of Pythagoras.

CLEOPATRA: Has she [indicating the slave] become proficient in the philosophy of Pythagoras?

MUSICIAN: Oh, she is but a slave. She learns as a dog learns.

CLEOPATRA: Well, then, I will learn as a dog learns; for she plays better than you.[23]

Some of the earliest work in artificial-intelligence research had ventured down the path of having a computer learn as a dog learns, using forerunners of neural networks. In their 1966 book, *Artificial Intelligence Through Simulated Evolution*, Lawrence Fogel, Alvin Owens, and Michael Walsh suggested that "it would appear worthwhile to replace the process of modeling man as he now exists with the process of modeling evolution," recognizing that the outcome would doubtless be different from what nature has come up with so far.[24] The circuitry available at that time, however, was not powerful enough to support such a proposal. The more Cartesian approaches continued to predominate, without making substantial progress toward the ultimate goal of building a thinking machine. Doing the job in the traditional engineering way has proved too difficult to manage and coordinate. Engineering requires breaking the problem down into manageable pieces, then fitting the pieces back together again, exactly the process that theories of emergence say cannot work:

Imagine a collection of tens of thousands of people doing these modules, which is how we'd have to engineer it. If you engineer something that way, it has to decompose, and it has to go through these fairly standardized interfaces. There's every reason to believe that the brain is not that neatly partitioned.[25]

There's another approach besides this strict engineering approach which can produce something of that complexity, and that's the evolutionary approach. We humans were produced by a process that wasn't engineering. We now have computers fast enough to simulate the process of evolution within the computer. So we may be able to set up situations in which we can cause intelligent programs to evolve within the computer.[26]

Over the coming years, the new maths and, ultimately, bit evolution itself are destined to play a more and more central role in artificial-intelligence research. Although the processing capacity of a human brain is a subject of debate, parallel supercomputers are growing toward the lower end of the range. Systems are currently on order that link together as many as nine thousand processors, each of which will approach the power of a Cray 1 supercomputer. Such a laboratory machine provides the sort of environment from which we would typically expect a major scientific advance such as bit evolution to come. Housed at a prestigious university or national laboratory, staffed by experienced experts, and dedicated to the task of breeding intelligence, such an installation would follow in the organizational footsteps of the most successful scientific establishments of the Industrial Age.

This established method of Big Science, however, is strikingly at odds with the new idea of invention being like a distributed gold rush, in which tens of thousands of investigators crawl over potentially fertile ground, accepting the reality that most of them will come up empty-handed. The important question in this context is whether full-fledged bit evolution could get itself started (perhaps has gotten itself started already) among tens of thousands of amateurs, "in the wild" so to speak, rather than among a tightly coupled group of experts.

Such a step requires both fertile ground and large numbers of amateur investigators. The amateur investigators are already in place. Every high school student with a modern personal computer has the hardware capacity to participate. The fertile ground is also coming into place. It is the new trove of data about ecologies and the earth that is now becoming available for the first time. Even the ability to exchange genetic material is in place, although it is risky to do so in a totally unfettered way. All that is missing is the human element: knowledge about how to apply the new intermaths and the ability to cooperate on a large scale, in parallel.

17

LISTENING TO LIFE

During Thoreau's lifetime the planet was being wired up for the first time, but he had no personal use for such bandwidth. Why run a telegraph from Maine to Texas when "Maine and Texas, it may be, have nothing important to communicate"?[1] Certainly there was nothing in Texas, or even Maine, that impinged on the daily behavior at Walden Pond: no Chernobyl, no theme-park developers, and only an occasional irksome act of government. As for the rest of the world, it held neither novelty nor relevance because nothing ever changed. Thoreau stood ready personally to predict the behavior of Spain a year ahead of time:

> News which I seriously think a ready wit might write a twelve-month, or twelve years, beforehand with sufficient accuracy. As for Spain, for instance, if you know how to throw in Don Carlos and the Infanta, and Don Pedro and Seville and Granada, from time to time in the right proportions,—they may have changed the names a little since I saw the papers,—and serve up a bull-fight when other entertainments fail, it will be true to the letter, and give us as good an idea of the exact state of ruin of things in Spain as the most succinct and lucid reports under this head in the newspapers: and as for England, almost the last significant scrap of news from that quarter was the revolution of 1649.[2]

Thoreau was the ultimately meticulous listener to life in the small: the "self-appointed inspector of snowstorms and rain-storms," who once measured and counted sections of houstonia plants to arrive triumphantly at a census of three thousand blossoms per square foot. Yet there *were* global effects in his life. Although he did not speculate on the causes, he noted that "we are accustomed to say in New England that few and fewer pigeons visit us every year."[3] Perhaps he should have sent out a telegraph query to Texas requesting data about bird migration patterns there. Unfortunately, even if the Texas telegraph station happened to be on the migration route of the pigeons, there likely would have been no Thoreau there to gather the data. Like Johannes Kepler, Henry David was one of a kind.

The difficulties of listening to the wider patterns of life are formidable. The Egyptians, for example, have been trying to do so since the dawn of history. The simple goal of predicting the size of the Nile flood goes back to biblical times. Formal records of these floods are available from the seventh century, but no real progress was made. While physical scientists were finding ways to predict successfully the behavior of the planets and falling bodies, and a host of other material behaviors, the patterns of the Nile valley remained a mystery. Sometimes a very high year follows directly on the heels of a very low one. Sometimes the differences have been more systematic: The years 1905–1952 were 30 percent below the average of the prior decades. It was only during World War II that the flow of moisture from the South Atlantic across central Africa to the upper Nile regions was first charted. In terms of predicting the height of the annual flood, the best indicators in the 1920s turned out to be, *mirabile dictu*, the temperature at Dutch Harbor, Alaska; the temperature at Samoa; and the barometric pressure at Port Darwin, Australia. (It is no longer true.)[4]

Simultaneous with these first studies of moisture patterns across Africa, and while John Maynard Keynes was still worrying that computers and equations were being used too eagerly in trying to predict the flow of goods and services in America and Europe, scientists in Egypt were worrying that computers there could not be used enough to try to predict the flow of the Nile because

the Computers, those essential people whose importance is not fully recognized, but whose work nonetheless is the basis of river regulation and projects, are, as a class, in danger of becoming extinct in Egypt.[5]

Scientists needed these computers to do more than just listen to the patterns of rainfall and the subsequent flooding. They were trying to grapple with an environment in which humans were prominent participants: The Nile is an ecosystem populated with "river engineers" who build dams and actively engage in other "river regulation and projects." The job of the computers was to try to understand the interaction of the human and the river behaviors in the Nile Valley. It took an Egyptian computer several months to determine how a single year's flood profile (the river's behavior) would be altered by a single hypothetical set of new dams (the river engineers' behavior). Working through all combinations of potential flood levels and potential dam sites was out of the question. Even using one of the most powerful electronic computers in England in the late 1950s, it took half an hour to process a single scenario. It took all of 1958 for the government of Sudan to test, using the most advanced Monte Carlo mathematical techniques, a full set of dam proposals against a full set of historical flood levels. Meanwhile, the Egyptian river engineers went ahead and started building the Aswân High Dam.

Today the world is being wired up anew, allowing ones and zeros to course about the planet just as dashes and dots started to do in Victorian times. These information links are quickly being filled with data about life. Satellite information about Walden Pond and about the Nile Valley, and about everything in between, is becoming routinely available to anyone with a home computer and a network connection. It is not necessary to tramp eight or ten miles to keep an appointment with a data set. Organizations such as the Consortium for International Earth Science Information Network (http://www.ciesin.org) have been established specifically to bring together "data on actions involving a human component, such as agriculture, industry, and population [with] physical science data on topics like ice levels, global temperatures, and related phenomena."[6] Tens of billions of dollars are spent each year gathering this kind of data. Amounts equivalent to Thoreau's entire lifetime of journal entries may be downloaded in minutes, as illustrated in figure 17.1.

The sudden availability of all these new data puts us at the same sort of historic threshold that the first Greek and Babylonian scientists successfully crossed. We have heretofore unfathomed behavior awaiting our exploration, as they had. We can choose which techniques and vocabulary to use, as they could. Should we use numbers? Should we use circles and lines? Should we use something completely new? And where should we look first? It is only in retrospect that we will know

Figure 17.1. When computers and data were both scarce, intermaths were not economically viable. Today the world is awash in data that can be downloaded into a home computer over the Internet. Among the first data sets to become available were those containing terrain information about the planet. In less than an hour, a home computer can load the data for a sector of geography (in this case northern Colorado) and process it into a dimensional representation.

Now data about the changing patterns of social and biological behavior is joining the early physical data on the Internet. This new data offers a limitless diet of free training data for intermath formulations. Without it, they could not learn. Earth image courtesy of NASA.

for sure which patterns are the important ones. Galileo focused on certain patterns of star and planet behavior for the same reason we focus on certain patterns of carbon dioxide behavior: They are the behaviors that have turned out to be important in ways their original discoverers could not have fully anticipated when they first started to listen for them:

It is to be supposed that the first observers of Heaven knew no more but one motion common to all the stars, as is this [daily] one; yet I believe that in few days they perceived that the Moon was inconstant in keeping company with the other stars; but yet, withal, many years must have passed before they distinguished all the planets. . . . Many more years ran out before the stations and retrogressions of the three superior planets were known, as, also, their approximations and recessions from the Earth, which were the necessary occasions of introducing the eccentrics and epicycles, things unknown even to Aristotle, for he makes no mention thereof.[7]

Keeling discovered very early that CO_2 in the Earth's atmosphere cycles daily. CO_2 in the air increases measurably at night when plants shut down photosynthesis for the day, and then hits a low in the sunny afternoon as the plants go full steam turning CO_2 into vegetables. A few years later Keeling observed a second cycle: a hemispherical seasonal cycle of CO_2, low in summer and peaking in the winter for the same reason CO_2 peaks at night: no greens at work to eat it. . . . Recently, other researchers have spotted in Keeling's meticulous recordings a fourth trend: the seasonal cycle is increasing in amplitude.[8]

Given the data available to them up in the sky, the Greeks learned how to anticipate the daily motions. Given our new data riches, our goal must be higher: in Thoreau's words, "to anticipate, not the sunrise and the dawn merely, but, if possible, Nature herself!"[9] It sounds like a job for Big Science, for some form of internationally funded SuperComputing SuperCollector that could consolidate this new data about life and turn it into a form we can understand and, to the extent possible, predict. The two French university professors, Laplace and Tarantola, have given us two competing visions of how this Big Science might work:

An Intellect who at any given instant knew all the forces that animate nature and the mutual positions of the beings who compose it, were this Intellect but vast enough to submit his data to analysis, could condense into a single formula the movement of the greatest body in the universe and that of the lightest atom; to such an Intellect nothing would be uncertain, for the future, even as the past, would be ever before his eyes.[10]

As soon as you write an equation, it is wrong, because reducing a complex reality to an equation is just too simplistic a view of things. Large parallel computers, with large amounts of memory, may allow us to develop an entirely new sort of physics where, instead of reducing the facts to equations, we can just store in the computer the facts. Then we can extrapolate and we can predict. That's what physics is about: extrapolating and predicting.[11]

The numbers and equations approach of Laplace has the advantage of its four hundred year head start. There already exist predictive differential equation models in most of the physical sciences. More to the point, there exists an educational system dedicated to training new generations of scientists in the associated vocabulary of numbers and equations. The challenge for Laplace's Intellect in the coming decade is twofold: first, to combine ("condense") the known equations of the individual physical sciences and, second, to extend the reach of equational vocabulary into the realms of biological and social behavior. Both appear to be insuperably difficult.

Progress toward interdisciplinary integration of physical science models is certainly being made. Because the behavior of the oceans has a large effect on the weather in the atmosphere, for example, oceanographers and meteorologists are now "coupling" their models so that each reflects the changing behavior of the other. The latest models reflect the fact that the ocean transports as much tropical heat to the poles as the atmosphere does, and it stores fifty times as much carbon dioxide.[12] Even in these fields, however, there is resistance to breaking down barriers among multiple disciplines.

Global weather forecasters, for example, have long focused on the ocean pattern known as El Niño off the coast of Peru as a factor in weather worldwide. They have worked with oceanographers to understand and predict it. Recently, a geologist noted a possible relationship between El Niño and shifting plate tectonics in the ocean floor near Australia, east of Port Darwin. Underseas volcanoes may be a source of the warmer water that drives El Niño. Meteorologists and oceanographers,

however, have not shown interest in integrating geology into their thinking, because it is hard and their current explanations already seem ade-
quate.[13] Even in closely related fields such as meteorology, oceanography,
and geology, it is tedious to marry equational theories. In more distant
fields, such as biology and ecology, there has been little progress at all.

The power of the Tarantola approach is that it sidesteps the need for
an overarching Intellect to invent equations that bridge conflicting disciplines. In his approach, a very large computer would simply hold the
data and provide it on request. The approach, which is the physical
science analog of the memory-based reasoning technology of the cognitive scientists, holds great promise in areas in which the total amount
of data is manageable. The planet as a whole, however, disgorges a trillion pieces of data per day per satellite.

In between these two visions lies the possibility of a whole new form
of distributed Big Science, a parallel form in which the ship of science
is carried ashore by an army of Galilean ants rather than by a single
Laplacian Intellect or a single SuperCollecting SuperComputer. The
potential for amateur discovery lies in the unused capacity of millions
of home computers, which might collectively evolve the ability to listen to life and help us to understand what the data mean. These home
computers are, in aggregate, far more powerful than any national data
center. In addition, the high school–age users of these computers are
still partially free from indoctrination in the old sequential ways of
thought, the old ways of seeing and processing information. When
dealing with prodigious amounts of data, the importance of thinking
and seeing in new ways may exceed the importance of raw computing
power. Recall the artificial-intelligence researcher who wished there
were equations for creativity, humor, and common sense, "but, sadly, I
don't believe they exist." Those who have yet to be fully steeped in the
maths of the Industrial Age may, to their benefit, rejoice rather than be
sad when no such equation rears its head. The ecologist Marty Condon describes the ability of fifth graders to find patterns in fruit fly
wing markings that she had overlooked:

> As a scientist, you're trained not to see certain things, not to look in
> places where you've never found useful information. There's a real
> advantage to opening things up to people who don't have these
> kinds of preconceptions.[14]

By rearranging the wing patterns into new posies, first this way and
then that, the fifth graders found an unsuspected species among Con-

don's samples, a species that now carries the name of their elementary school.

Much of what we need to forget in life we learned in kindergarten. It is there, for example, that we learned to think of "sharing" in terms of using a scarce piece of hardware, like a toy truck or supercomputer center, one at a time sequentially, as opposed to sharing a piece of software like a song all together in parallel. Economists call resources like toy trucks "rival goods," adding to the sense of individual competition. (Goods that a second person can enjoy without denying enjoyment to the first are called "nonrival" goods.) Charles Babbage scoffed at the idea of ten thousand people cooperating in a task, yet thousands of students in projects such as "Live From the Stratosphere" (http://quest.arc.nasa.gov/livefrom/stratosphere.html) are already beginning to work together electronically, perhaps because they are too young to know it is impossible.[15]

Beginning to find patterns in the vast amounts of data becoming available about life on earth may require teams of thousands of computers singing the songs of the new maths in parallel each night. It also requires giving up individual credit for a discovery just as the individual elementary school students were willing to do. When useful patterns and predictions well up out of the intermosh pit, they will not be the result of any one individual's effort. Evolutionary computations require diversity: The wrong approaches are as essential to evolutionary progress as the ones that ultimately combine and win through:

> Error is the mark of the higher organisms, and is the schoolmaster by whose agency there is upward evolution.[16]

Earth-Observing Satellites will produce trillions of pieces (bytes) of data per day. In addition to being fed into national supercomputer centers, these data could also be broadcast, much like a television broadcast. Spread out over twenty-four hours, these terabytes in raw form would flow at a rate of a few dozen megabytes per second.

No home computer can keep up with such data rates, even if the data were preprocessed and compressed, so each would have to drink selectively. A home computer watching Walden Pond might take in just the data for this one sector and ignore all the rest. Those watching a bird migration might take data for a patch of Central America as well. Those watching the Nile might take Samoa and Port Darwin, just to see if the old relationship is returning. The data stream need not be limited to satellite images. All available data about behavior on the earth, from election results to stock tickers to yesterday's newspaper, are potentially grist for the mill. The Global Learning and Observation to Benefit the Environment (GLOBE) project (http://www.globe.gov) is already underway to allow thousands of students to study and share satellite data electronically. Also underway is the CoVis project, which allows students to share scientific data online and to "develop their science understanding by practicing science as it is practiced by scientists."[17]

The goal of a collaborative use of intermaths by students is baldly more radical than CoVis, of course. Its goal is to practice science in a way that it is *not* being practiced at all by scientists still grounded in the sequential maths of the Industrial Age. Given the power of today's personal computers, it would take only a few hundred students working in a coordinated way to emulate, for example, the system that Hillis used to breed a world-class sorting program. The computers used in that sorting program had, to be sure, a different balance between processing power and communications. Although each of the sixteen thousand processors was far weaker than a modern home computer, each had a far easier time intercommunicating because they all lived together in the same physical cabinet. Hence, the system did very little computation and learning between breeding and mating cycles.

Today's home computers are much more isolated and, like isolated Appalachian hollows, must interbreed within themselves for many generations before receiving new genetic material from outside. On the other hand, a fast personal computer is much more powerful than each processor in the original sorting experiment, so it can keep a whole valleylike subpopulation going within its own resources. Home computers will have another advantage that the Connection Machine processors did not have: individual human owners to coach them along and contribute clever ideas and diversity of their own. Participants need not all sing in tune, nor even sing the same tune. It is the old sequential mode of thought that puts the premium on uniformity. Genetic computing experiments of approximately this magnitude have already been proposed by the ecologist and artificial-life researcher Thomas Ray.[18]

Of particular interest will be cliques of such computers that, over the course of weeks or months (or years) of otherwise unused computer time, become good at predicting their data. The longer training period suggests that the patterns are subtle; the gradual improvement through training indicates that the patterns are really there. The next step would be to share, or "publish," successful predictions. As purportedly accurate predictions become available, other computers studying similar topics have a choice of whether to continue to take all their input from the raw data stream or to substitute another group's published prediction. A computation that includes Spain could, in essence, take up Thoreau's offer to predict the country's behavior for the next twelvemonth and eliminate the need to process all the raw data from Spain itself.

Publishers will inevitably claim predictive power beyond what they actually deliver. In that sense, they would be like managers of financial investment funds who implicitly claim to be able to predict the future behavior of some aspect of a seemingly incomprehensible mass of business and market data. Over time, some of those predictions turn out to be better than others. Those funds find themselves incorporated into more and more portfolios, and even into other funds. The fact that this year's source of good predictions may not be the best source next year does not invalidate the overall system. The market simply adapts. Those whose predictive power declines are gradually culled and replaced by those whose abilities are on the upswing.

The ultimate step, for which we are not yet fully prepared, is for participating computers to share their genetic material universally. In this environment, computers and teams of computers would continually try out new building blocks that have proved valuable elsewhere. They would incorporate what works for them as well and let the rest die off, rather like the way some bacteriologists are now viewing the whole global population of bacteria as a single superorganism evolving off a single corpus of genetic material.[19] Such an environment, of course, breaks down the current distinction between program development and program utilization. In a genetic environment, every computer becomes an integral part of the program-development process. Traditionally, the computers that are used to develop and test software are firewalled from the computers that ultimately use it. Genetic programming requires that all participating computers be prepared for the surprises, including crashes and loss of disk files, that go along with any program-development process. A process of interbreeding that is powerful enough to produce a world-class sorting program is also powerful enough potentially to produce a world-class computer virus. The benefit of breeding, of course, is that computing power is finally mobilized to develop its own programs, rather than just running the ones that are produced by the processes of human thought.

How long would it take for this seemingly hopeless adolescent mishmash, this tangled web of city and country prejudices, to start producing valuable predictions of the earth's behavior and thus to compete successfully with equational techniques? Could the first coherent and lasting results emerge after ten million hours of total running time? We do not yet know. Experiments breeding solutions to structural analysis problems have shown that simply introducing genetic methods within a single processor slowed the solution time down by a factor of five.[20] The need to communicate among computers, of course, creates a much greater bottleneck. Balancing these inefficiencies is the fact that large metropolitan areas are now adding personal computers at a rate of more than a million a year each, so factors of five or even five hundred are not insuperable.

The 1990s may see only a few thousand early experimenters using spare computing capacity to pan for patterns in global data. Success at this level will depend on being shrewd about which data lodes to stake out. Rich claims are those for which little competing theory exists because copious data have just become available and for which the impact of human action is clearly manifest. River systems like the Nile or the Mississippi provide a framework for thinking about the subject, although the fruitful early targets will undoubtedly be smaller in scale and subject to more rapid change.

There are no satellite images of the Nile from the time of Pharaoh, but there are many images of the great Mississippi flood of 1993. The Mississippi is one of the most intensively managed rivers in the world. Human-constructed levees discourage its traditional tendency to flood and to change its borders on an annual basis. Small dikes projecting partway into the river from one bank serve to shift the flow toward the other bank and motivate the river to scour its bed deeper, thereby avoiding the need to dredge in order to get big ships through. Two hundred flood-control dams buffer the spring floods. Channels that have been cut through meanders shorten the river by more than a hundred miles.

Of even greater interest than the Mississippi are the great river systems that have not been heavily engineered in the past but are about to be in the near future. Even in a normal year, large portions of Bangladesh, for example, are flooded by the three great rivers that pass through it. In the worst years, virtually the entire country is impacted. A massive engineering intervention is contemplated, to narrow the rivers and to cure them of their tendency to shift their paths from year to year. Proponents foresee a vast improvement in the quality of life. Critics expect the river system to laugh at any invasion of static concrete walls and go about its business roughly as it always has. Nobody knows for sure what will happen as dams and levees are put into place. All of it, however, will likely happen under the watchful gaze of the satellites.

> Large dams have only been with us for a few decades, and are really essentially huge experiments on the river systems of the world. . . . There seems to be a growing sense of unreality about the enormity of these effects, and we seem to be not learning from the mistakes that have occurred in the past.[21]

On a more local scale, hundreds of privately owned American dams now come under the jurisdiction of a 1986 law requiring environmental review as part of the process of licensing. Ten years later, the license-renewal process has now begun for many of these dams. On the Deerfield River in Vermont and central Massachusetts, for example, the owners of ten small dams are making modifications to encourage the fish population. It is these more local ecologies that can provide fertile ground for an Information Age science project.[22]

Not all of the out-of-control floods of the modern world are happening in river valleys, of course. We are also being flooded by text information, much of which is readily available in electronic form but little of which has yet been analyzed to understand its patterns. This text represents still another interesting opportunity for amateur use of the new intermaths. Lewis Richardson suggested what can be done at the scale of the individual news report. He suggested that politicians say the same things over and over and over again. His hypothetical speech by the defense minister of "Jedesland" was one example.

Meanwhile, the linguist George Zipf has suggested powerful ways of finding stories on similar topics within huge volumes of text. Commonality of individual word use follows a predictable pattern now known as Zipf's law.[23] The rarer the word in text overall, the more likely it is to be important when it is used. Rare words, such as those not known to spell checkers, are invariably good indicators of what a piece of text is about. Two text files that have the same words rejected by the spell checker are almost sure to be on the same general subject. Thus, the word *Chernobyl,* which was virtually nonexistent in English-language text prior to the 1980s, is a specific indicator of the subject matter of the stories it appears in. So is the word *Zipf.* A computer does not need to know what the subject matter is to know that something new is afoot when such words start appearing. Zipf's law is already at the heart of at least one commercially available information-retrieval service. It is one technique that is available to look for patterns and repetition in the news.

An activity that has not existed in the past but is about to become significant is electronic advertising on the Internet. Can the patterns of advertising messages be correlated with patterns of social behavior elsewhere in society? Assuming that advertising "works," how is its impact felt? Richardson pointed to advertising as a possible form of propaganda that might influence war moods among the citizenry. Modern economists point to advertising as a potential means of undercutting the validity of supply–demand curves because it allows manufacturers, who control supply, potentially to manipulate demand as well. Such patterns are well worth looking for each night when the computer would otherwise be doing nothing.

The process of analyzing advertising text on the Internet is illustrated by the FIDO program (http://www.continuumsi.com/Fido), which creates an index of products currently being offered for sale electronically. FIDO is able to recognize text that offers products for sale because it has learned to do so, using Internet data to train on. The cognitive scientist Marc Goodman started with the text from just a few Internet sites. He hand-labeled some of the product descriptions and then used a learning program to find the rest of the products at that site. When FIDO could do so without making mistakes, the scientists sent it on to a new site, where products were described in a different way. Gradually, FIDO learned to separate descriptions of products for sale from all other text on the Internet. It has now trained on almost a hundred thousand pages of text.[24]

There is a common denominator, of course, among all these investigators: the first Greek astronomers, the elementary school discoverers of the fruit fly species, the developers of FIDO, the discoverer of carbon dioxide patterns, and even Thoreau himself. They were all pioneers who went out and listened to data that had not been listened to before. They learned what others had not learned because they listened where others had not bothered to listen or where data had never before existed. The scientists at the Prediction Company focused first on financial data, partly because, even in the 1980s, financial data were available in volume to train on. They are using it to hone their intermath formulations for other applications like global climate or epidemics:

We are interested in [financial forecasting] because our dream is to produce prediction machinery that will allow us to predict lots of

different things . . . anything generating a lot of data we don't understand well.[25]

The availability of new public data about our planet represents the
Information Age's first big Gold Rush. In the process of mining the
data and sharing the evolving programs that explore it, today's infor-
mational forty-niners may do more than find golden patterns. They
may give birth to bit evolution itself and do it well before the artificial-
intelligence experts get there. It all seems slightly heretical, and it is. It
is at least as heretical as the new ways of thought and the new algebraic
maths of Descartes, material that, he freely acknowledged, "turns away
the young from the study of the old and true Philosophy. . . . An
imprudent youth can deduce from it certain opinions which are
opposed to the other disciplines and faculties and above all the orthodox Theology."[26]

THE
ΛFTERMATH

During the 1970s, a mathematician set out to match an autistic savant at the mind task of determining the day of the week of any date in the past or future. Despite enormous amounts of practice and the memorization of a full-page table, the mathematician could not match the savant in speed. And then he could. All of a sudden, he no longer needed to step through the operations he had been practicing so diligently. The correct answer just happened. Instead of being first nature to him, it had become second nature. Using terminology popular at the time, a psychologist surmised that the entire task had migrated from the left brain to the right brain. Once a product of traditional sequential thought, it had simply transferred to new ground.[1]

The reality was likely different. The faster parallel formulation had likely been in mind all along. It just was not competitive. Like a tangled web of home computers, it was initially put to shame by the big data center on the other side of town. Normally, the human process terminates at this early stage, choking off the supply of training data before it has had time to work its magic. This mathematician kept going, however, giving the inherently more sophisticated parallel formulation a chance to finish learning. In the end, the Cartesian side of things was left with nothing to do but falsely take credit for having shown the way.

Now this same extraordinary contest, and same unconvincing explanation, has taken hold in computing. This time, however, the economics are all on the side of the parallel formulations. Training data are getting cheaper and more abundant every year, and the sequential formulations of human scientists and programmers are not. Electronics circuits vastly prefer to operate in parallel, whereas humans, at least at the conscious level, do not. In addition, the cutting edge of science has shifted from the nonadaptive world of earth, air, fire, and water to the adaptive, evolving world of immune systems, market segments, and intelligences. The rational thought of place and pace does not take us very deeply into the perpetual–novelty world of pattern. It is not even the way we ourselves behave most of the time. As Arthur has noted,

> if one were to imagine the vast collection of decision problems economic agents [you and I] might conceivably deal with as a sea or an ocean, with the easier problems on top and more complicated ones at increasing depth, then deductive rationality would describe human behavior accurately only within a few feet of the surface.[2]

We would like to think that the new adaptive ways of processing information are just the logical next step in a chain of development, because thought specializes in logical next steps and chains of development. In reality, Part Three of the Book of Nature sends us all the way back to one of the earliest forks in the road of Western culture and bids us start afresh. Everything, including thought itself, is up for reconsideration.

It was the pre-Socratic philosopher Heraclitus who asserted that "all things flow," or "all is change." Starved for computing power, the tangled web of developing Greek science chose the "all" as a primal building block. Although they have been in the cultural mix all along, formulations based on "change" or "each" were simply not competitive. Much of the edifice of universal scientific law traces its ancestry back to the incorporation of "all" as a building block, as illustrated in figure 18.1. With it, astronomers came to dominate Part One of Galileo's Book of Nature. The physicists of Part Two continued the focus on compressed universal law and its ability to fit the strengths and weaknesses of human computers. Isaac Newton, like many of his followers, refused to let his work "bear on any subjects except those that could be treated by means of the calculations he knew how to make."[3] Mathematical scientists found it far more efficient to think in

"All is circle"

"All is equation"

"Each is change"

Figure 18.1. When civilization began, human thought was the only available resource for processing information. Today our information processing capacity is a trillion times greater, with almost all of the increase being electronic. These electronic circuits do not need the constant ("universal") programs and smoothly varying data that human minds prefer. For them, the jagged terrain of the real world is as absorbable as the artificial sphere of the geometer or the torus of the analyst. Using the new evolutionary intermaths, they have the ability to go where thought alone cannot.

terms of unchanging formulations like "all is circles riding atop circles" and, later, "all is sines riding atop cosines" instead of more data-intensive formulations like "each is change mating in parallel with other change to evolve spontaneously into new and novel change." Formulations that use building blocks like "change" and "each" have been uncompetitive for thousands of years because they require huge amounts of cheap computing power and cheap data. They are, however, the key to vast realms of knowledge inaccessible to "all" and hence to traditional methods of thought.

The choice for us as individuals today is whether we want to stay within the comfortable confines of Part Two or retrace our steps and start afresh with Part Three. The danger for us, and for our children, is that the choice may be locked into us for life by the time we graduate from high school. The parallel ways of pattern are antithetical to the sequential ways of place or pace. Once we learn one, it is hard to fully grasp the other. Descartes, Locke, and Goethe were right. Maths all by themselves can have a dominant effect on the way the mind develops. As the twentieth-century physicist Stanisław Ulam suggested, "mathematics plays a genetic role. It is one of the few ways to perfect the brain, to perhaps develop new connections in the brain. It has a peculiar sharpening value. Nothing could be more important."[4] And nothing could be more permanent. Once the ways of sequential geometry, algebra, and calculus have played this role, the results are beyond the reach of any delete key. Sequentialism is forever. Once our teachers have shaped our young minds to think in train, it takes enormous effort to accept, with Hillis, that

> if I look at [a genetically evolved] program, I'm unable to tell how it works. It's an obscure, weird program, but it does the job, because it comes from a line of hundreds of thousands of programs that did the job.[5]

Because of our early training, we often try to make sense out of this new world of pattern using the centuries-old languages of pace, much as Adam Smith used it to describe the realm of King Henry VIII. As the pace picks up, however, pace itself runs out of explanatory power:

> [The realm's] pace seems rather to have been gradually accelerated than retarded . . . not only to have been going on, but to have been going on faster and faster."[6]

I'm persuaded that the acceleration of technology-acceleration is even now distorting human institutions and expectations, whether or not we are approaching a metaphorical "event horizon" beyond which everything becomes unrecognizable.[7]

An *event horizon* or *singularity* is a point beyond which a vocabulary cannot penetrate. The new forms of autonomous computation even create a sense of an end of all human creativity: "The first ultra-intelligent machine is the last invention that man need ever make."[8] The Industrial Age language of control also conjures up a sense of foreboding that is summarized in the title of Kevin Kelly's powerful book *Out of Control*. Kelly's book is required reading for an appreciation of how pervasive the evolutionary computing techniques already are and how "each variety will, for certain, remain out of our exclusive control and carry its own agenda."[9] The process is not one that we can stop, any more than our ancestors could have nipped cultural evolution in the bud: "Having infiltrated computers, artificial life will henceforth never retreat from being in some computer, somewhere."[10] Rather than fight a rearguard action, Kelly argues persuasively that it is already time to start letting go and trusting intelligence in whatever form it presents itself:

> Investing machines with the ability to adapt on their own, to evolve in their own direction, and grow without human oversight is the next great advance in technology. Giving machines freedom is the only way we can have intelligent control. What little time [is] left in this century is rehearsal time for the chief psychological chore of the twenty-first century: letting go, with dignity.[11]

Even among the users of the new intermaths themselves, however, the incumbent language of hierarchy and control still lingers, because at our current transitional stage it is still humans who are writing the evolutionary programs. It is still possible to assert, with Ray, that "I'm god. I'm omniscient. I can get information on whatever attracts my attention without disturbing [my artificial ecology], without walking around crushing plants."[12]

Ray's Tierra system is indeed remarkable. He starts with a computer program that is preengineered to replicate itself within an environment of mutations. As the system fills with programs and some must die, those with the fewest errors are considered to be more fit and thus are more likely to survive. The result is a riot of evolving computational creatures. Parasites emerge that are shorter because they use parts of other programs to do their replicating work for them. Then, the host victims retaliate, learning to trick the parasites into creating new hosts instead of new parasites. Among the survivors is a self-replicating program that is a quarter the size of its primal ancestor, without resorting itself to parasitism.

> An amazing menagerie of software creatures, an entire ecosystem, spontaneously emerged through the process of evolution. Describing these creatures was an adventure, because they inhabited an alien universe, based on a physics and chemistry totally different from the rainforest life forms I knew and loved.[13]

Ray is indeed in control of at least his own copy of Tierra and can pull the plug on it if he chooses. However, this role of the human scientist in such formulations ultimately fades, just as the role of human scientists in formulating strategies for Prisoner's Dilemma has already faded away. In Part Three of the Book of Nature, the exclusive franchise of human thought as the mechanism for understanding the world no longer holds.

After Copernicus moved humankind off center stage of the physical universe, Descartes filled the void in two steps. First, he gave centrality to human thought. Second, he enlisted the mathematics curriculum to inculcate his new methods of thought. New notions of being soon came together to replace the ones destroyed by Copernicus. Now these notions have taken us about as far as they can. Electronic computers that evolve and adapt on their own are as terminal to old conceits as the heliocentric theory proved to be: "The problem is not simply that the Singularity represents the passing of humankind from center stage, but that it contradicts our most deeply held notions of being."[14] True. A new chapter in the Book of Nature inevitably requires fresh notions of being. The question is how to start looking for them.

One approach, espoused most eloquently by the Massachusetts Institute of Technology artificial-intelligence researcher Mitchel Resnick, is to start teaching the new parallel ways *before* we teach the old sequential ways instead of the other way around. His students start early in life to listen to the new intermaths in their own voice, as Kepler once learned to listen to data and Hillis learned to listen to neuron when neither was a fashionable thing to do. In his graceful book *Turtles, Termites, and Traffic Jams,* Resnick describes young students who are exposed to the techniques of the new intermaths before the full weight of the sequential (Resnick prefers the term *centralized*) thought processes have been inculcated. These are the students who will live comfortably in the new chapter of the Book of Nature that our computers will write with us. These are the students who will develop new notions of being to replace the ones that are based on the supposed omnipotence of human thought.

Resnick's tool of instruction is a computer language called Star-Logo, which has three important attributes. First, StarLogo is parallel. It allows young users to program thousands of agents called turtles and to let them all move around at once on a computer screen. Each can be given simple rules to follow, much as a cellular automata formulation does. In a trivial example, five turtles could be placed in the center of the screen and told to pick a direction individually and move ten steps in that direction. The result is not interesting, but with five thousand turtles, a clear circle forms on the screen. Thus, StarLogo is exactly the tool Galileo needed to follow up on his idea of myriad individual stars forming an expanding circular universe. Galileo could only ask his readers to see this parallel result in their imaginations. Contemporary students can watch it happen directly and see how a very large number of objects acting independently and in parallel can create orderly and coherent behavior without ever being explicitly told to do so.

Second, StarLogo is responsive. Each individual turtle is able to sense its surroundings and to alter its behavior on the basis of what it finds out. Thus, students can experiment with how turtles of two specific kinds can interact. Red and green turtles, for example, might prefer to live on patches of the screen where at least 30 percent of their neighbors, living on adjacent patches, are like them. When such proves to be the case, they stay put. Otherwise, they move to an empty patch. The result is that the red and green turtles segregate, although that was not at all their intent. Turtles who wanted just a few similar neighbors end up with, on average, 70 percent similar neighbors.[15] In this way, students can learn firsthand that one set of intents at the individual level can lead to a dramatically different set of results emerging at the group level. The maths of the Industrial Age have taught different lessons.

Third, StarLogo has an active environment. The patches of the computer screen can be programmed just as the turtles are. Thus, students can mimic the behavior of an ant colony foraging for food. Ants who find food create a pheromone trail that attracts other ants. The colony does not get stuck in this behavior, however, because the environment gradually dissipates the pheromone, causing the trail to fade away soon after the food supply is exhausted. The whole system adapts. Isaac Newton was not capable of thinking in this adaptive, evolutionary way. He could compute the changes to planetary orbits if the Annual Motion were doubled and the year became half as long, but the results here on earth "would be pernicious. . . . The cold Winter would overtake us, before our Corn and Fruits could possibly be ripe."[16] Indeed, when such changes are instantaneous, they wreak havoc. But if they are gradual, as the current increase in carbon dioxide seems to be, organisms potentially can adapt at the same time the environment is changing. By making turtles and patches peers, Star-Logo offers an experimental environment reminiscent of the Gaia hypothesis of James Lovelock.

The point of StarLogo is not that the Gaia hypothesis is correct or incorrect. Its point, and Resnick's point, is that what we learn in math class has a powerful effect on which alternative views of the world we are able to listen to and which we cannot even hear. In particular, the old equational maths can make us tone deaf to behaviors that work simultaneously in parallel and to behavior for which history matters. The scientist Hermann Helmholtz, for example, was frustrated by students whose initial preparation had been in liberal arts and grammar, areas in which rules routinely have exceptions. Helmholtz felt he could not make good scientists until he had purged them of this silliness:

> What strikes me in my own experience with students who pass from our classical schools to scientific and medical studies is first, a certain laxity in the application of strictly universal rules. The grammatical rules, in which they have been exercised, are for the most part followed by long lists of exceptions; accordingly they are not in the habit of relying implicitly on the certainty of a legitimate deduction from a strictly universal law.[17]

These long lists of exceptions are, of course, the voice of history speaking. Helmholtz could not, or would not, listen to this voice. He wanted a world of "i before e, *punkt*." Science and computing since the Renaissance have focused on universal behavior, for which, by definition, history does not matter. This focus is one of the sources of the oft-noted estrangement between the sciences and the humanities. As pioneering scientists listen to the world of the new emergent vocabularies, however, they are unveiling a chapter for which history matters just about everywhere, for which "evolutionary biology, with its interest in historical processes, is in some respects as closely allied to the humanities as it is to the exact sciences,"[18] for which "as economics pushes on beyond 'statics' it becomes less like science and more like history,"[19] and for which there is much less of the "grand unifying theory [and] the pleasures of theorems and proof. Instead the uncertain embrace of history and sociology and biology."[20]

The lessons of StarLogo and the other intermaths are prerequisite to the grander adventure of collective analysis of the new riches of data about our planet. They provide entree to the new world where electronic circuits are our intellectual peers and partners, riding their own autonomous wave of bit evolution. This is the world after thought.

As Henry David Thoreau listened for the whistle blast of the train across the pond, he sensed a world where the limits imposed by old human muscle analogies were finally being overcome. Perhaps, he thought, with the arrival of "this traveling demigod, this cloud-compeller . . . the earth had got a race now worthy to inhabit it."[21]

It had for sure got a race that was qualitatively different from the horse-drawn coaches that had come before, because, in Schumpeter's words, "Add as many mail coaches as you please, you will never get a railroad by so doing."[22] The same is true of the limits of the old human mind analogies. Run Part Two of the Book of Nature as fast as you please—even at the speed of light if you wish—you will never get Part Three by so doing. Part Three will only be authored by a partnership of sequential human minds and autonomous parallel electronic circuits because "so long as we admit only discursive symbolism as a bearer of ideas, 'thought' in this restricted sense must be regarded as our only intellectual activity."[23] And it is simply not enough anymore.

ACKNOWLEDGMENTS

fter Thought is based on some of the world's youngest science, and some of its oldest. Both were made wonderfully accessible to me. At the Boston Athenaeum, Catharina Slautterback, Trevor Johnson, and Stephen Nonack made their most treasured mathematical volumes available both for research and for reproduction. At the Rare Book Room of the Boston Public Library, Roberta Zonghi, Giuseppe Bisaccia, and Eugene Zepp guided me through the library's extraordinary holdings of early science texts and reproduced key diagrams. The MIT library's policy of accessibility to scholars was also indispensable, as was the help of Michelle Kincade in organizing the research material as it grew.

Without the help and patient explanations of my former colleagues at Thinking Machines Corporation, I would never have understood the full import of the new intermaths. Danny Hillis introduced me to the potential of pure parallelism. Corporate Fellow Stephen Wolfram first pointed out how partial differential equations were designed for humans, not electronic circuits. David Waltz focused me on the role of data, emphasizing that a good algorithm is one that improves its performance as it is given more data. Kurt Thearling read early drafts and made indispensable suggestions of new material to include. The breadth of knowledge represented by the dozens of additional colleagues and visiting researchers who also helped me understand this field is a tribute to co-founder Sheryl Handler, who assembled the team. I am grateful to them all. Responsibility for any errors is, of course, mine alone.

Professor Stephen Graubard of Brown University, editor of *Daedalus* magazine, provided essential early encouragement for my line of research, as has my very supportive editor at Basic Books, Susan Rabiner. I am grateful for her wise and insistent counsel throughout the project.

♫OTES

Chapter 1: Reassigning the Tasks of the Mind

1. W. D. Hillis, "What is massively parallel computing, and why is it so important?" *Daedalus* 121, no. 1 (winter 1992): 2.
2. G. Sturt, *The Wheelwright's Shop* (Cambridge, England: University Press, 1923), p. 70.
3. F. A. P. Barnard (1869), quoted in P. Kidwell and P. Ceruzzi, *Landmarks in Digital Computing* (Washington, D.C.: Smithsonian Institution Press, 1994), p. 24.
4. N. Negroponte, *Being Digital* (New York: Knopf, 1995).
5. S. Wolfram, "Cellular automata and partial differential equations," Thinking Machines seminar series, 15 August 1986.
6. H. Thoreau, "Walden," in B. Atkinson, ed., *Walden and Other Writings* (New York: Modern Library, 1937), p. 238.
7. Sturt, *The Wheelwright's Shop*, p. 70.
8. J. Bronowski, *The Ascent of Man* (Boston: Little, Brown, 1973), p. 59.
9. Sturt, *The Wheelwright's Shop*, p. 70.
10. L. Margulis, quoted in J. Brockman, *The Third Culture: Beyond the Scientific Revolution* (New York: Simon and Schuster, 1995), p. 136.
11. Sturt, *The Wheelwright's Shop*, p. 75.
12. A. Eddington, *The Nature of the Physical World* (New York: Macmillan, 1929), p. xiii.
13. J. Keynes, quoted in C. Lehmann-Haupt, "The making of an economist, part 2," *New York Times*, 14 February 1994, C13.

14. J. Schumpeter, "The common sense of econometrics," in R. Clemens, ed., *Essays on Entrepreneurs, Innovations, Business Cycles, and the Evolution of Capitalism* (New Brunswick, N.J.: Transaction Publishers, 1989), p. 35.

15. B. Anderson, *Imagined Communities: Reflections on the Origin and Spread of Nationalism*, rev. ed. (London: Verso, 1991), p. 165.

16. A. Whitehead, quoted in G. Hodgson, *Economics and Evolution: Bringing Life Back into Economics* (Ann Arbor: University of Michigan Press, 1993), p. 196.

17. J. Bailey, "The ghosts of computers past: Understanding data parallel architecture in the context of the human computing era," in H. Simon, ed., *Scientific Applications of the Connection Machine* (Singapore: World Scientific, 1989), p. 19.

18. S. Langer, *Philosophy in a New Key* (New York: Mentor Books, 1951), pp. 76, 86.

19. J. Holland et al., *Induction: Processes of Inference, Learning, and Discovery* (Cambridge, Mass.: MIT Press, 1986), pp. 289ff.

20. G. Miller and P. Todd, "Evolutionary wanderlust: Sexual selection with directional mate preferences," Thinking Machines seminar series, 2 March 1993.

21. M. Minsky, quoted in D. Crevier, *AI: The Tumultuous History of the Search for Artificial Intelligence* (New York: Basic Books, 1993), p. 9.

22. K. Kelly, "The gene in the machine," *New York Times*, 15 May 1995, A17.

23. D. Farmer, quoted in Brockman, *The Third Culture*, p. 370.

Chapter 2: The Master Thought Process of the Modern World

1. G. Galilei, *Dialogues Concerning Two New Sciences*, trans. H. Crew and A. deSalvio (New York: Macmillan, 1914), p. 215.

2. K. Mendelssohn, *Science and Western Domination* (London: Thames and Hudson, 1976), pp. 8, 10.

3. Goethe, quoted in F. Cajori, *Mathematics in Liberal Education* (Boston: Christopher Publishing House, 1928), p. 104.

4. P. Krugman, quoted in D. Warsh, "The man who put cities on the intellectual map," *Boston Globe*, 22 May 1994, 73.

5. Simplicius, quoted in P. Duhem, *To Save the Phenomena: An Essay on the Idea of Physical Theory from Plato to Galileo,* trans. E. Doland and C. Maschler (Chicago: University of Chicago Press, 1969), p. 3.

6. J. von Neumann, "Method in the physical sciences," in A. Taub, gen. ed., *John von Neumann: Collected Works*, vol. 6 (New York: Pergamon Press, 1963), p. 492.

7. M. Friedman, *Essays in Positive Economics* (Chicago: University of Chicago Press, 1953), p. 9.

8. R. Cramer, quoted in P. Ceruzzi, "When computers were human," *Annals of the History of Computing* 13, no. 3 (1991): 243.

9. H. Goldstine, *The Computer from Pascal to von Neumann* (Princeton, N.J.: Princeton University Press, 1972), p. 142.

10. W. Smith, "Notes on the special developments of the computing ability,"

in E. Harsburgh, *Modern Instruments and Methods of Calculation* (London: G. Bell and Sons, 1915), p. 63.

11. M. Delambre, quoted in R. Woodhouse, *A Treatise on Astronomy Theoretical and Practical* (Cambridge, England: J. Smith, 1821), p. 866.

12. T. Kuhn, *The Structure of Scientific Revolutions*, 2d ed., enlarged (Chicago: University of Chicago Press, 1970), p. 52.

13. P. David, "Clio and the economics of QWERTY," *American Economic Review Proceedings* 75 (1985): 332–37.

14. R. Davis, quoted in Crevier, *AI*, p. 157.

Chapter 3: The Book of Nature

1. E. Wigner, *Symmetries and Reflections: Scientific Essays of Eugene P. Wigner* (Cambridge, Mass.: MIT Press, 1970), p. 222.

2. C. Babbage, *The Ninth Bridgewater Treatise* (London: John Murray, 1837), p. 48.

3. G. Galilei, "The assayer," quoted in H. Blumenberg, *The Genesis of the Copernican World*, trans. R. Wallace (Cambridge, Mass.: MIT Press, 1987), p. 409.

4. G. Galilei, *Dialogue on the Great World Systems in the Salusbury Translation*, ed. G. de Santilla (Chicago: University of Chicago Press, 1953), p. 306.

5. J. Donne, quoted in M. Nicolson, *Breaking the Circle*, rev. ed. (New York: Columbia University Press, 1960), p. 120.

6. I. Newton, *Principia Mathematica,* trans. F. Cajori (Berkeley: University of California Press, 1934), p. xiv.

7. E. Hille, "Ordinary differential equations," *Encyclopedia Britannica*, vol. 7 (London: Encyclopedia Britannica, 1911), p. 407.

8. D. Strassman, "Feminist thought and economics; or, what do the Visigoths know?" *American Economic Review* 84, no. 2 (May 1994): 153.

9. R. Boyle, quoted in N. Hanson, *Patterns of Discovery* (Cambridge, England: University Press, 1958), p. 193.

10. R. McCormack, "One hour with Seymour Cray," *High Performance Computing and Communications Week* 2, no. 46 (26 November 1993): 7.

11. G. Williams, quoted in Brockman, *The Third Culture*, p. 43.

12. K. Boulding, "What is evolutionary economics?" *Journal of Evolutionary Economics* 1 (1991): 17.

13. F. Bacon, quoted in O. Gregory, *A Treatise on Astronomy* (London: Kearsley, 1803), p. 140.

14. S. Kauffman, "Requirements for evolvability in complex systems: Orderly dynamics and frozen components," in S. Forrest, ed., *Emergent Computation* (Amsterdam: Elsevier Science, 1990), p. 136.

15. S. Forrest, "Emergent computation: Self-organizing, collective, and cooperative phenomena in natural and artificial computing networks," in Forrest, ed., *Emergent Computation*, p. 1.

16. P. Laplace, quoted in T. Dantzig, *Number the Language of Science*, 4th ed. (New York: Macmillan, 1959), p. 136.

17. A. Tarantola, unpublished interview.

18. M. Kimmelman, "One provocateur inspired by another," *New York Times*, 11 August 1995, C26.

19. J. Jacobs, *The Death and Life of Great American Cities* (New York: Random House, 1961), p. 45.

20. Regiomontanus, quoted in J. Klein, *Greek Mathematical Thought and the Origin of Algebra*, trans. E. Braun (Cambridge, Mass.: MIT Press, 1968), p. 261.

21. R. Descartes, quoted in Klein, *Greek Mathematical Thought,* p. 272.

22. J. Gunn et al., *Hierarchical Algorithm for Computer Modeling of Protein Tertiary Structure: Folding of Myoglobin to 6.2 Angstrom Resolution*, Columbia University preprint, 29 October 1993, p. 1.

23. A. Kekule, quoted in *Nicholas Copernicus: Complete Works*, trans. E. Rosen (Baltimore: Johns Hopkins University Press, 1978), p. 336.

24. Bellarmine, quoted in Duhem, *To Save the Phenomena*, p. 107.

25. Galilei, quoted in Duhem, *To Save the Phenomena*, p. 109.

26. Quoted in F. Cajori, *A History of the Conceptions of Limits and Fluxions in Great Britain from Newton to Woodhouse* (Chicago: Open Court Publishing, 1919), p. 283.

27. S. Ulam, quoted in D. Campbell, "Nonlinear science," *Los Alamos Science*, no. 15 (1987, special issue): 259.

28. R. Descartes, "Objections against the meditations and replies," trans. E. Haldane and G. Ross, in R. Hutchins, ed., *Great Books of the Western World*, vol. 31 (Chicago: Encyclopedia Britannica, 1952), p. 289.

Chapter 4: The First Fiction

1. F. Nietzsche, quoted in Dantzig, *Number the Language of Science*, p. 139.

2. D. Cooper, *Computer Science: Past, Present, and Future* (Swansea, Wales: University College of Swansea, 1968), p. 16.

3. Aristotle, "On the universe," J. Barnes, ed., *The Complete Works of Aristotle: The Revised Oxford Translation* (Princeton, N.J.: Princeton University Press, 1984), p. 634.

4. Claudian, quoted in D. Price, "Gears from the Greeks: The Antikythera mechanism—a calendar computer from ca. 80 BC," *Transactions of the American Philosophical Society*, n.s., vol. 64, part 7 (November 1974): 57.

5. Homer, *The Iliad*, trans. R. Lattimore (Chicago: University of Chicago Press, 1962), p. 79.

6. B. Bowden, ed., *Faster than Thought: A Symposium on Digital Computing Machines* (London: Sir Isaac Pitman and Sons, 1955), p. 211.

7. F. Bacon, quoted in Gregory, *A Treatise on Astronomy*, p. 140.

8. Copernicus, N. "On the revolutions of the heavenly spheres," trans. C. Wallis, in Hutchins, ed., *Great Books of the Western World*, vol. 16, pp. 514, 526.

9. J. Kepler, *The New Astronomy*, trans. W. Donahue (Cambridge, England: University Press, 1992), p. 514.

10. Rheticus, quoted in Duhem, *To Save the Phenomena*, p. 65.

11. J. Jandun, quoted in Duhem, *To Save the Phenomena*, p. 43.

12. Potano, quoted in Duhem, *To Save the Phenomena*, p. 54.

13. J. Cobb, Jr., and D. Griffin, *Process Theology: An Introductory Exposition* (Philadelphia: Westminster Press, 1976), p. 129.

14. H. Carter, *A View of Early Typography* (Oxford: Clarendon Press, 1969), p. 40.

15. J. Petreius, in N. Swerdlow, "Johannes Petreius's letter to Rheticus," *Isis* 83 (June 1992): 274.

16. P. de Medina, *A Navigator's Universe: The Libro de Cosmographia of 1538*, trans. U. Lamb (Chicago: University of Chicago Press, 1972), p. 181.

17. Price, "Gears from the Greeks," p. 54.

18. C. Thomas-Stanford, *Early Editions of Euclid's Elements*, trans. author (London: Charles Thomas-Stanford, 1926), plate 1a.

19. R. Zorach, "The new mediaeval aesthetic," *Wired*, January 1994, 48.

Chapter 5: An Emergent Fable of Astronomers and Stars

1. Donne, quoted in Nicolson, *Breaking the Circle*, p. 120.

2. Kepler, *The New Astronomy*, p. 508.

3. Fontenelle, quoted in I. B. Cohen, ed., *Isaac Newton's Papers & Letters on Natural Philosophy* (Cambridge, Mass: Harvard University Press, 1958), p. 456.

4. Galilei, *Two New Sciences*, p. 20.

5. Galilei, *Dialogue on the Great World Systems*, p. 462.

6. C. Hinshelwood, *The Vision of Nature* (Cambridge, England: University Press, 1961), p. 28.

7. Regiomontanus, *Disputationem Ioannis*, paraphrased in C. Kren, "Planetary latitudes: The *Theorica Gerardi* and Regiomontanus," *Isis* 68 (June 1977): 200.

8. O. Neugebauer, *A History of Ancient Mathematical Astronomy* (Berlin: Springer-Verlag, 1975), p. 3.

9. Ibid., 56.

10. G. Owen, *The Universe of the Mind* (Baltimore: Johns Hopkins University Press, 1971), p. 17.

11. Kepler, *The New Astronomy*, p. 573.

12. Ibid.

13. T. Hobbes, quoted in Blumenberg, *The Genesis of the Copernican World*, p. 44.

14. B. Hasslacher, "Parallel billiards and monster systems," *Daedalus* 121, no. 1 (winter 1992): 57.

15. L. d'Etaples, quoted in Duhem, *To Save the Phenomena*, p. 57.

16. A. Gore, *Earth in the Balance: Ecology and the Human Spirit* (Boston: Houghton Mifflin, 1992), p. 162.

Chapter 6: The Computer Within Living Memory

1. C. Babbage, quoted in F. Cajori, *A History of Mathematical Notations* (La Salle, Ill.: Open Court Publishing, 1928–29), p. 429.

2. Galilei, *Two New Sciences*, p. 189.

3. Ibid., 194.

4. Galilei, *Dialogue on the Great World Systems*, p. 463.

5. R. Descartes, "Rules for the direction of the mind," trans. E. Haldane and G. Ross, in R. Hutchins, ed., *Great Books of the Western World*, vol. 31, p. 18.

6. H. Goldstine, and J. von Neumann, "On the principles of large scale computing machines," in Taub, gen. ed., *Collected Works*, vol. 5, p. 20.

7. Descartes, "Rules for the direction of the mind," p. 32.

8. Aristotle, quoted in R. Sorabji, *Aristotle on Memory* (Providence, R.I.: Brown University Press, 1972), p. 55.

9. Descartes, "Rules for the direction of the mind," p. 35.

10. Ibid., 17.

11. E. Grosholz, "Descartes' unification of algebra and geometry," in S. Gaukroger, ed., *Descartes: Philosophy, Mathematics, and Physics* (Brighton, England: Harvester Press, 1980), p. 160.

12. Descartes, "Rules for the direction of the mind," p. 10.

13. Ibid., 5.

14. Ibid., 7.

15. Ibid., 7.

16. R. Descartes, quoted in C. Larmore, "Descartes' empirical epistemology," in Gaukroger, ed., *Descartes*, p. v.

17. Descartes, "Rules for the direction of the mind," p. 20.

18. Ibid., 16.

19. Ibid., 7.

20. Ibid., 13.

21. E. Dijkstra, "The humble programmer," in *Communications of the ACM*, October 1972, p. 865.

22. R. Descartes, *The Method, Meditations, and Philosophy*, trans. J. Veitch (New York: Tudor Publishing, 1947), p. 161.

23. Aristotle, "On the heavens," in Barnes, ed., *The Complete Works*, p. 481.

24. I. Kant, quoted in J. Kemp, *The Philosophy of Kant* (London: Oxford University Press, 1968), p. 32.

25. C. Langton, "Artificial life," in C. Langton, ed., *Artificial Life: SFI Studies in the Science of Complexity* (Reading, Mass.: Addison-Wesley, 1988), p. 41.

26. Descartes, "Rules for the direction of the mind," p. 34.

27. J. Wallis, quoted in Klein, *Greek Mathematical Thought*, p. 219.

28. R. Descartes, *The Geometry*, trans. D. Smith and M. Latham (La Salle, Ill.: Open Court Publishing, 1952), p. 9.

29. Descartes, "Rules for the direction of the mind," p. 29.

30. J. Locke, quoted in Cajori, *Mathematics in Liberal Education*, p. 52.

Chapter 7: Listening to Data

1. J. Kepler, quoted in M. Caspar, *Kepler*, trans. C. Hellman (London: Abelard-Schuman, 1959), p. 62.

2. J. Kepler, "Epitome of Copernican astronomy," trans. C. Wallis, in Hutchins, ed., *Great Books of the Western World*, vol. 16, p. 955.

3. Kepler, *The New Astronomy*, p. 589.

4. Ibid., 589.

5. Ibid., 207.

6. Ibid., 469.

7. Ibid., 411.

8. Ibid., 615.

9. Ibid., 283–84.

10. W. Pauli, *The Influence of Archetypal Ideas on Kepler's Theories* (New York: Pantheon Books, 1955), p. 156.

11. H. Butterfield, *The Origins of Modern Science* (New York: Macmillan, 1961), p. 63.

12. Galilei, *Dialogue on the Great World Systems*, p. 350.

13. Ibid., 469.

14. Kepler, *The New Astronomy*, pp. 285–86.

15. Ibid., 482.

16. Ibid., 453.

17. Ibid., 576.

18. Nicolson, *Breaking the Circle*, p. 154.

19. J. Mill, quoted in A. Lugg, "The process of discovery," *Philosophy of Science* 52 (March 1985): 209.

20. W. Whiston, quoted in W. Rouse Ball, *An Essay on Newton's "Principia"* (London: Macmillan, 1893), p. 9.

21. I. Newton, quoted in Rouse Ball, *Essay on Newton's "Principia,"* p. 17.

22. Newton, *Principia Mathematica*, p. 29.

23. Glaisher, quoted in Rouse Ball, *Essay on Newton's "Principia,"* p. 61.

24. Galilei, *Dialogue on the Great World Systems*, p. 222.

25. J. Flamsteed, quoted in I. B. Cohen, *Introduction to Newton's "Principia"* (Cambridge, Mass.: Harvard University Press, 1971), p. 175.

26. Ibid.

27. J. Keynes, quoted in D. Patinkin, "Keynes and econometrics: On the interaction between the macroeconomic revolutions of the interwar period," *Econometrica* 44, no. 6 (November 1976): 1102.

28. A. Einstein, quoted in Brockman, *The Third Culture*, p. 340.

29. J. Farrar, *An Elementary Treatise on Astronomy* (Cambridge, England: Hilliard, Metcalf, 1827), p. 134.

30. Conduitt, quoted in Rouse Ball, *Essay on Newton's "Principia,"* p. 26.

31. Newton, quoted in Cohen, *Introduction to Newton's "Principia,"* p. 79.

32. Cajori, in Newton, *Principia Mathematica,* p. xxxii.

33. Newton, *Principia Mathematica,* p. 6.

34. Ibid., 550.

35. R. Hooke, quoted in Rouse Ball, *Essay on Newton's "Principia,"* p. 70.

36. Newton, quoted in Rouse Ball, *Essay on Newton's "Principia,"* p. 158.
37. Ibid., 159.
38. J. Kepler, quoted in C. Baumgardt, *Johannes Kepler: Life and Letters* (New York: Philosophical Library, 1951), p. 139.
39. Galilei, *Dialogue on the Great World Systems*, p. 7.

Chapter 8: The Maths of the Industrial Age

1. Langer, *Philosophy in a New Key*, p. 82.
2. K. May, "Historiography: A perspective for computer scientists," in N. Metropolis et al., eds., *A History of Computing in the Twentieth Century* (New York: Academic Press, 1980), p. 17.
3. K. Wilson, "Science, industry, and the new Japanese challenge," *Proceedings of the IEEE* 72, no. 1, (January 1984): 10.
4. Quoted in F. Cajori, *A History of the Conceptions of Limits and Fluxions in Great Britain from Newton to Woodhouse* (Chicago: Open Court Publishing, 1919), p. 256.
5. J. Gowdy, "Higher selection processes in evolutionary economic change," *Journal of Evolutionary Economics* 2 (1992): 11.
6. *Bulletin of the Boston Public Library*, no. 1 (January–March 1922): 3.
7. E. Forbes, *Greenwich Observatory* (London: Taylor and Francis, 1975), p. 9.
8. J. Adams, *Scientific Papers*, W. Adams, ed. (Cambridge, England: University Press, 1896), pp. 328–29.
9. Mädler, quoted in M. Grosser, *The Discovery of Neptune* (Cambridge, Mass.: Harvard University Press, 1962), p. 56.
10. G. Adams, quoted in Grosser, *The Discovery of Neptune*, p. 79.
11. I. Grattan-Guinness, "Work for the hairdressers: The production of de Prony's logarithmic and trigonometric tables," *Annals of the History of Computing* 12, no. 3 (1990): 177.
12. G. Scheutz, *Specimens of Tables, Calculated, Stereomoulded, and Printed by Machinary* (London: Longman, Brown, 1857), p. vii.
13. Bowden, ed., *Faster than Thought*, p. 25.
14. Ibid.
15. L. Richardson, "The approximate arithmetical solution by finite differences of physical problems involving differential equations, with an application to the stresses in a masonry dam," *Philosophical Transactions of the Royal Society of London*, series A, 210 (February 1911): 325.
16. Goldstine, *The Computer from Pascal to von Neumann*, p. 130.
17. C. Babbage, quoted in J. Dubbey, *The Mathemetical Work of Charles Babbage* (Cambridge, England: University Press, 1978), p. 174.
18. G. de Prony, quoted in Grattan-Guinness, "Work for the hairdressers," p. 179.
19. A. Lovelace, quoted in Goldstine, *The Computer from Pascal to von Neumann*, p. 22.
20. C. Babbage, Boston Public Library Manuscript, Ms. E.210.19 v.2 (42) 20 March 1830, p. 1.

21. Scheutz, *Specimens of Tables,* p. 7.

22. J. P. Eckert, "The ENIAC," in Metropolis et al., eds., *A History of Computing,* p. 527.

23. C. Hodgson, *Mathematical and Scientific Library of Charles Babbage* (London: Hodgson and Son, 1872), p. 4.

24. Adams, *Scientific Papers,* p. xiv.

25. F. Moulton, *An Introduction to Celestial Mechanics,* 2d ed. (New York: Dover Publications, 1970), p. 30.

26. J. von Neumann, "The mathematician," in Taub, gen. ed., *Collected Works,* p. 2.

27. Bowden, ed., *Faster than Thought,* p. 27.

28. Goldstine, *The Computer from Pascal to von Neumann,* p. 142.

29. H. Goldstine and J. von Neumann, "Planning and coding problems for an electronic computing instrument," in Taub, gen. ed., *Collected Works,* p. 99.

30. D. Allen, *Relaxation Methods* (New York: McGraw-Hill, 1954), p. v.

31. S. Ulam, quoted in F. Ulam, ed., "Conversations with Rota," *Los Alamos Science,* no. 15 (special issue, 1987): 305.

32. N. Metropolis, "The age of computing: A personal memoir," *Daedalus* 121, no. 1 (winter 1992): 127.

33. S. Ulam, quoted in F. Ulam, ed., "Conversations with Rota," p. 311.

34. Descartes, quoted in Larmore, "Descartes' empirical epistemology," in Gaukroger, ed., *Descartes,* p. v.

35. Cohen, ed., *Isaac Newton's Papers & Letters,* p. 276.

36. G. Boole, quoted in Goldstine, *The Computer from Pascal to von Neumann,* p. 36.

37. F. Moulton, *Consider the Heavens* (New York: Doubleday Doran, 1940), p. 47.

38. C. Turbayne, *The Myth of Metaphor,* rev. ed. (Columbia: University of South Carolina Press, 1970), p. 47.

39. C. Babbage, *The Ninth Bridgewater Treatise* (London: John Murray, 1837), p. 32.

40. Laplace, quoted in Dantzig, *Number,* p. 136.

41. A. Hyman, "Introduction," in H. Buxton, *Memoir of the Life and Labours of the Late Charles Babbage,* A. Hyman, ed. (Cambridge, Mass., MIT Press, 1987), p. 7.

42. C. Babbage, *Passages from the Life of a Philosopher* (London: Longman, Green, 1864), p. 402.

43. Babbage, *The Ninth Bridgewater Treatise,* p. 48.

Chapter 9: The Advent of New Sciences and New Maths

1. Galilei, *Two New Sciences,* p. 215.

2. G. Galilei, "On motion," in *On Motion and on Mechanics,* trans. I. Drabkin (Madison: University of Wisconsin Press, 1960), p. 116.

3. S. Richardson, "Lewis Fry Richardson (1881–1953): A personal biography," *Journal of Conflict Resolution* 1, no. 3 (1957): 301.

4. D. Wilkinson, *Deadly Quarrels: Lewis F. Richardson and the Statistical Study of War* (Berkeley: University of California Press, 1980), p. 20.

5. L. Richardson, *Generalized Foreign Politics: A Study in Group Psychology* (Cambridge, England: University Press, 1939), p. 4.

6. Ibid., 3.

7. Ibid., 73.

8. Ibid., ii

9. *Nature* published eight notes: 18 May 1935, p. 830; 28 December 1935, p. 1025; 15 November 1941, p. 598; 19 August 1944, p. 240; 19 May 1945, p. 610; 27 July 1945, p. 135; 29 September 1951, p. 567; 24 November 1951, p. 920.

10. Richardson, *Generalized Foreign Politics*, p. 81.

11. L. Richardson, "Stability after the war," *Nature*, 19 August 1944, p. 240.

12. L. Richardson, "Could an arms race end without fighting?," *Nature*, 29 September 1951, 567.

13. Richardson, *Generalized Foreign Politics*, p. 86.

14. Ibid.

15. A. Rapaport, *The Origins of Violence: Approaches to the Study of Conflict* (New York: Paragon House, 1989), p. 375.

16. A. Rapaport, "Lewis F. Richardson's mathematical theory of war," *Journal of Conflict Resolution* 1, no. 3 (1957): 295.

17. Hanson, *Patterns of Discovery*, p. 46.

18. Rapaport, "Lewis F. Richardson's mathematical theory of war," p. 297.

19. R. Eckhardt, "Stan Ulam, John von Neumann, and the Monte Carlo method," *Los Alamos Science*, no. 15 (1987, special issue): 131.

20. A. Hall, "On an experimental determination of π," *The Messenger of Mathematics*, 2 (1873): 137.

21. Metropolis, "The age of computing," p. 123.

22. N. Metropolis, "The beginning of the Monte Carlo method," *Los Alamos Science*, no. 15 (1987, special issue): 127.

23. D. Shaw, quoted in S. Kaisler, *Parallel Computing Workshop Report* (1982), p. 30.

24. Kepler, *The New Astronomy*, p. 411.

25. Galilei, quoted in Duhem, *To Save the Phenomena*, p. 109.

26. Pontano, quoted in Duhem, *To Save the Phenomena*, p. 54.

27. Bellarmine, quoted in Duhem, *To Save the Phenomena*, p. 107.

28. S. Wolfram, "Cellular automata as models of complexity," *Nature,* 4 October 1984, 419.

29. R. Herman and K. Gardels, "Vehicular traffic flow," *Scientific American*, December 1963, 35.

30. Hasslacher, "Parallel billiards," p. 60.

31. Langer, *Philosophy in a New Key*, p. 86.

32. Hasslacher, "Parallel billiards," p. 61.

33. H. Goldstine and J. von Neumann, "On the principles of large scale computing machines," in Taub, gen. ed., *Collected Works*, vol. 5, p. 12.

34. Hasslacher, "Parallel billiards," p. 62.

Chapter 10: Listening to Neuron

1. J. Maxwell, quoted in Goldstine, *Computer from Pascal to von Neumann*, p. 34.
2. W. D. Hillis, *The Connection Machine* (Cambridge, Mass.: MIT Press, 1985), p. 3.
3. Ibid., 5.
4. Augustine, quoted in R. Quinones, *The Renaissance Discovery of Time* (Cambridge, Mass.: Harvard University Press, 1972), p. 14.
5. L. Richardson, *Weather Prediction by Numerical Process* (New York: Dover Publications, 1965), p. xi.
6. Ibid., 219.
7. C. Babbage, *On the Economy of Machinery and Manufactures* (New York: Augustus M. Kelley, 1963), p. 47.
8. Richardson, *Weather Prediction*, p. 219.
9. J. von Neumann, "Numerical integration of the barotropic vorticity equation," in Taub, gen. ed., *Collected Works*, vol. 6, p. 421.
10. B. de Spinoza, "Ethics," in R. Hutchins, ed., *Great Books of the Western World*, vol. 31, p. 373
11. Richardson, *Generalized Foreign Politics*, p. 3.
12. W. Wallace, *Galileo's Early Notebooks: The Physical Questions* (Notre Dame, Ind.: University of Notre Dame Press, 1977), p. 50.
13. Jacobs, *The Death and Life of Great American Cities*, p. 45.
14. W. D. Hillis, "The Connection Machine (Computer Architecture of the New Wave)," MIT A.I. Memo no. 646, 1981, p. 3.
15. Descartes, "Rules for the direction of the mind," p. 10.
16. O. McBryan, "New architectures: Performance highlights and new algorithms," *Parallel Computing* 7 (1988): 481.
17. Hillis, "The Connection Machine (Computer Architecture of the New Wave)," p. 24.
18. Galilei, *Two New Sciences*, p. 20.
19. Gunn, et al., *Hierarchical Algorithm*, p. 1.
20. J. Holland, quoted in J. Horgan, "From complexity to perplexity," *Scientific American*, June 1995, 105.

Chapter 11: The New Intermaths of the Information Age

1. Sturt, *The Wheelwright's Shop*, p. 74.
2. T. Sejnowski and C. Rosenberg, "Parallel networks that learn to pronounce English text," *Complex Systems* 1 (1987): 151.
3. Hertz, quoted in Dantzig, *Number*, p. 76.
4. P. Shea and F. Liu, "Operational experience with a neural network in the detection of explosives in checked airline luggage" (paper presented at the IJCNN 90 Conference, June 1990), 2.
5. M. Gardner, "The fantastic combinations of John Conway's new solitaire game 'life'," *Scientific American,* October 1970, 120.
6. Ibid., 121.

Chapter 12: The Patterns Within Life

1. H. Gleason, *Thoreau Country* (San Francisco: Sierra Club Books, 1975), p. xiv.
2. R. Southwell, *Relaxation Methods in Theoretical Physics* (Oxford: Clarendon Press, 1949), p. 2.
3. W. D. Hillis, "Co-evolving parasites improve simulated evolution as an optimization procedure," in Forrest, ed., *Emergent Computation*, p. 233.
4. S. Kirkpatrick et al., "Optimization by simulated annealing," *Science*, 13 May 1983, 676.
5. J. Koza, "Genetic programming: A paradigm for genetically breeding populations of computer programs to solve problems" (Stanford University Report no. STAN-CS-90–1314, 1990), 23.
6. Laplace, quoted in Dantzig, *Number*, p. 136
7. Tarantola, unpublished interview.
8. J. Scott, *The Scientific Work of René Descartes (1596–1650)* (London: Taylor and Francis, 1952), p. 28.
9. E. Mach, *Popular Scientific Lectures*, 3d ed., trans. T. McCormack (Chicago: Open Court Publishing, 1898), p. 193.
10. A. Aaboe, "Scientific astronomy in antiquity," in F. Hodson, ed., *The Place of Astronomy in the Ancient World* (London: Oxford University Press, 1974), p. 23.
11. Richardson, *Weather Prediction*, p. xi.
12. C. Stanfill and D. Waltz, "Toward memory-based reasoning," *Communications of the ACM* 29, no. 12 (December 1986): 1218.
13. Babbage, *Passages*, p. 36.
14. Hasslacher, "Parallel billiards,"p. 65.

Chapter 13: The Life Within Patterns

1. D. Hammerstrom, "Neural networks at work," *IEEE Spectrum*, June 1993, 26.
2. G. Johnson, "Sifting market patterns for profit," *New York Times*, 11 September 1995, D1.
3. W. Stevens, "Extinction of the fittest may be the legacy of lost habitats," *New York Times*, 27 September 1994, C3.
4. Holland et al., *Induction*, p. 104.
5. W. B. Arthur, "Inductive reasoning and bounded rationality," *American Economic Review* 84, no. 2 (May 1994): 408.
6. M. Resnick, *Turtles, Termites, and Traffic Jams* (Cambridge, Mass.: MIT Press, 1994), p. 124.
7. S. Kuznets, "Parts and wholes in economics," in D. Lerner, ed., *Parts and Wholes* (New York: Free Press of Glencoe, 1963), p. 58.
8. J. Gleick, "New appreciation of the complexity in a flock of birds," *New York Times*, 24 November 1987, C1.

9. Holland et al., *Induction*, p. 2.

10. W. B. Arthur, "On designing economic agents that behave like human agents," *Journal of Evolutionary Economics* 3 (1993): 2.

11. Holland et al., *Induction*, p. 171.

12. Richardson, *Generalized Foreign Politics*, p. 27.

13. Ibid., 3.

14. M. Browne, "Micro-machines help solve intractable problem of turbulence," *New York Times*, 3 January 1995, B13.

15. Whitehead, quoted in Hodgson, *Economics and Evolution*, p. 196.

Chapter 14: Computing the Patterns of Societies and Economies

1. C. Jelavich and B. Jelavich, *The Balkans* (Englewood Cliffs, N.J.: Prentice-Hall, 1965), p. 29.

2. S. Tambiah, "Ethnic conflict in the world today," *American Ethnologist*, no. 16 (1989): 340.

3. G. Silverberg and B. Verspagen, "Collective learning, innovation and growth in a boundedly rational, evolutionary world," *Journal of Evolutionary Economics* 4 (1994): 207ff.

4. A. Smith, *An Enquiry into the Nature and Causes of the Wealth of Nations*, E. Cannon, ed. (Chicago: University of Chicago Press, 1976), p. 100.

5. A. Smith, "The principles which lead and direct philosophical enquiries: Illustrated by the history of astronomy," in I. Ross, ed., *Adam Smith: Essays on Philosophical Subjects* (Oxford: Clarendon Press, 1980), p. 66.

6. T. Veblen, quoted in Hodgson, *Economics and Evolution*, p. 126.

7. W. Blake, quoted in M. Boden, *The Creative Mind: Myths and Mechanisms* (New York: Basic Books, 1991), p. 262.

8. R. Thompson, *Theories of Ethnicity: A Critical Appraisal* (New York: Greenwood Press, 1989), p. 43.

9. A. Phillips, "Mechanical models in economic dynamics," *Economica* Vol. 17 (August 1950): 283.

10. Ibid., 284.

11. Ibid., 293.

12. Ibid., 305.

13. Richardson, *Generalized Foreign Politics*, p. 85.

14. A. Marshall, quoted in Hodgson, *Economics and Evolution*, p. 99.

15. Marshall, quoted in D. Warsh, "In which the salad course comes, and goes," *Boston Globe*, 6 March 1994, 85.

16. Marshall, quoted in D. Warsh, "The Colorado Trail," *Boston Globe*, 30 January 1994, 49.

17. Smith, *Wealth of Nations*, vol. 2, p. 411.

18. Anderson, *Imagined Communities*, p. 165.

19. Ibid., 185.

20. J. Keynes, *The General Theory of Employment, Interest, and Money* (San Diego, Calif.: Harcourt Brace Jovanovich, 1953), p. 305.

21. R. Lucas and T. Sargent, "After Keynesian macroeconomics," in R. Lucas and T. Sargent, eds., *Rational Expectations and Econometric Practice* (Minneapolis: University of Minnesota Press, 1981), p. 296.

22. J. Keynes, "Professor Tinbergen's method," in D. Muggridge, ed., *The Collected Works of John Maynard Keynes*, vol. 14 (London: Macmillan, 1973), p. 309.

23. Ibid., 318.

24. Keynes, *The General Theory*, pp. 297–98.

25. P. Samuelson, *Foundations of Economic Analysis* (Cambridge, Mass.: Harvard University Press, 1963), p. 6.

26. W. B. Arthur and G. McNicoll, "Large-scale simulation models in population development," *Population and Development Review*, December 1975, 254.

27. K. Popper, quoted in T. Mayer, *Truth vs. Precision in Economics* (Brookfield, Vt.: Edward Elgar, 1993), p. 26.

28. F. Hayek, quoted in Hodgson, *Economics and Evolution*, p. 154.

29. G. Becker, *The Economic Approach to Human Behavior* (Chicago: University of Chicago Press, 1976), p. 14.

30. Ibid., 5.

Chapter 15: Computing the New Realities of the Information Age

1. H. Simon, *The Sciences of the Artificial* (Cambridge, Mass.: MIT Press, 1969), p. 106.

2. A. Whitehead, *Adventures of Ideas* (New York: Free Press, 1933), p. 92.

3. J. Flores, "Que assimilated, brother, yo soy asimilao: The structuring of Puerto Rican identity in the U.S.," *Journal of Ethnic Studies* 13, no. 3 (1985): 11.

4. Hodgson, *Economics and Evolution*, p. 69.

5. J. Schumpeter, paraphrased in K. Iwai, "Towards a disequilibrium theory of long-run profits," *Journal of Evolutionary Economics* 1 (1991): 20.

6. R. LeVine, *Culture, Behavior, and Personality* (Chicago: Aldine Publishing, 1973), p. 146.

7. Resnick, *Turtles, Termites, and Traffic Jams*, p. 66.

8. Samuelson, *Foundations of Economic Analysis*, p. 19.

9. Casson, quoted in Gowdy, "Higher selection processes in evolutionary economic change," p. 11.

10. P. Anderson, "More is different: Broken symmetry and the nature of the hierarchical structure of science," *Science*, 4 August 1972, 393–95.

11. Hodgson, *Economics and Evolution*, p. 253.

12. G. Dosi, "Some thoughts on the promises, challenges and dangers of an 'evolutionary perspective' in economics," *Journal of Evolutionary Economics* 1 (1991): 6.

13. P. Romer, quoted in P. Robinson, "Paul Romer," *Forbes ASAP* (1995): 68.

14. Boulding, "What is evolutionary economics?" p. 14.

15. W. B. Arthur, "Positive feedbacks in the economy," *Scientific American*, February 1990, 93.

16. Gowdy, "Higher selection processes in evolutionary economic change," p. 11.

17. M. Shurmer and P. Swann, "An analysis of the process generating *de facto* standards in the PC spreadsheet software market," *Journal of Evolutionary Economics* 5 (1995): 119ff.

18. R. Marks, "Breeding hybrid strategies: Optimal behaviour for oligopolists," *Journal of Evolutionary Economics* 2 (1992): 18.

19. Ibid., 22.

20. P. Davies, quoted in Brockman, *The Third Culture*, p. 310.

21. J. Holland, *Hidden Order: How Adaptation Builds Complexity* (Reading, Mass.: Helix Books, 1995), p. 84.

22. Friedman, *Essays in Positive Economics*, p. 21.

23. Galilei, *Dialogue on the Great World Systems*, p. 249.

24. P. Krugman, quoted in D. Warsh, "What difference will it make?" *Boston Globe*, 9 October 1994, A1.

25. Kuznets, "Parts and wholes in economics," p. 70.

26. S. Wright, quoted in Hodgson, *Economics and Evolution*, p. 215.

27. M. Strober, "Rethinking economics through a feminist lens," *American Economic Review* 84, no. 2 (May 1994): 144.

28. T. Bergstrom, "On the evolution of altruistic ethical rules for siblings," *American Economic Review* 85, no. 1 (March 1995): 58–59.

29. W. B. Arthur, "On designing economic agents that behave like human agents," *Journal of Evolutionary Economics* 3 (1993): 3.

Chapter 16: Computing the Patterns of Bodies and Minds

1. O. W. Holmes, quoted in Cajori, *Mathematics in Liberal Education*, p. 117.

2. S. Kauffman, "Requirements for evolvability in complex systems: Orderly dynamics and frozen components," in Forrest, ed., *Emergent Computation*, p. 137.

3. Ibid., 137.

4. Ibid., 141.

5. H. Hertz, quoted in Dantzig, *Number*, p. 76.

6. D. Freedman, "AI helps researchers find meaning in molecules," *Science*, 13 August 1993, 844.

7. Gunn et al., *Hierarchical Algorithm*, p. 1.

8. Freedman, "AI helps researchers," p. 844.

9. Gunn et al., *Hierarchical Algorithm*, p.1.

10. D. Farmer, "A Rosetta stone for connectionism," in Forrest, ed., *Emergent Computation*, p. 168.

11. Brockman, *The Third Culture*, p. 211.

12. Farmer, "A Rosetta stone for connectionism," p. 171.

13. C. Langton, quoted in Brockman, *The Third Culture*, p. 349.

14. Organizers of the Dartmouth Conference, quoted in Crevier, *AI*, p. 26.

15. H. Simon, quoted in D. MacKenzie, "The automation of proof: A historical and sociological exploration," *IEEE Annals of the History of Computing* 17, no. 3 (1995): 12.

16. MacKenzie, "The automation of proof," p. 12.

17. Ibid., 14.

18. Sturt, *The Wheelwright's Shop*, p. 70.

19. Crevier, *AI*, p. 209.

20. S. Omohundro, "Geometric learning tasks," in Forrest, ed., *Emergent Computation*, p. 309.

21. D. Lenat, quoted in Crevier, *AI*, p. 240.

22. D. Lenat, "Artificial intelligence: A crucial storehouse of commonsense knowledge is now taking shape," *Scientific American*, September 1995, 80.

23. G. B. Shaw, quoted in Mayer, *Truth vs. Precision in Economics*, p. 27.

24. L. Fogel et al., *Artificial Intelligence Through Simulated Evolution* (New York: Wiley, 1966), p. 9.

25. W. D. Hillis, quoted in Brockman, *The Third Culture*, p. 382.

26. Ibid.

Chapter 17: Listening to Life

1. Thoreau, "Walden," in Atkinson, ed., *Walden and Other Writings*, p. 47.

2. Ibid., 85.

3. Thoreau, "Walking," in Atkinson, ed., *Walden and Other Writings*, p. 629.

4. H. Hurst, *The Nile: A General Account of the River and the Utilization of Its Waters* (London: Constable, 1952), p. 60.

5. Ibid., vii.

6. "CIESIN's gateway," The Innovation Network, http://www.ciesin.org, 1995.

7. Galilei, *Dialogue on the Great World Systems*, p. 462.

8. K. Kelly, *Out of Control: The New Biology of Machines, Social Systems, and the Economic World* (Reading, Mass.: Addison-Wesley, 1994), p. 157.

9. Thoreau, "Walden," in Atkinson, ed., *Walden and Other Writings*, p. 15.

10. Laplace, quoted in Dantzig, *Number*, p. 136.

11. Tarantola, unpublished interview.

12. R. Malone et al., "Climate, the ocean, and parallel computing," *Los Alamos Science*, no. 21 (1993): 206.

13. W. Broad, "Hot vents in the sea floor may drive El Niño," *New York Times*, 25 April 1995, C7.

14. M. Condon, quoted in, "Struggling with insect research? Ask a seventh grader for help," *New York Times*, 29 August 1995, C5.

15. D. Chandler, "From afar, kids do science on the 'net," *Boston Globe*, 18 September 1995, 28.

16. A. Whitehead, *Process and Reality: Corrected Edition*, D. Griffin and D. Sherburne, eds. (New York: Free Press, 1978), p. 168.

17. Pea, quoted in Chandler, "From afar," p. 28.

18. F. Flam, "Ecologist plans to let cyberlife run wild in internet reserve," *Science*, 20 May 1994, 1085.

19. Kelly, *Out of Control*, p. 372.

20. S. Kumar, "Concurrent genetic algorithms for structural optimization on a massively parallel computer," Thinking Machines seminar series, 17 June 1994.

21. W. Shenouda, "Resettlement of population in the high Aswân dam project," *Seventh International Conference on Large Dams*, (Paris: International Commission on Large Dams, 1991), p. 100.

22. W. Stevens, "New rules for old dams can revive rivers," *New York Times*, 28 November 1995, C1.

23. G. Zipf, *Selected Studies of the Principle of Relative Frequency in Language* (Cambridge, Mass.: Harvard University Press, 1932).

24. M. Goodman, personal communication.

25. D. Farmer, quoted in Kelly, *Out of Control*, p. 431.

26. Descartes, "Objections against the meditations, and replies," p. 289.

The AfterMath

1. B. Rimland, "Matching wits with twin savants," *Psychology Today* (August 1978), 74.

2. W. B. Arthur, "Inductive reasoning and bounded rationality," *American Economic Review* 84, no. 2 (May 1994): 406.

3. E. de Gamaches, quoted in Duhem, *Aim and Structure*, p. 49.

4. S. Ulam, quoted in F. Ulam, ed., "Conversations with Rota," p. 311.

5. Hillis, quoted in Brockman, *The Third Culture*, p. 384.

6. Smith, *Wealth of Nations*, p. 100.

7. V. Vinge, "Technological singularity," *Whole Earth Review*, winter 1993, 88.

8. Ibid., 90.

9. Kelly, *Out of Control*, p. 419.

10. Ibid., 412.

11. Ibid., 127.

12. T. Ray, quoted in Kelly, *Out of Control*, p. 297.

13. T. Ray, "How I created life in a virtual universe," *Bionomic Perspectives*, spring 1993, 3.

14. Vinge, "Technological singularity," p. 94.

15. Resnick, *Turtles, Termites, and Traffic Jams*, p. 86.

16. I. Newton, quoted in Cohen, ed., *Isaac Newton's Papers & Letters*, p. 371.

17. H. Helmholtz, quoted in Cajori, *Mathematics in Liberal Education*, p. 103.

18. E. Mayr, quoted in Hodgson, *Economics and Evolution*, p. 248.

19. J. Hicks, quoted in D. Hendry, "Econometrics—alchemy or science?" *Economica* 47 (Nov. 1980), 402.

20. F. Hahn, quoted in Hodgson, *Economics and Evolution*, p. 266.

21. Thoreau, "Walden," in Atkinson, ed., *Walden and Other Writings*, p. 106.

22. J. Schumpeter, quoted in Gowdy, "Higher selection processes," p. 10.

23. Langer, *Philosophy in a New Key*, p. 82.

BIBLIOGRAPHY

Introduction and Place

Aaboe, A. "Scientific astronomy in antiquity." In F. Hodson, ed., *The Place of Astronomy in the Ancient World.* London: Oxford University Press, 1974.

Adams, T. *Typographia: Or the Printer's Instructor.* Philadelphia: Johnson, 1851.

Al-Kishi, J. *The Planetary Equatorium.* Translated by E. Kennedy. Princeton, N.J.: Princeton University Press, 1960.

Aristotle. "On the heavens." In J. Barnes, ed., *The Complete Works of Aristotle: The Revised Oxford Translation.* Princeton, N.J.: Princeton University Press, 1984.

——. "The physics." In J. Barnes, ed., *The Complete Works of Aristotle: The Revised Oxford Translation.* Princeton, N.J.: Princeton University Press, 1984.

Autolycus. *The Books of Autolycus: On a Moving Sphere and on Risings and Settings.* Translated by F. Bruin. Beirut: American University of Beirut, 1971.

Bailey, J. "First we reshape our computers, then our computers reshape us: The broader intellectual impact of parallelism." *Daedalus* 121, no. 1 (winter 1992).

——. "The ghosts of computers past: Understanding data parallel architecture in the context of the human computing era." In H. Simon, ed., *Scientific Applications of the Connection Machine.* Singapore: World Scientific, 1989.

Baumgardt, C. *Johannes Kepler: Life and Letters.* New York: Philosophical Library, 1951.

Blumenberg, H. *The Genesis of the Copernican World.* Translated by R. Wallace. Cambridge, Mass.: MIT Press, 1987.

Brahe, T. *Tycho Brahe's Description of His Instruments and Scientific Work as Given in Astronomiae Instauratae Mechanica.* Translated by H. Raeder. Copenhagen: Ejnar Munksgaard, 1946.

Brearley, H. *Time Telling Through the Ages.* New York: Doubleday Page, 1919.

Brewster, D. *Memoirs of the Life, Writings, and Discoveries of Sir Isaac Newton.* Edinburgh: Thomas Constable, 1855.

Briggs, H. *The Effects of Errors in Surveying.* London: Charles Griffin, 1912.

Bronowski, J. *The Ascent of Man.* Boston: Little, Brown and Company, 1973.

Butterfield, H. *The Origins of Modern Science 1300–1800.* New York: Macmillan, 1951.

Cajori, F. *A History of the Conceptions of Limits and Fluxions in Great Britain from Newton to Woodhouse.* Chicago: Open Court Publishing, 1919.

———. *A History of Mathematical Notations. Vols. 1, 2.* La Salle, Ill.: Open Court Publishing, 1928–29.

———. *Mathematics in Liberal Education.* Boston: Christopher Publishing House, 1928.

———. *The Teaching and History of Mathematics in the United States.* Washington, D.C.: Government Printing Office, 1890.

Callahan, J. *Four Views of Time in Ancient Philosophy.* Cambridge, Mass.: Harvard University Press, 1948.

Carder, J. *Art Historical Problems of a Roman Land Surveying Manuscript: The Codex Arcerianus A, Wolfenbütel.* New York: Garland Publishing, 1978.

Carter, H. *A View of Early Typography.* Oxford: Clarendon Press, 1969.

Caspar, M. *Kepler.* Translated by C. Hellman. London: Abelard-Schuman, 1959.

Christianson, J. "Tycho's treatise on the comet of 1577." *Isis* 70 (March 1979).

Cipolla, C. *Clocks and Culture: 1300–1700.* New York: Walker, 1967.

Clagett, M. "The medieval Latin translations from the Arabic of the *Elements* of Euclid, with special emphasis on the versions of Adelard of Bath." *Isis* 44, parts I, II, nos. 135–136 (June 1953).

Clair, C. *A Chronology of Printing.* London: Cassell, 1969.

Cohen, I. B. *Introduction to Newton's "Principia."* Cambridge, Mass.: Harvard University Press, 1971.

Cohen, I. B., ed. *Isaac Newton's Papers & Letters On Natural Philosophy.* Cambridge, Mass.: Harvard University Press, 1958.

Cooper, D. *Computer Science: Past, Present, and Future.* Swansea, Wales: University College of Swansea, 1968.

Copernicus, N. "On the revolutions." In E. Rosen, trans., *Nicholas Copernicus: Complete Works.* Baltimore: Johns Hopkins University Press, 1978.

———. "On the revolutions of the heavenly spheres." Translated by C. Wallis. In R. Hutchins, ed., *Great Books of the Western World.* Vol. 16. Chicago: Encyclopedia Britannica, 1939.

Crone, E., et al., eds. *The Principal Works of Simon Stevin.* Amsterdam: Swets and Zeitlinger, 1961.

Davis, J., and H. Merrick. *Direction of a Line.* Ann Arbor, Mich.: Geroge Wahr, 1910.

Descartes, R. *The Geometry.* Translated by D. Smith and M. Latham. La Salle, Ill.: Open Court Publishing, 1952.

———. *The Method, Meditations, and Philosophy.* Translated by J. Veitch. New York: Tudor Publishing, 1947.

———. "Objections against the meditations, and replies." Translated by E. Haldane and G. Ross. In R. Hutchins, ed., *Great Books of the Western World.* Vol. 31. Chicago: Encyclopedia Britannica, 1952.

———. "Rules for the direction of the mind." Translated by E. Haldane and G. Ross. In R. Hutchins, ed., *Great Books of the Western World.* Vol. 31. Chicago: Encyclopedia Britannica, 1952.

Dilke, O. *The Roman Land Surveyors.* Newton, England: Abbot, David and Charles, 1971.

Dreyer, J. *A History of Astronomy from Thales to Kepler.* 2d ed. New York: Dover Publications, 1953.

———. *Tycho Brahe: A Picture of Scientific Life and Work in the Sixteenth Century.* New York: Dover Publications, 1963.

Duhem, P. *The Aim and Structure of Physical Theory.* Translated by P. Wiener. New York: Atheneum Press, 1962.

———. *To Save the Phenomena: An Essay on the Idea of Physical Theory from Plato to Galileo.* Translated by E. Doland and C. Maschler. Chicago: University of Chicago Press, 1969.

Eisenstein, E. *The Printing Press as an Agent of Change: Communications and Cultural Transformations in Early Modern Europe.* 2 vols. Cambridge, England: University Press, 1979.

Ellis, B. "The origin and nature of Newton's laws of motion." In R. Colodny, ed., *Beyond the Edge of Certainty: Essays in Contemporary Science and Philosophy.* Englewood Cliffs, N.J.: Prentice-Hall, 1965.

Feyerabend, P. "Problems of empiricism." In R. Colodny, ed., *Beyond the Edge of Certainty: Essays in Contemporary Science and Philosophy.* Englewood Cliffs N.J.: Prentice-Hall, 1965.

Fraser, D. *Newton's Interpolation Formulas.* London: Layton, 1930.

Gade, J. *The Life and Times of Tycho Brahe.* Princeton, N.J.: Princeton University Press, 1947.

Galilei, G. *Dialogue on the Great World Systems in the Salusbury Translation.* Edited by G. de Santilla. Chicago: University of Chicago Press, 1953.

———. *Dialogues Concerning Two New Sciences.* Translated by H. Crew and A. Salvio. New York: Macmillan, 1914.

———. "On mechanics." Translated by S. Drake. In *On Motion and On Mechanics.* Madison: University of Wisconsin Press, 1960.

———. "On motion." Translated by I. Drabkin. In *On Motion and On Mechanics.* Madison: University of Wisconsin Press, 1960.

Gaukroger, S. "Descartes' project for a mathematical physics." In S. Gaukroger, ed., *Descartes: Philosophy, Mathematics, and Physics.* Sussex, England: Harvester Press, 1980.

Gerulaitis, L. *Printing and Publishing in Fifteenth Century Venice.* Chicago: American Library Association, 1974.

Gingerich, O. "Astronomy in the age of Columbus." *Scientific American*, November 1992.

———. *The Great Copernicus Chase.* Cambridge, Mass.: Sky Publishing, 1992.

Gleason, H. *Thoreau Country.* San Francisco: Sierra Club Books, 1975.

Goldschmidt, E. *The Printed Book of the Renaissance.* Cambridge, England: University Press, 1950.

Goldstein, B. *The Astronomy of Levi ben Gerson (1288–1344): A Critical Edition of Chapters 1–20 with Translation and Commentary.* New York: Springer-Verlag, 1985.

Gore, A. *Earth in the Balance: Ecology and the Human Spirit.* Boston: Houghton Mifflin, 1992.

Goudsmit, S., and R. Claiborne. *Time.* New York: Time, 1966.

Graves, F. *A History of Education During the Middle Ages and the Transition to Modern Times.* New York: Macmillan, 1920.

Grosholz, E. "Descartes' unification of algebra and geometry." In S. Gaukroger, ed., *Descartes: Philosophy, Mathematics, and Physics.* Sussex, England: Harvester Press, 1980.

Hamilton, F. *Books Before Typography.* United Typothetae of America, 1918.

Hamilton, H., and W. Falconer, trans. *The Geography of Strabo.* London: Bohn, 1854.

Hanson, N. *Patterns of Discovery.* Cambridge, England: University Press, 1958.

Haskins, C. *Studies in the History of Mediaeval Science.* Cambridge, Mass.: Harvard University Press, 1924.

Heath, T. *Aristarchus of Samos: The Ancient Copernicus.* Oxford: Clarendon Press, 1913.

———. *Diophantus of Alexandria: A Study in the History of Greek Algebra.* New York: Dover Publications, 1964.

———. *A History of Greek Mathematics.* Oxford: Clarendon Press, 1921.

Hinshelwood, C. *The Vision of Nature.* Cambridge, England: University Press, 1961.

Hobson, E. *John Napier and the Invention of Logarithms.* Cambridge, England: University Press, 1914.

Homer. *The Iliad.* Translated by R. Lattimore. Chicago: University of Chicago Press, 1962.

Jacobs, J. *The Death and Life of Great American Cities.* New York: Random House, 1961.

Jaki, S. "Introductory essay." In P. Duhem, *To Save the Phenomena: An Essay on the Idea of Physical Theory from Plato to Galileo.* Translated by E. Doland and C. Maschler. Chicago: University of Chicago Press, 1969.

Johnson, G. "Sifting hidden market patterns for profit." *New York Times*, 11 September 1995.

Jones, A. "The adaptation of Babylonian methods in Greek numerical astronomy." *Isis* 82 (1991).

Kennedy, E. "Late medieval planetary theory." *Isis* 57, no. 189 (1966).

Kepler, J. "Epitome of Copernican astronomy." Translated by C. Wallis. In R. Hutchins, ed., *Great Books of the Western World*. Vol. 16. Chicago: Encyclopedia Britannica, 1939.

———. *The New Astronomy*. Translated by W. Donahue. Cambridge, England: University Press, 1992.

Kidwell, P., and P. Ceruzzi. *Landmarks in Digital Computing*. Washington, D.C.: Smithsonian Institution Press, 1994.

Klein, J. *Greek Mathematical Thought and the Origin of Algebra*. Translated by E. Braun. Cambridge, Mass.: MIT Press, 1968.

Knorr, W. *Textual Studies in Ancient and Medieval Geometry*. Boston: Birkhäuser, 1989.

Koyre, A. *Metaphysics and Measurement*. Cambridge, Mass.: Harvard University Press, 1968.

Kren, C. "Planetary latitudes: The *Theorica Gerardi* and Regiomontanus." *Isis* 68 (June 1977).

Kuhn, T. *The Structure of Scientific Revolutions*. 2d ed., enlarged. Chicago: University of Chicago Press, 1970.

Landes, D. *Revolution in Time*. Cambridge, Mass.: Belknap Press, 1983.

Langer, S. *Philosophy in a New Key*. New York: Mentor Books, 1951.

Larmore, C. "Descartes' empirical epistemology." In S. Gaukroger, ed., *Descartes: Philosophy, Mathematics, and Physics*. Sussex, England: Harvester Press, 1980.

Lehmann-Haupt, C. "The making of an economist, part 2." *New York Times*, 14 February 1994.

Lloyd, G. "Saving the appearances." *The Classical Quarterly* 28 (1978).

Lloyd, H. *Some Outstanding Clocks over Seven Hundred Years 1250–1950*. London: Leonard Hill, 1958.

Locke, J. *An Essay Concerning Human Understanding*. Edited by A. Pringle-Pattison. Oxford: Clarendon Press, 1924.

Lugg, A. "The process of discovery." *Philosophy of Science* 52 (March 1985).

MacPike, E. *Helvelius, Flamsteed, and Halley: Three Contemporary Astronomers and Their Mutual Interactions*. London: Taylor and Francis, 1937.

Mahoney, M. "The beginnings of algebraic thought in the seventeenth century." In S. Gaukroger, ed., *Descartes: Philosophy, Mathematics, and Physics*. Sussex, England: Harvester Press, 1980.

Maull, N. "Cartesian optics and the geometrization of nature." In S. Gaukroger, ed., *Descartes: Philosophy, Mathematics, and Physics*. Sussex, England: Harvester Press, 1980.

McCluskey, S. "Early Christian astronomy." *Isis* 81 (March 1990).

McCormack, R. "One hour with Seymour Cray." *High Performance Computing and Communications Week* 2, no. 46 (26 November 1993).

McMurtrie, D. *The Book: The Story of Printing and Bookmaking*. London: Oxford University Press, 1943.

Medina, P. de. *A Navigator's Universe: The Libro de Cosmographia of 1538*. Translated by U. Lamb. Chicago: University of Chicago Press, 1972.

Mendelssohn, K. *Science and Western Domination*. London: Thames and Hudson, 1976.

Middleton-Wake, C. *The Invention of Printing*. London: John Murray, 1897.

Munsell, J. *Outline of the History of Printing*. Albany, N.Y.: Munsell, 1839.

Nahm, M., ed. *Selections from Early Greek Philosophy*. New York: Appleton-Century-Crofts, 1964.

Napier, J. *The Construction of the Wonderful Canon of Logarithms*. Translated by W. MacDonald. Edinburgh: William Blackwood, 1889.

Napier, M. *Memoirs of John Napier of Merchiston*. Edinburgh: William Blackwood, 1834.

Negroponte, N. *Being Digital*. New York: Knopf, 1995.

Neugebauer, O. *A History of Ancient Mathematical Astronomy*. Berlin: Springer-Verlag, 1975.

Newton, I. *Principia Mathematica*. Translated by F. Cajori. Berkeley: University of California Press, 1934.

Newton, R. "Astronomy in ancient literate societies." In F. Hodson, ed., *The Place Of Astronomy in the Ancient World*. London: Oxford University Press, 1974.

Nicolson, M. *Breaking the Circle*. Rev. ed. New York: Columbia University Press, 1960.

Nicolson, M., and G. Rousseau. *"This Long Disease My Life": Alexander Pope and the Sciences*. Princeton, N.J.: Princeton University Press, 1968.

Ong, W. *Ramus: Method, and the Decay of Dialogue*. Cambridge, Mass.: Harvard University Press, 1958.

Owen, G. *The Universe of the Mind*. Baltimore: Johns Hopkins University Press, 1971.

Pauli, W. *The Influence of Archetypal Ideas on Kepler's Theories*. New York: Pantheon Books, 1955.

Pedersen, O., and M. Pihl. *Early Physics and Astronomy: A Historical Introduction*. New York: American Elsevier, 1974.

Penrose, F. *A Method of Predicting by Graphical Construction Occultations of Stars by the Moon, and Solar Eclipses for Any Given Place*. London: Macmillan, 1869.

Peters, C., and E. Knobel. *Ptolemy's Catalogue of Stars: A Revision of the Almagest*. Washington, D.C.: Carnegie Institution of Washington, 1915.

Price, D. "Gears from the Greeks: The Antikythera mechanism—a calendar computer from ca. 80 BC." *Transactions of the American Philosophical Society*, n.s., 64, part 7 (November 1974).

Prior, A. *Papers on Time and Tense*. Oxford: Clarendon Press, 1968.

Proctor, R. *Old and New Astronomy*. London: Longmans, Green, 1892.

Ptolemy, C. "The almagest." Translated by R. Taliaferro. In R. Hutchins, ed., *Great Books of the Western World*. Vol. 16. Chicago: Encyclopedia Britannica, 1939.

Putnam, G. *Books and Their Makers During the Middle Ages*. New York: Putnam's Sons, 1896.

Quinn, J. *The Doctrine of Time in St. Thomas*. Washington, D.C.: Catholic University of America Press, 1960.

Quinones, R. *The Renaissance Discovery of Time.* Cambridge, Mass.: Harvard University Press, 1972.

Regiomontanus. *On Triangles.* Translated by B. Hughes. Madison: University of Wisconsin Press, 1967.

Romilly, J. de. *Time in Greek Tragedy.* Ithaca, N.Y.: Cornell University Press, 1968.

Rouse Ball, W. *An Essay on Newton's "Principia."* London: Macmillan, 1893.

Ruby, J. "The origins of scientific 'law'." *Journal of the History of Ideas* 47, no. 3 (July–September 1986).

Sachs, A. "Babylonian observational astronomy." In F. R. Hodson, ed., *The Place of Astronomy in the Ancient World.* London: Oxford University Press, 1974.

Schuster, J. "Descartes' Mathesis Universalis: 1619–28." In S. Gaukroger, ed., *Descartes: Philosophy, Mathematics, and Physics.* Sussex, England: Harvester Press, 1980.

Scott, J. *The Scientific Work of René Descartes.* London: Taylor and Francis, 1952.

Sorabji, R. *Aristotle on Memory.* Providence, R.I.: Brown University Press, 1972.

Stewart, D. *An Account of the Life, Writings, and Inventions of John Napier.* Perth: Morison, 1778.

Stillwell, M. *The Awakening of Interest in Science During the First Century of Printing 1450–1550.* New York: Bibliographical Society of America, 1970.

Sturt, G. *The Wheelwright's Shop.* Cambridge, England: University Press, 1923.

Swerdlow, N. "Johannes Petreius's letter to Rheticus." *Isis* 83 (June 1992).

———. "Translating Copernicus." *Isis* 72 (March 1981).

Swerdlow, N., and O. Neugebauer. *Mathematical Astronomy in Copernicus' De Revolutionibus.* New York: Springer-Verlag, 1984.

Thomas-Stanford, C. *Early Editions of Euclid's Elements.* London: Charles Thomas-Stanford, 1926.

Thoreau, H. "Walden." In B. Atkinson, ed., *Walden and Other Writings.* New York: Modern Library, 1937.

———. "Walking." In B. Atkinson, ed., *Walden and Other Writings.* New York: Modern Library, 1937.

Thorndike, L. *Science and Thought in the Fifteenth Century.* New York: Columbia University Press, 1929.

Turbayne, C. *The Myth of Metaphor.* Rev. ed. Columbia: University of South Carolina Press, 1970.

Wallace, W. *Galileo's Early Notebooks: The Physical Questions.* Notre Dame, Ind.: University of Notre Dame Press, 1977.

Warner, D. "What is a scientific instrument, when did it become one, and why?" *British Journal of the History of Science,* March 1990.

Watts, I. *The First Principles of Astronomy and Geography.* 8th ed. London: Longman, 1772.

Westman, R. "The Melanchthon circle, Rheticus, and the Wittenberg interpretation of the Copernican theory." *Isis* 66 (June 1975).

Whiteside, D. *The Mathematical Principles Underlying Newton's Principia Mathematica.* Glasgow: University of Glasgow, 1970.

Wigner, E. *Symmetries and Reflections: Scientific Essays of Eugene P. Wigner.* Cambridge, Mass.: MIT Press, 1970.

Williams, S. *The History of Ancient Education.* Syracuse, N.Y.: Bardeen, 1903.
———. *The History of Medieval Education.* Syracuse, N.Y.: Bardeen, 1903.

Wilson, C. "Kepler's derivation of the elliptical path." *Isis* 59, no. 19 (spring 1968): 1.

Wilson, J. "On the Platonist doctine of the idea-numbers." *The Classical Review* 18 (June 1904).

Yeomans, D. "The origins of North American astronomy: Seventeenth century." *Isis* 68 (September 1977).

Zeller, M. *The Development of Trigonometry from Regiomontanus to Pitiscus.* Ann Arbor: University of Michigan, 1944.

Zorach, R. "The new mediaeval aesthetic." *Wired,* January 1994.

Pace

Adams, J. *Scientific Papers.* Edited by W. Adams. Cambridge, England: University Press, 1896.

Airy, G. *An Elementary Treatise on Partial Differential Equations.* London: Macmillan, 1866.

Alexander, T. "Cray's way of staying super-duper." *Fortune,* 18 March 1985.

Allen, D. *Relaxation Methods.* New York: McGraw-Hill, 1954.

"A problem as big as a planet." *The Economist,* 5 November 1994.

Arneson, E. "The early art of terrestrial measurement and its practice in Texas." *The Southwestern Historical Quarterly* 29 (October 1925).

Babbage, C. *The Exposition of 1851.* London: John Murray, 1851.
———. *The Influence of Signs in Mathematical Reasoning.* Cambridge, England: Smith, 1826.
———. *The Ninth Bridgewater Treatise.* London: John Murray, 1837.
———. *On the Economy of Machinary and Manufactures.* New York: Augustus M. Kelley, 1863.
———. *Passages from the Life of a Philosopher.* London: Longman, Green, 1864.
———. *Reflections on the Decline of Science in England.* London: Fellowes, 1830.

Bailey, J. *Implementing Fine-Grained Scientific Algorithms on the Connection Machine Supercomputer.* Thinking Machines Corporation TR90-1, 1990.

Barnett, T., and R. Somerville. "Advances in short term climate prediction." *Reviews of Geophysics and Space Physics* 21, no. 5 (June 1983).

Bird, G. "Direct simulation and the Boltzmann equation." *The Physics of Fluids* 13, no. 11 (November 1969).
———. "Monte Carlo simulation of gas flows." *Annual Review of Fluid Mechanics* 10 (1978).

Bliss, G. *Mathematics for Exterior Ballistics.* New York: Wiley, 1944.

Boole, G. *An Investigation of the Laws of Thought.* Boston: Dover Publications, 1951.

————. *A Treatise of Differential Equations.* 5th ed. New York: Chelsea Publishing, 1959.

Booth, B. "Simulating real-world performance." *Computer-aided Engineering,* October 1993.

Bowden, B., ed. *Faster than Thought: A Symposium on Digital Computing Machines.* London: Sir Isaac Pitman and Sons, 1955.

Bowie, W. *Determination of Time, Longitude, Latitude, and Azimuth.* 5th ed. Washington, D.C.: Government Printing Office, 1913.

Brown, C. "Mathematical models." In E. Harsburgh, ed., *Modern Instruments and Methods of Calculation.* London: Bell and Sons, 1915.

Browne, M. "Micro-machines help solve intractable problem of turbulence." *New York Times,* 3 January 1995.

Brownlee, S. "Forecasting: How exact is it?" *Discover,* April 1985.

Bryant, P. "Arithemtic in the cradle." *Nature* (27 August 1992).

Buckner, W. *Calculated Tables of Ranges for Navy and Army Guns.* New York: Van Nostrand, 1865.

Burks, A. "From ENIAC to the stored-program computer." In N. Metropolis et al., eds., *A History of Computing in the Twentieth Century.* New York: Academic Press, 1980.

Burks, A., H. Goldstine, and J. von Neumann. "Preliminary discussions of the logical design of an electronic computing instrument." In A. Taub, gen. ed., *John von Neumann: Collected Works,* Vol. 5. New York: Pergamon Press, 1963.

Buxton, H. *Memoir of the Life and Labours of the Late Charles Babbage Esq. F.R.S.* Edited by A. Hyman. Cambridge Mass.: MIT Press, 1987.

Buzbee, B. "Gaining insight from supercomputing." *Proceedings of the IEEE* 72, no. 1 (January 1984).

Buzbee, B., and D. Sharp. "Perspectives on supercomputing." *Science* (8 February 1985).

Campbell, D. "Nonlinear science." *Los Alamos Science,* no. 15 (1987, special issue).

Caseau, P. "Digital modelling: Ten years from now." *Speedup* 7, no. 1 (June 1993).

Ceruzzi, P. *Beyond the Limits: Flight Enters the Computer Age.* Cambridge, Mass.: MIT Press, 1989.

————. "When computers were human." *Annals of the History of Computing* 13, no. 3 (1991).

Dantzig, T. *Number the Language of Science.* 4th ed. New York: Macmillan, 1959.

Davidson, H. "Some predictions on the performance of future supercomputers for simulation and control." Lawrence Livermore National Laboratory UCRL-89969, October 1983.

Dick, S., and L. Doggett, eds. *Sky with Ocean Joined.* Washington, D.C.: U. S. Naval Observatory, 1983.

Dijkstra, E. "The humble programmer." *Communications of the ACM,* October 1972.

Dodd, K. *Mathematics in Aeronautical Research.* London: Oxford University Press, 1964.

Dubbey, J. *The Mathematical Work of Charles Babbage.* Cambridge, England: University Press, 1978.

Eckert, J. "The ENIAC." In N. Metropolis et al., eds., *A History of Computing in the Twentieth Century.* New York: Academic Press, 1980.

————. "A survey of digital computer memory systems." *Proceedings of the I.R.E.,* October 1953.

Eckhardt, R. "Stan Ulam, John von Neumann, and the Monte Carlo method." *Los Alamos Science,* no. 15 (1987, special issue).

Eddington, A. *The Nature of the Physical World.* New York: Macmillan, 1929.

Efron, B., and R. Tibshirani. "Scientific data analysis in the computer age." *Science* (26 July 1991).

Egolf, T. "Scientific applications of the Connection Machine at the United Technologies Research Center." In H. Simon, ed., *Scientific Applications of the Connection Machine.* Singapore: World Scientific, 1989.

Farrar, J. *An Elementary Treatise on Astronomy.* Cambridge, England: Hilliard, Metcalf, 1827.

Focardi, S. "Simulation: Towards a scientific society." *Speedup* 7, no. 1 (June 1993).

Forbes, B. "Three-dimensional modeling of reacting heat flows in horseshoe vortex combustors." The American Association of Mechanical Engineers, 84-GT-170, 1984.

Forbes, E. *Greenwich Observatory.* London: Taylor and Francis, 1975.

Fordham, H. *Some Notable Surveyors & Map-Makers of the Sixteenth, Seventeenth, & Eighteenth Centuries and Their Work: A Study in the History of Cartography.* Cambridge, England: University Press, 1929.

Fourier, J. *The Analytical Theory of Heat.* Translated by A. Freeman. New York: Dover Publications, 1955.

Frisch, U., B. Hasslacher, and Y. Pomeau. "A lattice gas automaton for the Navier Stokes equation." Los Alamos Preprint *LA-UR-85-3503,* 25 September 1985.

Fulghum, D. "U.S. labs reorient to new endeavors." *Aviation Week & Space Technology,* 7 December 1992.

Gardner, M. "The fantastic combinations of John Conway's new solitaire game 'life'." *Scientific American,* October 1970.

————. "On cellular automata, self-reproduction, the Garden of Eden and the game 'life'." *Scientific American,* February 1971.

Gloudeman, J. "The anticipated impact of supercomputers on finite-element analysis." *Proceedings of the IEEE* 72, no. 1 (January 1984).

Goldstein, S. *Lectures on Fluid Dynamics.* London: Interscience Publishers, 1960.

Goldstein, S., ed. *Modern Developments in Fluid Dynamics.* Oxford: Clarendon Press, 1938.

Goldstine, H. *The Computer from Pascal to von Neumann.* Princeton, N.J.: Princeton University Press, 1972.

—. *A History of Numerical Analysis from the 16th Through the 19th Century.* New York: Springer-Verlag, 1977.

Goldstine, H., and J. von Neumann. "On the principles of large scale computing machines." In A. Taub, gen. ed., *John von Neumann: Collected Works*, Vol. 5. New York: Pergamon Press, 1963.

—. "Planning and coding problems for an electronic computing instrument." In A. Taub, gen. ed., *John von Neumann: Collected Works*, Vol. 5. New York: Pergamon Press, 1963.

Grattan-Guinness, I. "Work for the hairdressers: The production of de Prony's logarithmic and trigonometric tables." *Annals of the History of Computing* 12, no. 3 (1990).

Gregory, O. *A Treatise on Astronomy, in Which the Elements of the Science Are Deduced in a Natural Order, from the Appearances of the Heavens to an Observer on the Earth; Demonstrated on Mathematical Principles, and Explained by an Application to the Various Phenomena.* London: Kearsley, 1803.

Grosser, M. *The Discovery of Neptune.* Cambridge, Mass.: Harvard University Press, 1962.

Hall, A. "On an experimental determination of π." *The Messenger of Mathematics*, 2 (1873).

Hammersley, J., and D. Handscomb. *Monte Carlo Methods.* New York: Barnes and Noble, 1965.

Harlow, F. "Early work in numerical hydrodynamics." *Los Alamos Science*, no. 15 (1987, special issue).

Hasslacher, B. "Discrete fluids part I: Background for lattice gas automata." *Los Alamos Science*, no. 15 (1987, special issue).

—. "Discrete fluids part II: The simple hexagonal model." *Los Alamos Science*, no. 15 (1987, special issue).

—. "Parallel billiards and monster systems." *Daedalus* 121, no. 1 (winter 1992).

Hecht, J. "Optical design enters the computer age." *Computers in Physics*, November–December 1987.

Herman, R., and K. Gardels. "Vehicular traffic flow." *Scientific American*, December 1963.

Herrmann, E. *Exterior Ballistics 1935.* Annapolis, Md.: U.S. Naval Institute, 1935.

Hillis, W. D. "Co-evolving parasites improve simulated evolution as an optimization procedure." In S. Forrest, ed., *Emergent Computation.* Amsterdam: Elsevier Science, 1990.

—. *The Connection Machine (Computer Architecture of the New Wave).* MIT A.I. Memo no. 646, 1981.

—. *The Connection Machine.* Cambridge, Mass.: MIT Press, 1985.

—. "Intelligence as an emergent behavior; or, the songs of Eden." *Daedalus* 117 (winter 1988).

—. "What is massively parallel computing, and why is it so important?" *Daedalus* 121, no. 1 (winter 1992).

Hopper, G., and J. Mauchly. "Influence of programming techniques on the design of computers." *Proceedings of the I.R.E.*, October 1953.

Hyman, A. *Charles Babbage: Pioneer of the Computer.* Princeton, N.J.: Princeton University Press, 1982.

Johan, Z., et al. "An efficient communications strategy for finite element methods on the Connection Machine CM–5 system." *Computer Methods in Applied Mechanics and Engineering* 113 (1994).

Johnson, O. "Three-dimensional wave equation computations on vector computers." *Proceedings of the IEEE* 72, no. 1 (January 1984).

Kahn, R. "A new generation in computing." *IEEE Spectrum,* November 1983.

Kaisler, S. *Parallel Computing Workshop Report,* 1982.

Kays, W., and A. London. *Compact Heat Exchangers.* New York: McGraw-Hill, 1955.

Kelvin, L. "Nineteenth century clouds over the dynamical theory of heat and light." *The London, Edinburgh, and Dublin Philosophical Magazine* 2, no. 7 (July 1901).

Kendall, R., et al. "The impact of vector processors on petroleum reservoir simulation." *Proceedings of the IEEE* 72, no. 1 (January 1984).

Kerr, R. "The race to predict next week's weather." *Science* (1 April 1983).

Kidwell, P. "American scientists and calculating machines: From novelty to commonplace." *Annals of the History of Computing* 12, no. 1 (1990).

Kiekebusch, B., et al. "Interactive aerodynamic design tools." *Speedup* 7, no. 1 (June 1993).

Kirkpatrick, S., et al. "Optimization by simulated annealing." *Science* (13 May 1983).

Kolata, G. "The finite element method: A mathematical revival." *Science* (24 May 1974).

———. "Solving linear systems faster." *Science* (14 June 1985).

Lamb, H. *The Evolution of Mathematical Physics.* Cambridge, England: University Press, 1924.

———. *A Treatise on the Mathematical Theory of the Motion of Fluids.* Cambridge, England: University Press, 1879.

Lerner, E. "The great weather network." *IEEE Spectrum,* February 1982.

Levy, S. "Kay + Hillis." *Wired,* January 1994.

Ludgate, P. "Automatic calculating machines." In E. Harsburgh, ed., *Modern Instruments and Methods of Calculation.* London: Bell and Sons, 1915.

Mach, E. *Popular Scientific Lectures.* 3d ed. Translated by T. McCormack. Chicago: Open Court Publishing, 1898.

———. *The Science of Mechanics: A Critical and Historical Account of Its Development.* Translated by T. McCormack. Chicago: Open Court Publishing, 1919.

Majocchi, R. "Computer applications in car design." *Speedup* 7, no. 1 (June 1993).

Malone, R., et al. "Climate, the ocean, and parallel computing." *Los Alamos Science,* no. 21 (1993).

Mason, A., ed. *The Journal of Charles Mason and Jeremiah Dixon.* Philadelphia: American Philosophical Society, 1969.

Mathematical and Scientific Library of Charles Babbage. London: Hodgson and Son, 1872.

May, K. "Historiography: A perspective for computer scientists." In N. Metropolis et al., eds., *A History of Computing in the Twentieth Century.* New York: Academic Press, 1980.

McBryan, O. "New architectures: Performance highlights and new algorithms." *Parallel Computing* 7 (1988).

Metropolis, N. "The age of computing: A personal memoir." *Daedalus* 121, no. 1 (winter 1992).

———. "The beginning of the Monte Carlo method." *Los Alamos Science,* no. 15 (1987, special issue).

Mitchell, R. "Fantastic journeys in virtual labs." *Business Week,* 19 September 1994.

Molvig, K., and R. Iannucci. "Digital physics." *Machine Design,* 12 December 1994.

Molvig, K., et al. *Flow Simulation Validations of Lattice Gas Aerodynamics.* Exa Corporation, February 1992.

———. *Lattice Gas Aerodynamics.* Exa Corporation, January 1992.

Moulton, F. *Consider the Heavens.* New York: Doubleday Doran, 1940.

———. *An Introduction to Celestial Mechanics.* 2d rev. ed. New York: Dover Publications, 1970.

Norrie, C. "Supercomputers for superproblems: An architectural introduction." *IEEE Computer,* March 1984.

Paulos, J. *Innumeracy: Mathematical Illiteracy and Its Consequences.* New York: Vintage Books, 1988.

Pedetti, R. "Peculiar uses of FEM in structural engineering." *Speedup* 7, no. 1 (June 1993).

Peterson, V. "Application of supercomputers to computational aerodynamics." NASA Technical Memorandum 85965, June 1984.

Rapaport, A. "Lewis F. Richardson's mathematical theory of war." *Journal of Conflict Resolution* 1, no. 3 (1957).

———. *Mathematical Models in the Social and Behavioral Sciences.* New York: Wiley, 1983.

———. *The Origins of Violence: Approaches to the Study of Conflict.* New York: Paragon House, 1989.

Ricardo, D. *The Principles of Political Economy and Taxation.* London: Dent and Sons, 1973.

Richardson, L. "The approximate arithmetical solution by finite differences of physical problems involving differential equations, with an application to the stresses in a masonry dam." *Philosophical Transactions of the Royal Society of London,* series A, 210 (February 1911).

———. *Arms and Insecurity.* London: Atlantic Books, 1960.

———. "Chaos, international and molecular." *Nature,* 27 July 1946.

———. "Could an arms-race end without fighting?" *Nature,* 29 September 1951.

———. "The distribution of wars in time." *Journal of Royal Statistical Society* 107, parts 3–4 (1944).

———. "Distribution of wars in time." *Nature*, 19 May 1945.

———. *Forms Whereon to Write the Numerical Calculations Described in "Weather Prediction by Numerical Process."* London: Cambridge University Press, 1922.

———. "A freehand graphic way of determining stream lines and equipotentials." *The London, Edinburgh, and Dublin Philosophical Magazine* 15, 6th ser. (January–June 1908).

———. "Frequency of occurrence of wars and other fatal quarrels." *Nature*, 15 November 1941.

———. "Generalized foreign politics." *British Journal of Psychology* (monograph supplements) 23 (1939).

———. *Generalized Foreign Politics: A Study in Group Psychology.* Cambridge, England: University Press, 1939.

———. "Mathematical psychology of war." *Nature*, 18 May 1935.

———. "Mathematical psychology of war." *Nature*, 28 December 1935.

———. "A purification method for computing the latent columns of numerical matrices and some integrals of differential equations." *Philosophical Transactions A* 242, no. 852 (4 July 1950).

———. "Stability after the war." *Nature*, 19 August 1944.

———. *Weather Prediction by Numerical Process.* New York: Dover Publications, 1965.

Richardson, S. "Lewis Fry Richardson (1881–1953): A personal biography." *Journal of Conflict Resolution* 1, no. 3 (1957).

Rigaud, S. *Correspondence of Scientific Men of the Seventeenth Century. Vol. 1.* Hildesheim, Germany: Georg Olms Verlagsbuchhandlung, 1965.

———. *Correspondence of Scientific Men of the Seventeenth Century. Vol. 2.* Hildesheim, Germany: Georg Olms Verlagsbuchhandlung, 1965.

Roche, J. "Harriot's 'Regiment of the Sun'." *British Journal for the History of Science* 14, no. 48 (November 1981).

Sanger, D. "The surge in supercomputers." *New York Times*, 1 March 1985.

Scheuerer, G. "An overview of the present status and future requirements for industrial CFD." *Speedup* 7, no. 1 (June 1993).

Scheutz, G. *Specimens of Tables, Calculated, Stereomoulded, and Printed by Machinary.* London: Longman, Brown, 1857.

Shaw, F. *An Introduction to Relaxation Methods.* New York: Dover Publications, 1953.

Shimomura, T., et al. "Calculations using lattice gas techniques." *Los Alamos Science*, no. 15 (1987, special issue).

Smith, A. *An Enquiry into the Nature and Causes of the Wealth of Nations.* Edited by E. Cannon. Chicago: University of Chicago Press, 1976.

———. "The principles which lead and direct philosophical enquiries: Illustrated by the history of astronomy." In I. Ross, ed., *Adam Smith: Essays on Philosophical Subjects.* Oxford: Clarendon Press, 1980.

Somerville, Mrs. *Mechanism of the Heaven.* London: John Murray, 1831.

Southwell, R. V. *The Place of Engineering Science in University Studies: An Inaugural Address Delivered Before the University of Oxford.* Oxford: Clarendon Press, 1930.

———. *Relaxation Methods in Engineering Science: A Treatise on Approximate Computation.* London: Oxford University Press, 1949.

———. *Relaxation Methods in Theoretical Physics.* Oxford: Clarendon Press, 1949.

———. *Relaxation Methods in Theoretical Physics.* Vol. 2. Oxford: Clarendon Press, 1956.

Sugarman, R., and P. Wallich. "The limits to simulation." *IEEE Spectrum*, April 1983.

Taylor, E. *The Haven-Finding Art: A History of Navigation from Odysseus to Captain Cook.* London: Hollis and Carter, 1956.

———. *The Mathematical Practitioners of Tudor & Stuart England.* Cambridge, England: University Press, 1954.

Taylor, E., and M. Richey. *The Geometrical Seaman.* London: Hollis and Carter, 1962.

Tezduyar, T., et al. "Parallel finite-element computation of 3D flows." *IEEE Computer*, October 1993.

Toffoli, T. "Cellular automata as an alternative to (rather than an approximation of) differential equations in modelling physics." In D. Farner et al., eds., *Cellular Automata.* Amsterdam: North-Holland, 1984.

Traub, K. *Digital Physics Simulation of Flow over a Backward-Facing Step.* Exa Corporation, May 1994.

Tropp, H. "The Smithsonian computer history project." In N. Metropolis et al., eds., *A History of Computing in the Twentieth Century.* New York: Academic Press, 1980.

Ulam, F., ed. "Conversations with Rota." *Los Alamos Science*, no. 15 (1987, special issue).

Ulam, S. "Von Neumann." In N. Metropolis et al., eds., *A History of Computing in the Twentieth Century.* New York: Academic Press, 1980.

Vishniac, G. "Simulating physics with cellular automata." In D. Farner et al., eds., *Cellular Automata.* Amsterdam: North-Holland, 1984.

von Neumann, J. "Blast wave calculation." In A. Taub, gen. ed., *John von Neumann: Collected Works*, Vol. 6. New York: Pergamon Press, 1963.

———. "The future of high-speed computing." In A. Taub, gen. ed., *John von Neumann: Collected Works*, Vol. 5. New York: Pergamon Press, 1963.

———. "The impact of recent developments in science on the economy and on economics." in A. Taub, gen. ed., *John von Neumann: Collected Works*, Vol. 6. New York: Pergamon Press, 1963.

———. "The mathematician." In A. Taub, gen. ed., *John von Neumann: Collected Works*, Vol. 1. New York: Pergamon Press, 1961.

———. "Memorandum: The use of variational methods in hydrodynamics." In A. Taub, gen. ed., *John von Neumann: Collected Works*, Vol. 6. New York: Pergamon Press, 1963.

———. "Method in the physical sciences." In A. Taub, gen. ed., *John von Neumann: Collected Works*, Vol. 6. New York: Pergamon Press, 1963.

———. "The NORC and problems in high speed computing." In A. Taub, gen. ed., *John von Neumann: Collected Works*, Vol. 5. New York: Pergamon Press, 1963.

————. "Numerical integration of the barotropic vorticity equation." In A. Taub, gen. ed., *John von Neumann: Collected Works*, Vol. 6. New York: Pergamon Press, 1963.

————. "Proposal and analysis for a new numerical method for hydrodynamical shock." In A. Taub, gen. ed., *John von Neumann: Collected Works*, Vol. 6. New York: Pergamon Press, 1963.

————. "Recent theories of turbulence." In A. Taub, gen. ed., *John von Neumann: Collected Works*, Vol. 6. New York: Pergamon Press, 1963.

————. "The role of mathematics in the sciences and in society." In A. Taub, gen. ed., *John von Neumann: Collected Works*, Vol. 6. New York: Pergamon Press, 1963.

————. "Statistical methods in neutron diffusion." In A. Taub, gen. ed., *John von Neumann: Collected Works*, Vol. 5. New York: Pergamon Press, 1963.

Waddell, J. *Bridge Engineering*. New York: Wiley, 1925.

Waltz, D. "Massively parallel AI." Paper presented at AAAI conference, August 1990.

Whipple, F. "Calculating machines." In E. Harsburgh, ed., *Modern Instruments and Methods of Calculation*. London: Bell and Sons, 1915.

Whitworth, J. *Miscellaneous Papers on Mechanical Subjects*. London: Longman, Brown, 1858.

Wilkinson, D. *Deadly Quarrels: Lewis F. Richardson and the Statistical Study of War*. Berkeley: University of California Press, 1980.

Williamson, C., Jr. "A history of the finite element method to the middle 1960's." Thesis, Boston University, 1976.

Williamson, D., and P. Swartzrauber. "A numerical weather prediction model: Computational aspects on the Cray–1." *Proceedings of the IEEE* 72, no. 1 (January 1984).

Wilson, G. "The life and times of cellular automata." *New Scientist*, 8 October 1988.

Wilson, K. "Science, industry, and the new Japanese challenge." *Proceedings of the IEEE* 72, no. 1 (January 1984).

Wolfram, S. "Preface." In D. Famer et al., eds., *Cellular Automata*. Amsterdam: North-Holland, 1984.

————. "Cellular automata as models of complexity." *Nature* (4 October 1984).

Woodhouse, R. *A Treatise on Astronomy Theoretical and Practical*. Cambridge, England: Smith, 1821.

Wynn, K. "Addition and subtraction by human infants." *Nature* (27 August 1992).

Zabusky, N. "Computational synergetics." *Physics Today*, July 1984.

Pattern and AfterMath

Anderson, B. *Imagined Communities: Reflections on the Origin and Spread of Nationalism*. Rev. ed. London: Verso, 1991.

Anderson, P., "More is different: Broken symmetry and the nature of the hierarchical structure of science." *Science*, 4 August 1972.

Arthur, W. B. "Inductive reasoning and bounded rationality." *American Economic Review* 84, no. 2 (May 1994).

———. "On designing economic agents that behave like human agents." *Journal of Evolutionary Economics* 3 (1993).

———. "Positive feedbacks in the economy." *Scientific American*, February 1990.

Arthur, W. B., and G. McNicoll. "Large-scale simulation models in population development." *Population and Development Review*, December 1975.

Becker, G. *The Economic Approach to Human Behavior.* Chicago: University of Chicago Press, 1976.

Bently, G. "Ethnicity and practice." *Comparative Studies in Society and History*, no. 29 (1987).

Bergstrom, T. "On the evolution of altruistic ethical rules for siblings." *American Economic Review* 85, no. 1 (Mar. 1995).

Boden, M. *The Creative Mind: Myths and Mechanisms.* New York: Basic Books, 1991.

Bolter, J. *Writing Space: The Computer, Hypertext, and the History of Writing.* Hillsdale, N.J.: Erlbaum, 1991.

Booker, L., et al. "Classifier systems and genetic algorithms." *Artificial Intelligence* 40, nos. 1–3 (September 1989).

Borland, J., and X. Yang. "Specialization, product development, evolution of the institution of the firm, and economic growth." *Journal of Evolutionary Economics* 5 (1995).

Boulding, K. "What is evolutionary economics?" *Journal of Evolutionary Economics* 1 (1991).

Broad, W. "Hot vents in the sea floor may drive El Niño." *New York Times*, 25 April 1995.

Brockman, J. "'Order for free': A conversation with Stuart Kauffman." *Edge*, September 1991.

———. *The Third Culture: Beyond the Scientific Revolution.* New York: Simon and Schuster, 1995.

Chandler, D. "From afar, kids do science on the 'net'." *Boston Globe*, 18 September 1995.

Churchill, W. *Fantasies of the Master Race.* Monroe, Me.: Common Courage Press, 1992.

"CIESIN's gateway." The Innovation Network, http://www.ciesin.org, 1995.

Cimoli, M., and G. Dosi. "Technological paradigms, patterns of learning and development: An introductory roadmap." *Journal of Evolutionary Economics* 5 (1995).

Clery, D. "ERS–1: A cautionary tale of data overload." *Science* (13 August 1993).

Cobb, J., Jr., and D. Griffin. *Process Theology: An Introductory Exposition.* Philadelphia: Westminster Press, 1976.

Compiani, M. "Learning and bucket brigade dynamics in classifier systems." In

S. Forrest, ed., *Emergent Computation.* Amsterdam: Elsevier Science, 1990.

Crevier, D. *AI: The Tumultuous History of the Search for Artificial Intelligence.* New York: Basic Books, 1993.

Daly, H. "Against free trade: Neoclassical and steady-state perspectives." *Journal of Evolutionary Economics* 5 (1995).

David, P. "Clio and the economics of QWERTY." *American Economic Review Proceedings* 75 (1985).

Dawkins, R. *The Blind Watchmaker.* New York: Norton, 1986.

Dosi, G. "Some thoughts on the promises, challenges and dangers of an 'evolutionary perspective' in economics." *Journal of Evolutionary Economics* 1 (1991).

Dosi, G., and Y. Kaniovski. "On 'badly behaved' dynamics." *Journal of Evolutionary Economics* 4 (1994).

Dosi, G., and R. Nelson. "An introduction to evolutionary theories in economics." *Journal of Evolutionary Economics* 4 (1994).

Dreyfus, H. "What computers still can't do." *The Key Reporter,* winter 1993–94.

"Electronics applied to water storage on Nile." *Times of London,* 22 March 1957.

Farmer, D. "A Rosetta stone for connectionism." In S. Forrest, ed., *Emergent Computation.* Amsterdam: Elsevier Science, 1990.

Fierher, T. "Dialect and dialectic: Negritude as critique and emulation of the western world." *Plantation Societies in the Americas* 3, no. 1 (October 1981).

Fisher, L. "Shifting lead at forefront of computing." *New York Times,* 11 September 1995.

Flam, F. "Ecologist plans to let cyberlife run wild in internet reserve." *Science* (20 May 1994).

Flores, J. "Que assimilated, brother, yo soy asimilao: The structuring of Puerto Rican identity in the U.S." *Journal Of Ethnic Studies* 13, no. 3 (1985).

Fogel, L., et al. *Artificial Intelligence Through Simulated Evolution.* New York: Wiley, 1966.

Forrest, S. "Emergent computation: Self-organizing, collective, and cooperative phenomena in natural and artificial computing networks." In S. Forrest, ed., *Emergent Computation.* Amsterdam: Elsevier Science, 1990.

————. "Genetic algorithms: Principles of natural selection applied to computation." *Science* (13 August 94).

Forrest, S., and J. Miller. "Emergent behavior in classifier systems." In S. Forrest, ed., *Emergent Computation.* Amsterdam: Elsevier Science, 1990.

Foss, N. "Theories of the firm: Contractual and competence perspectives." *Journal of Evolutionary Economics* 3 (1993).

Freedman, D. "AI helps researchers find meaning in molecules." *Science* (13 August 1993).

Friedman, M. *Essays in Positive Economics.* Chicago: University of Chicago Press, 1953.

Gibbs, W. "Creative evolution." *Scientific American*, October 1993.

Gleick, J. "New appreciation of the complexity in a flock of birds." *New York Times*, 24 November 1987.

Goodwin, R. "Schumpeter, Keynes, and the theory of economic evolution." *Journal of Evolutionary Economics* 1 (1991).

Gowdy, J. "Higher selection processes in evolutionary economic change." *Journal of Evolutionary Economics* 2 (1992).

Greening, D. "Parallel simulated annealing techniques." In S. Forrest, ed., *Emergent Computation*. Amsterdam: Elsevier Science, 1990.

Grossman, D. *Sleeping on a Wire: Conversations with Palestinians in Israel.* Translated by H. Watzman. New York: Farrar, Straus, and Giroux, 1993.

Gunn, J., et al. *Hierarchical Algorithm for Computer Modeling of Protein Tertiary Structure: Folding of Myoglobin to 6.2 Angstrom Resolution,* Columbia University preprint, 29 October 1993.

Hammerstrom, D. "Neural networks at work." *IEEE Spectrum*, June 1993.

Hammerton, D. "The Nile river: A case study." In R. Oglesby et al., eds., *River Ecology and Man*. New York: Academic Press, 1972.

Harnad, S. "The symbol grounding problem." In S. Forrest, ed., *Emergent Computation*. Amsterdam: Elsevier Science, 1990.

Hendry, D. "Econometrics: Alchemy or science?" *Economica* 47 (November 1980).

Hetherington, N. "Isaac Newton's influence on Adam Smith's natural laws in economics." *Journal of the History of Ideas* 44 (July–September 1983).

Hinton, G. "How neural networks learn from experience." *Scientific American*, September 1992.

Hodgson, G. *Economics and Evolution: Bringing Life Back into Economics*. Ann Arbor: University of Michigan Press, 1993.

Holland, J. *Adaptation in Natural and Artificial Systems*. Ann Arbor: University of Michigan Press, 1975.

———. "Complex adaptive systems." *Daedalus* 121, no. 1 (winter 1992).

———. "Concerning the emergence of tag-mediated lookahead in classifier systems." In S. Forrest, ed., *Emergent Computation*. Amsterdam: Elsevier Science, 1990.

———. "Escaping brittleness: The possibilities of general-purpose learning algorithms applied to parallel rule-based systems." In Michalski, Carborell, and Mitchell, eds., *Machine Learning II*. Los Altos: Kaufman, 1986.

———. *Hidden Order: How Adaptation Builds Complexity*. Reading, Mass.: Helix Books, 1995.

Holland, J., et al. *Induction: Processes of Inference, Learning, and Discovery*. Cambridge, Mass.: MIT Press, 1986.

Horgan, J. "From complexity to perplexity." *Scientific American*, June 1995.

Howell, P., and J. Allan, eds. *The Nile: Sharing a Scarce Resource*. Cambridge, England: University Press, 1994.

Hurst, H. *The Nile: A General Account of the River and the Utilization of its Waters*. London: Constable, 1952.

Iwai, K. "Towards a disequilibrium theory of long-run profits." *Journal of Evolutionary Economics* 1 (1991).

Jelavich, C., and B. Jelavich. *The Balkans.* Englewood Cliffs, N.J.: Prentice-Hall, 1965.

Johnson, G. "Sifting market patterns for profit." *New York Times*, 11 September 1995.

Kauffman, S. "Requirements for evolvability in complex systems: Orderly dynamics and frozen components." In S. Forrest, ed., *Emergent Computation.* Amsterdam: Elsevier Science, 1990.

Kaufman, H. "The emergent kingdom: Machines that think like people." *The Futurist*, Jan. 1994.

Kelly, K. "The gene in the machine," *New York Times*, 15 May 1995.

———. *Out of Control: The New Biology of Machines, Social Systems, and the Economic World.* Reading, Mass.: Addison-Wesley, 1994.

Keynes, J. *The General Theory of Employment, Interest, and Money.* San Diego, Calif.: Harcourt Brace Jovanovich, 1953.

———. "Professor Tinbergen's method." In D. Muggridge, ed., *The Collected Works of John Maynard Keynes.* Vol. 14. London: Macmillan, 1973.

Kimmelman, M. "One provocateur inspired by another," *New York Times,* 11 August 95.

Kirkpatrick, S., et al. "Optimization by simulated annealing." *Science* (13 May 1983).

Koza, J. *Genetic Programming: A Paradigm for Genetically Breeding Populations of Computer Programs to Solve Problems.* Stanford University Report no. STAN-CS-90-1314, 1990.

Kreps, D. *Game Theory and Economic Modeling.* Oxford: Clarendon Press, 1990.

Krugman, P. "Complex landscapes in economic geography." *American Economic Review* 84, no. 2 (May 1994).

———. "How I work." *The American Economist* 37, no. 2 (fall 1993).

Kuznets, S. "Parts and wholes in economics." In D. Lerner, ed., *Parts and Wholes.* New York: Free Press of Glencoe, 1963.

Lane, D. "Artificial worlds and economics, part I." *Journal of Evolutionary Economics* 3 (1993).

———. "Artificial worlds and economics, part II." *Journal of Evolutionary Economics* 3 (1993).

Langton, C. "Artificial life." In C. Langton, ed., *Artificial Life: SFI Studies in the Science of Complexity.* Reading, Mass.: Addison-Wesley, 1988.

———. "Computation at the edge of chaos: Phase transitions and emergent computation." In S. Forrest, ed., *Emergent Computation.* Amsterdam: Elsevier Science, 1990.

Lenat, D. "Artificial intelligence." *Scientific American*, September 1995.

Lesourne, J. "From market dynamics to evolutionary economics." *Journal of Evolutionary Economics* 1 (1991).

LeVine, R. *Culture, Behavior, and Personality.* Chicago: Aldine, 1973.

Lucas, R., and T. Sargent. "After Keynesian macro-economics." In R. Lucas and T. Sargent, eds., *Rational Expectations and Econometric Practice.* Minneapolis: University of Minnesota Press, 1981.

MacKenzie, D. "The automation of proof: A historical and sociological exploration." *IEEE Annals of the History of Computing* 17, no. 3 (1995).

Mageed, Y. "The integrated river basin development: The challenges to the Nile basin countries." In J. Lundqvist et al., eds., *Strategies for River Basin Management.* Boston: Reidel, 1985.

Malone, R., et al. "Climate, the ocean, and parallel computing." *Los Alamos Science*, no. 21 (1993).

Malone, T., et al. "Electronic markets and electronic hierarchies." *Communications of the ACM* 30, no. 6 (June 1987).

Marks, R. "Breeding hybrid strategies: Optimal behaviour for oligopolists." *Journal of Evolutionary Economics* 2 (1992).

Marshall, A. *Principles of Economics.* 8th ed. New York: Macmillan, 1948.

Marshall, E. "Fitting Planet Earth into a user-friendly database." *Science* (13 August 1993).

Maxion, R. "Towards diagnosis as an emergent behavior in a network ecosystem." In S. Forrest, ed., *Emergent Computation.* Amsterdam: Elsevier Science, 1990.

Mayer, T. *Truth vs. Precision in Economics.* Brookfield, Vermont: Edward Elgar, 1993.

Miller, G., and P. Todd. "Evolutionary wanderlust: Sexual selection with directional mate preferences." Thinking Machines seminar series, Cambridge, Mass., 2 March 1993.

Mirowski, P. *Against Mechanism.* Totowa, N.J.: Rowman and Littlefield, 1988.

Mitchell, M., and D. Hofstadter. "The emergence of understanding in a computer model of concepts and analogy-making." In S. Forrest, ed., *Emergent Computation.* Amsterdam: Elsevier Science, 1990.

Moffat, A. "Theoretical ecology: Winning its spurs in the real world." *Science* (25 February 1994).

Morton, O. "Unshackled: A survey of biotechnology and genetics." *The Economist*, 25 February 95.

Moyson, F., and B. Manderick. *The Collective Behavior of Ants: An Example of Self-organization in Massive Parallelism.* MIT AI Memo 88-7, January 1988.

Muth, J. "Rational expectations and the theory of price movements." In R. Lucas and T. Sargent, eds., *Rational Expectations and Econometric Practice.* Minneapolis: University of Minnesota Press, 1981.

Nelson, R. "Recent evolutionary theorizing about economic change." *Journal of Economic Literature* 33 (March 1995).

———. *Understanding Technical Change as an Evolutionary Process.* Amsterdam: North-Holland, 1987.

Nelson, R., and S. Winter. *An Evolutionary Theory of Economic Change.* Cambridge, Mass.: Belknap Press, 1982.

O'Brien, D. *The Classical Economists.* Oxford: Clarendon Press, 1975.

Omohundro, S. "Geometric learning tasks." In S. Forrest, ed., *Emergent Computation.* Amsterdam: Elsevier Science, 1990.

Parker, J. "Turn up the lights: A survey of cities." *The Economist*, 29 July 1995.

Patinkin, D. "Keynes and econometrics: On the interaction between the macroeconomic revolutions of the interwar period." *Econometrica* 44, no. 6 (November 1976).

Phillips, A. "Mechanical models in economic dynamics." *Economica* 17 (August 1950).

Pictet, O., et al. "Real-time trading models for foreign exchange rates." *Speedup* 7, no. 1 (June 1993).

Polanyi, M. *The Tacit Dimension.* Garden City, N.Y.: Doubleday, 1966.

Ray, T. "How I created life in a virtual universe." *Bionomic Perspectives*, spring 1993.

Reiss, T., and R. Hinderliter. "Money and value in the sixteenth century: The *Monete Cudende Ratio* of Nicholas Copernicus." *Journal of the History of Ideas* 40 (April 1979).

Reiter, C. "Toy universes." *Science 86* (June 1986).

Resnick, M. "Changing the centralized mindset." *Technology Review*, July 1994.
———. *Overcoming the Centralized Mindset: Towards an Understanding of Emergent Phenomena.* MIT E&L Memo no. 11, November 1990.
———. *Turtles, Termites, and Traffic Jams.* Cambridge, Mass.: MIT Press, 1994.

Rimland, B. "Matching wits with twin savants," *Psychology Today*, August 1978.

Robinson, P. "Paul Romer." *Forbes ASAP*, 1995.

Romer, P. "The origins of endogenous growth." *Journal of Economic Perspectives* 8, no. 1 (winter 1994).

Samuelson, P. *Foundations of Economic Analysis.* Cambridge, Mass.: Harvard University Press, 1963.

Schumpeter, J. "The common sense of econometrics." In R. Clemens, ed., *Essays on Entrepreneurs, Innovations, Business Cycles, and the Evolution of Capitalism.* New Brunswick, N.J.: Transaction Publishers, 1989.

Sejnowski, T., and C. Rosenberg. "Parallel networks that learn to pronounce English text." *Complex Systems* 1 (1987).

Semmler, W. "Information, innovation and diffusion of technology." *Journal of Evolutionary Economics* 4 (1994).

Shea, P., and F. Liu. "Operational experience with a neural network in the detection of explosives in checked airline luggage." Paper presented at IJCNN 90 Conference, June 1990.

Sheiber, S. "Lessons from a restricted Turing test." *Communications of the ACM* 37, no. 6 (June 1994).

Shen, H. *Modeling of Rivers.* New York: Wiley, 1979.

Shenouda, W. "Resettlement of population in the high Aswân dam project." *Seventeenth International Conference on Large Dams.* Paris: International Commission on Large Dams, 1991.

Shurmer, M., and P. Swann. "An analysis of the process generating *de facto* standards in the PC spreadsheet software market." *Journal of Evolutionary Economics* 5 (1995).

Siegfried, T. "Maybe people are just the bugs in the ultimate computer program." *Dallas Morning News*, 8 February 1993.

———. "A new age dawning in science?" *Dallas Morning News*, 28 September 1992.

———. "Opening the door to computer physics." *Dallas Morning News*, 26 October 1992.

Silverberg, G., and B. Verspagen. "Collective learning, innovation and growth in a boundedly rational, evolutionary world." *Journal of Evolutionary Economics* 4 (1994).

Simon, H. *The Sciences of the Artificial.* Cambridge, Mass.: MIT Press, 1969.

Stanfill, C. "Memory-based reasoning." *Encyclopedia of Artificial Intelligence.* 2d ed. New York: Wiley, 1992.

Stanfill, C., and D. Waltz. "Toward memory-based reasoning." *Communications of the ACM* 29, no. 12 (December 1986).

Stevens, W. "Effects of El Niño reach across ocean and linger a decade." *New York Times*, 9 August 1994.

———. "Extinction of the fittest may be the legacy of lost habitats." *New York Times*, 27 September 1994.

Strassman, D. "Feminist thought and economics; or, what do the Visigoths know?" *American Economic Review* 84, no. 2 (May 1994).

Strober, M. "Rethinking economics through a feminist lens." *American Economic Review* 84, no. 2 (May 1994).

"Struggling with insect research? Ask a seventh grader for help." *New York Times*, 29 August 1995.

Tambiah, S. "Ethnic conflict in the world today." *American Ethnologist*, no. 16 (1989).

Thearling, K. *Evolving MIMD Programs: Some Experiments with Multi-Cellular Artificial Life.* Thinking Machines Seminar, Cambridge, Mass., 31 May 1994.

Thompson, R. *Theories of Ethnicity: A Critical Appraisal.* New York: Greenwood Press, 1989.

Veblen, T. "Economics and evolution." In *Veblen on Marx, Race, Science, and Economics.* New York: Capricorn Books, 1969.

Vinge, V. "Technological singularity." *Whole Earth Review*, winter 1993.

Waldrop, M. "FAA fights back on plastic explosives." *Science* (13 January 1989).

Wegmann, E. *Design and Construction of Masonry Dams.* New York: Wiley, 1922.

Whitehead, A. *Adventures of Ideas.* New York: Free Press, 1933.

———. *Process and Reality: Corrected Edition.* Edited by D. Griffin and D. Sherburne. New York: Free Press, 1978.

———. *Science and the Modern World.* New York: Free Press, 1967.

Wilson, S. "Perceptron redux: Emergence of structure." In S. Forrest, ed., *Emergent Computation.* Amsterdam: Elsevier Science, 1990.

Wilson, W. *The Declining Significance of Race: Blacks and Changing American Institutions.* Chicago: University of Chicago Press, 1980.

Wolynes, P. "Protein folding as an information processing problem." Paper presented at Florida State University Workshop on Challenges in Structural Biology, 24 January 1992.

————. "Will computer design become a matter of evolution?" *Computers in Physics* 6, no. 3 (May–June 1992).

Wurtz, D., et al. "Analysis and prediction of currency exchange rates." *Speedup* 7, no. 1 (June 1993).

Zipf, G. *Selected Studies of the Principle of Relative Frequency in Language.* Cambridge, Mass.: Harvard University Press, 1932.

ιNDEX